COMMENTARY

ON THE

PROPHETS OF THE OLD TESTAMENT,

BY THE LATE

DR. GEORG HEINRICH AUGUST VON EWALD,

Professor of Oriental Languages in the University of Göttingen.

𝕿ranslated by

J. FREDERICK SMITH.

VOL. II.

YESAYA, 'OBADYA, AND MIKHA.

Wipf & Stock
PUBLISHERS
Eugene, Oregon

Wipf and Stock Publishers
199 W 8th Ave, Suite 3
Eugene, OR 97401

Commentary on the Prophets of the Old Testament, Volume 2
By Ewald, Georg Heinrich von
ISBN: 1-59752-651-7
Publication date 3/17/2006
Previously published by Williams and Norgate, 1876

In the present volume a few of the author's references to his untranslated works have been quoted in English for the convenience of the English reader. The numerous *paronomasiai* of Isaiah and Micah have had at times to receive in our tongue a form slightly different from that they bear in the German, but in almost every case the German has then been quoted. The Table of Chronological Arrangements of "Isaiah" at the end of the volume was drawn up with the hope that it might prove useful to readers of the prophet and of one of the best of his *exegetai*.—TR.

CONTENTS OF VOL. II.

ERRATA.

Page 41, line 3, read פֵּאַר instead of פְ׳.

    „   41, line 16, read מַעֲשֵׂה instead of מ׳.

    „   43, note, read Tʀ. instead of Tʀs.

    „   96, line 4, read הַשְּׂכִירָה instead of הַשְׂכ׳.

    „   115, line 24, read *Amîr* instead of *Amôr*.

    „   153, line 3, read *Tœmá* instead of *Tœmâ*.

    „   176, line 26, read ḥazama instead of ḥ—.

    „   176, line 28, read ḥizâm instead of ḥ—.

    „   198, line 9, read *whimper* instead of *whisper*.

    „   204, line 5, insert *as* after *though*.

    „   220, line 26, read לִצְבָּא instead of לְצְב׳.

    „   221, line 8, read דְבַר מִי instead of דב רמ׳.

    „   256, heading, read xxxiii. instead of xxiii.

PROPHETS OF THE OLD TESTAMENT.

2. YESAYA.

IN Yesaya we see prophetic literature, at the time when it most flourished, attain its highest summit; everything combined to raise him to this height, to which neither an earlier prophet as author could climb nor a later could again soar. Of the other prophets, all the more celebrated ones were distinguished by some special excellence and peculiar power, whether of speech or of deed; in Yesaya all the powers and all the beauties of prophetic speech and deed combine to form a symmetrical whole; he is distinguished less by any special excellence than by the symmetry and the perfection of all his powers. And as amongst all the older literary prophets he was manifestly the most productive and most successful in his public work, in speaking and writing, so there have been preserved far more of his writings, partly entire and partly fragmentary, than of any other of that series of prophets.

I. We cannot help supposing that Yesaya possessed, as the first condition of his peculiar historical greatness, a native power and animation of mind rarely possessed even by prophets. There are rarely combined in the same mind, the profoundest prophetic emotion and purest feeling, the most unwearied, successful and consistent activity amid all the confusions and changes of life, and lastly, that true poetic ease and beauty of style, combined with force and irresistible power; yet this triad of powers we find realized in Yesaya as in no

other prophet; and we must infer from the evident traces of
the constant co-operation of these three powers that the measure
of the original endowments of his mind was very great. We
further see him constantly located at the centre of the kingdom of Yuda, in Jerusalem itself, in close relations too with
the royal house, and entrusted with the most important public
affairs; and we understand how he, more than many other
prophets, could turn his prophetic eye in all directions from
this most favourable although most onerous position, and could
collect in wide survey all the spiritual relations of the age.
Finally, his activity was not of brief duration, nor was it
confined to his later years, nor restricted to little events, but
through a long life, which was devoted purely to the prophetic
impulses of his spirit, and which at the same time fell in the
midst of the most important world-events, continued, unchanged, and increased in inward power and outward means,
by the changes of fortunes, the length of years, and the magni-
tude of events. But to all this must be added that his life
falls exactly in the period when all prophecy, as well as all
literature, could be most freely and perfectly cultivated. Thus
everything combined to make of Yesaya the greatest prophet
of those centuries, whose work has also been immortalized for
all succeeding ages in his own writings. He occupies as prophet no less than as author that calm sunny height, which
a specially favoured mind takes possession of at the right time
in every ancient literature, a height which seems to wait for
him, and, when he has come and risen to it, seems to maintain and guard him to the end without intermission as its
proper occupier. It is true, Yesaya would have been impossible without Yôél and other great predecessors; he follows
them, and actively carries on their work : but just as the
inmost power of his mind is not dependent on his predecessors,
and he found much to dare and bear, so he stands above them
in his position after he has assumed it, and exhibits a spiritual
activity beyond which no successor could go in later times.
Everywhere Yesaya makes himself known as the regal prophet,

in his thoughts, the matter of his orations, and the style of his expression.

1. In thought Yesaya always hits the truth in its greatest* purity, and not only hits it, but also presents it boldly with pointed severity and victorious force ; and his thoughts turn not only upon the highest affairs of the kingdom, the nations, and his entire age, but also upon the eternal hope of the divine kingdom upon earth. It is not necessary to show this here in each single case ; the exposition of the particular passages will subsequently supply this : a few of the more general phenomena of this kind, however, must be elucidated now.

When Yesaya arose, there prevailed in Jerusalem pretty generally the notion, with which Yôél has made us familiar, of the special advantages of the holy city ; and during the long reign of 'Uzzia, which was externally successful, it had become in the case of the magnates of the land an indolent security, a proud trust in the indestructibility of their own good fortune, and an idle, luxurious enjoyment of life. 'Amôs, and to a certain extent Hoséa, had spoken against this false trust, but they lived far from Jerusalem, and it is hardly likely that their voices had produced great effect upon the proud capital. So far as we know, Yesaya is the first who in the midst of the capital laid bare almost all the popular opinions and dangerous errors of this kind in their radical perversity, and destroyed them with irresistible power ; and this long before the Assyrians threatened the kingdom of Yuda, ii. 2, v. 30 ; no subsequent prophet resisted so powerfully as he every form of human arrogance, nor pointed so over-poweringly to things inviolable and eternal.

When subsequently, under Hizqia, the foreign religions, and all kinds of superstition which had been tolerated or even favoured by previous kings, received no further protection, and the ancient Yahvé religion was more firmly adhered to by high and low, Yesaya's exertions had already obtained their first victory, and his mind might then have rested according to the common view. But, on the contrary, he now perceives with a clear incorruptible glance the dangers of a religion of hypocrisy and eye-service commended by authority, which under the appearance of serving the Highest with all assiduity and devotion only hides its carnal aims, and instead of giving itself up purely to the attractions of the pure spirit, less and less understands and follows it. In this respect, his utterances have a lasting import for all times and places where a higher spiritual religion has indeed fortunately public authority, but on account of this public authority, is constantly in danger of not being spiritually enough received, i. 11-17; xxix. 13, 14.

But although his keen glance thus recognises on all hands the large amount of vanity there is in human pursuits, and pierces through the great hidden deficiencies,—although on this account the baselessness of the existing relations, with the consequent necessity of an early general destruction, irresistibly forces itself upon his gaze when he looks into the veiled future, however mournful the picture may be,—he yet holds unchangeably fast by the eternal hope, and knows how much there is of good in the community of Yahvé which will approve itself by every sharp trial. Two truths especially cast a light for him into the darkness of the future, even in the most gloomy times : the one, that prosperity and salvation can be found in Yahvé alone, salvation for those who seek Him alone, prosperity without measure or end; the other, that only a remnant, indeed, a small, proved few of the community, can be preserved from the impending storms and trials, this few, however, being certainly and necessarily the basis of a new, reformed community, because in Yahvé's community there is an indestructible germ of good: two truths which 'Amôs and Hoséa had uttered, but which Yesaya was the first to exhibit with great power and decisiveness and to make the condition of his whole work, while they never left him without consolation and invigoration; he had even deposited them as an imperishable symbol in his own name *Yesaya (Yahvé's is salvation),* and in his son's name Sheâr Yashûb *(the remnant will be converted),* vii. 3 ; viii. 18, comp. viii. 13, sq.; xxxi.

1-6; vi. 11-13; xxviii. 5; x. 20-22; xi. 11, 16 (iv. 3). In the region of these forebodings and truths, there was, however, one conception, which the previous prophets had left untouched and consigned to him, and in which therefore he was able to show himself most original and independent. This was the precise idea as to the proper form which the longed for time of the purified and reformed future could alone assume. And in this respect the exalted regal mind of this prophet of Jerusalem was exhibited in its most illustrious light. He who from his own regal mind knew what unlimited power might be given to the individual soul to influence *many* and to inspire *all*, who besides saw daily in Jerusalem the traces of the former activity of a great mind like David,— he could conceive the future elevation of the community no otherwise than as sustained by *one* divine ruler. If, in fact, every spiritual elevation and awakening must proceed from the clearness and constancy of one exalted spirit, that was still more the case with that highest elevation which was longed for and striven for by ancient Israel; in the certainty that an individual was to be expected, the desire became distinct without losing itself in vague aberrations; in the idea of what an unlimitedly powerful spirit this individual must be, the desire found repose without falling into precipitation and impatience. Thus the Messianic desire necessarily assumed at last this form: but Yesaya was the first to arrive at it, and to give it the right shape. His happiest hope rests in the certainty, that this sure personal centre of the better future would not fail to appear; and his foreboding desire luxuriates in the pictures of his necessary greatness and exaltation; in foreboding desire he traces his character from his childhood through all the stages of his unique life up to the last; he beholds in him the true government and the fulfilment of all noble human endeavour; and he can surmise nothing beyond him save Yahvé and the consummation of his kingdom. But although Yesaya is the true author of this highest development of all divine hopes, even in his writings we can trace a growth in his manner of conceiving them: the oldest oration, ii. 2-5, 30; ix. 7—x. 4, contains nothing of the final conception of the Messianic king, whilst in the brief indications, vii. 14; viii. 10; ix. 5, sq., it appears as already known, but is expressed at length most powerfully and perfectly, xi. 1—5, 10, comp. xxxii. 1, sq. The contemporary and fellow countrymen of Yesaya, the author of Zakh. ix. and his junior Mikha, follow in this respect almost entirely the greater prophet, and after that time this special form, which the divine hopes had assumed, is never entirely lost.

Yesaya repeats the view of the earlier prophets concerning the Heathen, that their calamities must serve to make them look to the true God as the only real saviour. But he adds to this view its glorious consummation, by the happy presentiment which he expressed in the evening of his life, that after the conversion of the Heathen there would be no external difference at all between them and Israel, and no advantage would be possessed by these before those, but the same blessing will rest upon them all, xix. 18-25; an exalted view which stands almost solitary in the Old Testament.

With what sacred feelings he had looked upon the whole prophetic mission from the first, and still looked upon it, he explains in an introductory piece, ch. vi., with wonderful clearness and force, as no other prophet has done.

2. While no thought is too high or too far off for him, neither is there any phenomenon of his age which lies beyond the range of his eye, or is too difficult for the strength of his prophetic arm, every topic of prophetic discourse and teaching being commanded by him from his regal position; as a watchful, far-seeing, guard and watchman of his age, and standing as it were in the centre of the Hebrew world and of genuine religion (xxi. 11, sq.), his eye takes in and commands from his position everything that can provoke a prophet to speech and action, and there is nothing that escapes the truth of his thought or the weight of his words. His discourses comprehend the most varied topics, and yet they always issue from the same fundamental truth which inspires him. He contends

with the false prophets and magicians of every kind; but as with men who are far beneath the true prophetic dignity, and to silence whom a few words suffice, ii. 6; viii. 19: but if prophets, priests, and magnates, professing to worship Yahvé, tread the Temple with unholy feelings and behaviour, then he contends against them with every strongest weapon, and mercilessly strips them of all their false attire, i. 10-23; xxix. 9-14. He is content to present the divine truth, and when he has spoken what was necessary, he withdraws, calmly confident that the future will attest his words, viii. 16-18; xxx. 8: but when in place of the needful seriousness and collectedness in Yahvé, which he as a prophet had demanded, the people abandons itself to wild joy, as if to silence conscience, nothing then restrains him from speaking with the greater emphasis and severity, xxii. 1-14; or when a powerful party in the kingdom, from cowardice or embarrassment, will hide their crooked views and mischievous plans, precisely from him, because he was feared as the mouth of Yahvé, in reality therefore from Yahvé himself, he then searches the more inevitably into the secret which they wish to hide, places it before their eyes in all its pitiableness, and, without sparing, hurls all their pernicious purposes to the ground with terrible force, ch. xxviii.—xxxii. He overlooks no injustice in the realm, however and by whomsoever it may be committed, and directs his threatening words, when it is necessary, against the magnates and princes of the kingdom, priests and laymen, who by transgressions of various kinds continued to increase the evils of the kingdom and the sufferings of the people; indeed he directs his threats quite personally against one of the powerful friends of the king, xxii. 15, sq.; nor does the reigning Davîdic king stand too high for his divine word, he announces to him the truth even against his will and quite publicly, vii. 3-17, comp. iii. 12, but nevertheless would much rather work with him as dispenser of divine consolation and deliverance, ch. xxxvii.—xxxviii.; but, again, he does not spare, for instance, the ruler who in other respects willingly hears his words, but observes all his deeds with equal watchfulness, without preference as well as without enmity, and holds before him also the truthful mirror of evil foreboding as to the consequences, *e.g.* of pride and ambition in the midst of success, which is shown by the narrative, ch. xxxix., important in this respect although not intrinsically so. But while he speaks against the powerful without fear or hesitancy, moved purely by the divine truth, not less does he raise the weight of his words against everything that is perverse and ungodly in the great mass of the people, and in no case takes the side of the people against the legitimate reigning family when this is in danger, viii. 6, 11, sq. And lastly, he observes, not merely the internal affairs of the kingdom, he has an equally watchful eye for foreign affairs, and surveys the fortunes and destinies of all nations as far as his prophetic eye ranges; neither in this wide region can anything escape his clear spirit : whether it be the contact of such a nation with the inhabitants of Jerusalem, while this contact is very distant and is conceived by only the fewest as just barely possible, v. 26-30 ; or should an important question of this kind be immediately engaging the attention of the nation, xviii. 1-7. And in all cases he judges correctly with respect to foreign nations also and their relation to the Hebrews and the Yahvé-religion ; but if a foreign people has become unendurably insolent and cruel, he does not shrink from raising his indignant word and his forebodings of evil against it, even should it stand threateningly and with superior force in the midst of the land, x. 5-34 ; xxxvii. 22-35, and elsewhere. Thus as a true spiritual ruler he exercises his mastery over all subjects by the power of his thoughts and his public speech, and everything that is weak and perverse in the age vainly strives to hide itself from his invincible power. It is only by his observing the favourite custom of giving an external sign in addition to the truth that there is still observable in Yesaya also the marks of an age which was not yet prepared for the highest conceivable perfection of prophetic activity.

3. Lastly, his style everywhere bears the same impress of a regal mastery of his matter. It cannot be said that it is

strictly speaking elaborated and artistic, it bears a lofty simplicity and unconcern for outward charms, and resigns itself
freely to the guidance and requirement of each thought : but
everywhere it rolls onward in a full overwhelming stream, and
always accomplishes its purpose at the right point with simple
means.

It is of itself significant that Yesaya almost wholly dispenses
with the usual marks of the poetic style, *e.g.* the suffix מוֹ֫־, the
negative בַּל, and the like (xxx. 5 ; xxxii. 10) : he does not need
them, his style has sufficient poetic elevation and beauty. It
is quite otherwise with the pieces of his contemporaries, which
have been received into the same book, ch. xxiii. xxxiii., comp.
xvi. 4 *a*. It may be accepted as an exegetical law, that in all
cases the simpler expression answers best to the thought of this
prophet, since he never seeks his power in single words and
detached adornment ; a law of decisive importance in several
passages, *e.g.* xiv. 30. Similarly he does not make such
frequent use of plays upon the thoughts and words as other
prophets, *e.g.* xv. 1-9 ; xvi. 7-12 ; Mic. ch. i., not to mention
later prophets : his paronomasiæ are rare, but in all cases the
more telling, surprising the hearer with great entire thoughts
in the briefest form, v. 7 ; i. 23 ; xxx. 7, 16 ; xxxii. 19 ; x.
30, sq.

Yesaya always conducts and unfolds the thought of his
discourses in an elevated and sublime manner ; he accomplishes
much with a few brief words, which, however, are always transparent and easily understood ; at the right moment he collects
and moderates with a firm hand an overflowing impetuous
wealth of thought, which might easily lose itself in the unde-
fined ; and without becoming prolix he thoroughly exhausts
and finishes everything he handles. This strict collectedness
is most admirable in shorter oracles, which consisting of briefly
projected pictures and thoughts give rise to foreboding without
end, while they are yet presented in a complete and clear form, as
viii. 6—ix. 6 ; xiv. 29-32 ; xviii. 1-7 ; whilst at most in the long

piece ch. xxviii.—xxxii., the style flags here and there for the
moment to rise immediately with all the greater force. With
this compressed wealth of thought and style, a comparison is
rarely detached for the purpose of explaining and completing
it by itself, xxx. 13, sq. ; xxxi. 4, 5 : usually it forces its way
forthwith into the midst of the exposition of a matter, and is
closely interwoven with it, in fact, often one simile upon
another : and yet the many threads of discourse, which for the
moment are confused, are always soon reduced to perfect trans-
parency again ; which is a special peculiarity of this prophet, a
freedom of which he alone is master.—Similarly the structure
of his verse is always full and yet firmly defined : but in this
our prophet does not make it a matter of great importance to
weigh his words with the scrupulousness of an artist; not in-
frequently he repeats the same word in two members, xxxi. 8 ;
xxxii. 17 ; xi. 5 ; xix. 13, as if with his great inner power and
beauty he less needed a scrupulous perfection of the exterior.
The structure of his strophes is always easy and well-rounded.

But the thing of chief importance is, that we are wholly
unable to name a special peculiarity and favourite manner of
style in the case of Yesaya, as we find in the case of other prophets. He is not the specially lyric, or the specially elegiac, or
the specially rhetorical and monitory prophet, as, for instance,
Yôél, Hoséa, Mikha, in whose writings a special manner is
predominant : but every kind of style and every variation of
exposition is at his command to meet the requirements of his
subject : and this it is which in respect of style constitutes his
greatness, as well as generally one of his most prominent
excellences. His fundamental peculiarity is only the exalted
majestic repose of style, proceeding from the full and sure
command of his subject. This repose by no means requires
that the language should never be more violently agitated and
not blaze up where the subject requires it, with greater
vehemence coming home to the hearer : but even the most
extreme agitation which here and there occurs is bridled by

this repose in the back-ground, and does not pass beyond its proper limits, and soon returns with higher self-mastery to its regular flow, not again to leave it, ii. 9—iii. 1 ; xxviii. 11-23 ; xxix. 9-14. And just as little does this composure of style require that the subject shall be handled in the same smooth way without variation of delivery : on the contrary, Yesaya is a master in these variations which are recommended by the relation the hearers sustain to the thought : if he wishes to bring right home to his hearers a truth which lies beyond common minds and is unwillingly heard, and prove it to them by their own confessions, he resorts to popular instances from common life, v. 1-6 ; xxviii. 23-29 : if he wishes to call the attention of the overwise to a new truth and future prospect, he surprises them with a brief oracle, clothed in the form of an enigma, in order to leave its solution to their acuteness, vii. 14-16 ; xxix. 1-8 ; if the unhappy remediless state of his hearers' minds leads to nothing but grief, his language becomes for a while a lyric of moaning and lamentation, i. 21-23 ; xxii. 4, sq. ; if the infatuated guides of the nation mock, he surpasses them with their own weapons, and lays them low with the terrible seriousness of divine irony, xxviii. 10-13 ; also an incidental ironical word slips from the prophet with his superior vision, xvii. 3 *b* : thus his style exhibits every variation, it is tender and severe, instructive and minatory, mournful and then joyous with divine joy, sarcastic and serious, but it always returns at the right moment to its original elevation and repose, and never loses the ingrained fundamental characteristic of divine seriousness. Exhortation and correction is never painfully striven for and produced : but a brief, sharp word of admonition after the discussion of a matter produces a more telling effect, i. 16, sq. ; xxviii. 22, an appeal apparently incidentally flowing from the subject is more convincing and powerful, ii. 22 ; xxxi. 6.

The pre-eminent literary greatness of Yesaya is also exhibited in the fact, that he is not less capable of appreciating the best pieces of earlier prophets, and receives some of them

more or less altered into his own productions at fitting places,
ch. xv. sq. ; xxi. 11, sq. ; xiii., sq. In his case this is no mark
of the unproductiveness of his own mind, but rather an un-
envious acknowledgment which he paid to the writings of
prophets of even an earlier age, and a sign of his learning and
taste.

II. It may be expected that the entire life of this prophet
will have corresponded to this elevation of his mind, and the
traces which we are able to discern fully confirm the expectation.

We know no other prophet in whose case his entire life was
all along so closely connected with his prophetic calling, and
who in return reacted so powerfully upon the life of the whole
community. He does not separate himself from full intercourse
with the nation and politics, like Elia and Elisha, as a hermit,
or as head of a mere school, but on the contrary continues as a
citizen of his city and father of a family in the midst of the
commotions and temptations of the wider and the narrower
world, making, however, himself and his whole house living representatives and witnesses of the higher truths which animate
his mind, as if it were by no means sufficient merely to proclaim
them with his mouth. When his mind is filled with any great
thought, it is as if his spirit urged him to coin the thought into
a short, clear name, and to call himself, or one of his new-born
children, by this name, in order that the thought itself might
continue to exist, and take even firmer root, and thus all the
members of his house appear as living symbols and memorials
of the prophetic truths, vii. 3 ; viii. 3, sq., 18 ; not without a
significance of this kind is his wife also called the prophetess
simply, viii. 3. Or he enshrines a thought of this kind, which
does not immediately strike his contemporaries, in an enduring
name or in a brief formula, and writes it as an eternal memorial
and a witness for the future upon a public tablet, viii. 1, sq. ;
xxx. 8. Thus in all cases the eternal truths take the form of
lasting and distinct forms in his mind, which he cannot confine

to his own breast, but casts them into the midst of life, that the world may recognise and retain them.

It is a similar consequence of his intensely energetic action upon the world, that he delights to give a *sign, i.e.* some external guarantee for his words, and a *prognostic* or a kind of visible indication of the future, whether it is asked for or not, for the purpose of drawing the resisting world the more powerfully to faith; see further, vii. 11, sq.; xx. 3; comp. xxxviii. 7, sq., 22 (a more particular explanation of the latter instance of a special kind belonging to the historical books). Even when a sign of this kind cannot immediately appear, and so produce faith, he nevertheless promises it to promote the clearness and certainty of his discourse, vii. 14; xxxvii. 30, just as generally he delights in clear divine signs and witnesses of the truth, and gladly mentions them, xix. 20. Here also Yesaya is in all cases the man of action, who not only bears the future in his own spirit, but himself begins it, and hastens it as it were with divine action, conducting the world as by higher power to the knowledge of its truths, whether it will or not. Although, on the other hand, it is mournful when an age requires such external proofs.

How Yesaya stood in awe of no human power, and was then least to be alarmed when the greatest efforts were made to restrain him, has already been remarked, but should be especially remembered in this connexion.

Inasmuch as he thus powerfully influenced the life of the whole kingdom, it could not but be that times of great critical moment should come, when the weal or woe of the whole community depended upon his insight and firmness, and when his true power gained the opportunity of manifesting its real greatness. Such times were, *e. g.* those of the Syro-Ephráimitish war against Jerusalem, when he had to fight against the king Ahaz and his house, against false prophets, against the whole nation, and when, finding that the king would not hear him, he still in the midst of general confusion defended with the most wonderful steadfastness and distinctness the eternal truths against all, vii. 1—ix. 6; then those of the last movements of the Assyrians and their attack upon Jerusalem, when he never lost for a single moment his exalted presence of mind, and both spoke openly against the Assyrians, and inspired the people with new courage, pointing always to the source of true help alone, x. 4 —xi. 16; xvii. 12—xviii. 7; xiv. 24-27; ch. xxxvi. and xxxvii.

But if in the momentous and critical moments of the age, and in the great affairs of the kingdom itself, he not only continued unchanged, but then first unfolded his greatest and most uncommon energies and evinced himself as the genuine man of the divine spirit, it followed that gradually his reputation and the confidence placed in him must have grown in the whole nation, and before his death he would see some of the happy fruits of such a life. And as a fact we can with certainty gather this from the few fragments of his history. At first he must certainly have had for a long time to contend with great difficulties, with persecution and public threats, so that at times he had to fight against despair, vi. 9-13; viii. 11-20, a condition which from xxix. 11, we may consider to have lasted until the commencement of the reign of Hisqia. But in the course of the reign of this king, we see him rise to that high stage of public confidence, both with the king and the people, the extent of which may be estimated by the narrative of ch. xxxvi.—xxxix. And it may be said that all that higher tone and greater prosperity which mark the reign of Hisqia, as well as the victory over the Assyrians in Yuda, is his work, and that thus in his advanced years, reverenced as the true protector of the whole community, he witnessed a new moral elevation of the nation, and himself enjoyed a portion of the happy repose for which in earlier years he had long wished in vain in the midst of severe struggles. The last piece of his which has been preserved, ch. xix., breathes at its close a wonderfully happy repose, the unique glimpse of a mind as it were already in glory.

It follows plainly from viii. 11—13, 16, that a more intimate circle of disciples and friends also gradually collected about him ; indeed, everything indicates that in ch. xxiii. and xxxiii. we have pieces preserved from his disciples which were received into his book, just as manifestly Mikha, one of his junior contemporaries, appears to have been aroused to the prophetic work by his example.

III. That a prophet of this character would make great use of his pen to influence men and to consign to the future memorials of his truths as witnesses, must be supposed from his whole character and actions, and is proved by certain intimations by himself, viii. 1, 16 ; xxx. 8 ; that in this his disciples were of great service to him, follows from viii. 16. Indeed, we can discover in these passages, that his written productions were of a double nature : for the nation at large he often wrote single memorial sentences, or names, upon a publicly exhibited tablet in great characters, viii. 1 ; xxx. 8 *a,* comp. Hab. ii. 2 ; while for those to whom the reading of learned books was more familiar, he wrote his longer discourses in books properly speaking, xxx. 8 *b* ; viii. 16, comp. the books xxix. 11, sq., 18 : and it is evident that the records of the latter class only have been preserved to us. It is not only in itself probable but can be concluded with certainty from the passages quoted, that he did not merely take up his pen once or twice in his long prophetic life, but as often as ever the importance of his matter and the time itself urged him to make records.

We might therefore suppose that all the oracles of his which have been preserved were written down as soon as they had been orally delivered, and that after a time a larger book gradually grew out of a collection of them. Nevertheless, a number of indications do not altogether confirm this supposition. It may be justly objected to this view, that oracles concerning foreign nations, such as xiv. 29-32 ; ch. xv., sq. ; xxi. 11, sq., 13-17, were hardly first spoken and then put into writing, and that such short pieces as most of them are could not be very well committed to writing singly but only in a larger book with many other pieces. It is, however, certain from the historical notes with which several pieces are introduced, that at least such pieces can have been written down only a considerable time after the oral oration was made, vi. 1; vii. 1; xiv. 28; xx. 1-3; the oration, ch. i., although in its historical basis it belongs to a pretty late period, and must have been committed to writing much later than many other pieces, manifestly professes to be a kind of general preface and introduction to a collection of several separate oracles.

We must therefore suppose that Yesaya's writings were of two kinds. He might publish single pieces soon after he had orally spoken upon the subjects with which they deal; and of this class are plainly the two largest pieces which we possess in the present book, ii. 2—v. 30, together with ix. 7—x. 4, the oldest piece from Yesaya's hand, and the piece, ch. xxviii.— xxxii., from a considerably later time; each of these two larger pieces shows that it is a separate production, which might have been originally published by itself just as well as the books of 'Amôs and Mikha, which are not much larger; and in neither of these two longer pieces is there a historical word added which might indicate that each was written soon after the oral delivery. But he will not have immediately written down in this manner everything that he as a prophet said or did or thought; and after he had worked for a long time the resolve might arise in his mind to collect in a larger, more historically planned, book all his prophetic oracles, acts and thoughts, including those which had never yet been recorded; and of course the pieces which had been previously published separately might be received into a collection of this kind. That Yesaya's literary efforts took this form also, we have at least one proof in the instance of one larger collected work: this is also the work which, according to all indications, he wrote at the commencement of the reign of Hisqia. For the piece, ch. i., which must have stood at the head of a larger book of this kind as a prologue worthy of it, falls in this period as to its historical contents ; the historical notes, which further all betray the same hand, bring us beyond the death of Ahaz, vi. 1; vii. 1; xiv. 28; and the short oracles concerning foreign nations, which could moreover find a place only in a larger work of this kind, belong with respect to their historical basis also to this time. From the last years of 'Uzzia, when he came forward as prophet, to the death of Ahaz, Yesaya had already worked long enough as prophet to bring together into a larger book his entire previous work ; and although the tone of his mind at that time, as immediately appears in the first piece which he placed after ch. i., in the recollection of the moment of his call, ch. vi., was generally full of dark forebodings after such bitter experiences and in a time which threatened such severe and general ruin, yet the new reign of Hisqia promised a better future, so that a hortative reference to his past experiences and a severe lesson for the future was quite reasonable ; the longer book would thus indicate the boundary line of two important periods of time, and very probably greatly aided the reformation which began under Hisqia.

Accordingly by carefully examining every detail and slowly advancing from step to step, we may venture the attempt to restore the original form of the larger book just mentioned from the scattered pieces of the present book. Such an attempt would seem indeed to be wrecked on the fact that a very considerable number of Yesayanic pieces according to all appearances have been lost. We might suppose this as something very probable : but there are the most distinct evidences of it. No one who is closely acquainted with Yesaya's characteristics and has carefully examined the important piece, vii. 1—ix. 6, will be able to deny that acc. vii. 3; viii. 18, the names of the prophet himself, and his son Sheâr-Yashûb likewise, must have been explained in earlier pieces, and probably, considering their high significance, much more at length than we at present find is the case with his other son, viii. 3, sq.; the explanation of

2   2

the name Yesaya in its higher sense probably followed immediately after ch. vi., and that of his son's name, Sheâr-Yashûb,
must likewise have gone before, and therewith some of the
greatest prophetic truths must have found their explanation.
And since the oldest written piece, ii. 2—v. 30; ix. 7—x. 4,
says nothing at all about a Messiah, while the piece, vii. 1—
ix. 6, in reality presupposes this idea, which was as new as it
was important, we have every reason to suppose that the very
piece in which this truth first appeared has been lost.

Nevertheless so many and such varied literary productions
of Yesaya's own pen have been preserved, that we need not
despair of forming firm conceptions as to the various ages, the
order of succession, and the plan and art of his separate
writings, if we only correctly discover and apply all the means
of proof which are at our disposal. The result of all these
careful enquiries is, that Yesaya, as far as we can now see,
published books not less than seven times during the course of
his long prophetic career; and if these have not all been completely preserved, we still possess, in the book that bears his
name, far more literary remains of his than of any other prophet
before Yéremyá. It is now necessary to make ourselves acquainted with these books separately and in the order of their
succession.*

I. The oldest Book of Yesaya's.

Ch. ii. 2—v. 25; ix. 7—x. 4; v. 26-30.

These pieces belong to <u>one great oration,</u> as appears from
the combined evidence; the piece, ch. ix. 7—x. 4, especially
must originally have had its place before v. 26, since it is intelligible there alone,† although in a certain respect it is easily
separable.

---

* Comp. the essay in the *Jahrbb. der Bibl. Wiss.* vii. p. 28-53.

† As was said as early as 1837 in the third number of the *Zeitschrift für die
Kunde des Morgenlandes;* although there the insertion before v. 25 was accepted,
which is less suitable.

The discourse belongs to the time when the Assyrians had long made the Northern kingdom tributary, but otherwise had not appeared as conquerors in Palestine, and were looked upon, in Yuda especially, as very distant and little known nations, whose future appearance for the correction of the two weak kingdoms was surmised by the prophet only, v. 26-30. In Samaria, to which the oration once specially turns aside, ix. 7-20, the king Péqach began to divert the internal disunion and lawlessness into forays against Yuda in order at the same time to strengthen his exhausted kingdom in this way, ix. 9, 20; and we see from 2 Kings xv. 37 that these attacks had begun even under Yotham, although for a long time they were certainly confined to the border fortresses and adjoining lands of Yuda, and did not threaten Jerusalem until a later period, vii. 1. In Jerusalem itself the weak king Ahaz, who, acc. 2 Kings xvi. 2 was but twenty years of age, had then just ascended the throne, since the words

> " My people's rulers are a child
> and women rule over it,"

only poetically divide into two members the short sentence, *" my people's rulers are a child (i.e.,* a youthful, unwise king) *and women* in the palace *;"* and Ahaz was not simply young when he became king, but very weak and unmanly, as he is generally known to us, so that these words, as far as they permitted an allusion, could point to him alone.

At this time Jerusalem was in almost undisturbed possession of the same high prosperity and proud security to which it had become accustomed under the previous kings who had been powerful as regards the surrounding nations. The repose and the power of the kingdom of Yuda, the conquest of Ailah, on the Red Sea, by Uzzia, 2 Kings xiv. 22; xvi. 6, and especially the prudence of the previous kings, had favoured the intercourse of trade, and the whole land had become uncommonly rich and prosperous, ii. 7; besides, the ancient prophetic promises of a future still higher prosperity of Jerusalem, as

2 *

Yôél, *e.g.* had proclaimed them, could be boasted of.   But the
extended intercourse with foreigners had also brought with it
a great deal of foreign superstition, idolatry, and many frivolous
manners, ii. 6-8, 18; the rapidly increasing wealth and the
security of the land had been productive of pride, luxury, and
light-mindedness, and the women especially, who in any kingdom indicate the measure of morality, were spoilt by luxury
and high life, iii. 16—iv. 1 ; the injustice too of the powerful in
the kingdom, the corruption of the judges, and the persecution
of the inhabitants who could not help themselves, these evils
which had long lain hidden, were promoted most seriously by
the weakness of the young king, iii. 12-15; v. 1, sq.; x. 1-4.
In reference to the great dangers which lay in this apparently
prosperous and secure state of things, the prophet had long
ago spoken under the previous kings, and called attention to
the operation of Yahvé which was bringing all these things
to a great judgment; but his warning words had been ridiculed
by the proud, careless, and to some extent insolent people,
v. 18-21; iii. 8, sq.; people considered themselves in Jerusalem
as powerful and secure under the protection of the peace existing between the Assyrians and themselves and the external
worship of Yahvé.   It was in presence of the most recent and
serious dangers of the kingdom that the prophetic zeal of
Yesaya was kindled, whose eye penetrated through the hollow-
ness of these brilliant externalities : with tremendous force he
pointed to the certainty and necessity of a higher judgment
before which all human arrogance must grow pale, ii. 9-11,
12-22; iii. 16 ; v. 15, sq.; ix. 8, and evidently laboured precisely at this period of the commencement of a new reign in
Yuda with the greatest energy.   At the opening of a new reign
the most varied efforts and hopes naturally wake up with an
uncommon vigour; and a multitude of indications show to us
that the prophets, whenever this was possible, were more active
than usual at such times, which were so critical for the mainte-
nance and prosperity of the kingdom.   While Yesaya was

certainly at that period most active in public affairs, he also
resolved at the same time to labour by his pen for the first
time in his life; and thus this book originated, which according
to all the evidence is his oldest, and in which he might, with a
skilful hand, include much that he had publicly spoken at an
earlier period during the first sixteen or seventeen years of his
prophetic life. But it is easy to note in the whole tone and
in the overwhelming vehemence of this oratiou how certainly
it dates from the earliest years of the most powerful of all
prophets.

At that time the ancient and exalted belief of the inviola-
bility of their city still possessed the minds of the inhabitants
of Jerusalem; in fact, up to that time, external calamities had
rarely befallen the proud city and brought her to reflection:
this is the first written oration, not delivered incidentally and
far from the capital, as in the case of 'Amôs and Hoséa, but in
its midst by its own prophet, in which the entire persuasion
with respect to the city's safety receives a crushing blow, and
it is clearly announced, that the entire kingdom must decline
and the capital be destroyed, the possibility of which was then
presented in the distance by the Assyrians, at least to the un-
clouded eye of the prophet. This is the true state of the case,
and therein lies the subject-matter and purport of this long
and powerful oration, which is also planned with great art and
upon a large scale in order to exhaust the subject. That the
judgment of Yahvé will come, that it must come before the
ancient promises with respect to the blessed times of Jerusalem
can be fulfilled,—this is the first and most important position
which the prophet has to prove, and in the delineation of which
he can at first scarcely express himself in calm words, from
painful indignation at the infatuated arrogance of the time,
ii. 2—iv. 6. After a brief pause he then, as in an entirely different frame of mind to which he had brought himself, begins
to shew the necessity of the judgment according to the confessions of the men themselves who were aimed at in his

oration, v. 1-24, which in the first part of his oration he was
prevented from showing by his overpowering feeling; and in
the last part he casts a few additional glances, retrospective
and circumspective, including Samaria also, in order to return
to the fundamental truth of a great impending judgment.
The whole oration, therefore, falls into three smaller ones, the
style of which grows increasingly calmer and more self-pos-
sessed.

1.   *A judgment precedes the blessed time!* ch. ii. 2—iv. 6.

The blessed time promised by earlier prophets will indeed
come, but not before a severe judgment of all haughty men
who have fallen away from Yahvé! This thought is unfolded
in six somewhat lengthy strophes, of which the last only is
observably shorter and more rapid. At the head Yesaya places
one of the sublimest and most beautiful descriptions of the
blessed age from an earlier prophet (see under Yôél above,
vol. I. p. 114), to the certain hope of which he holds as fast as
any one, and in the image of which the nation as it now is may
mirror itself: but, alas, how far distant from it is this proud
Israel of to-day, against which Yahvé must rather be angry,
which must creep away to hide itself from his alarming
approach to judgment! ii. 2-11. Thus in the very first
strophe the oration which began so sweetly passes over into
the raging storm of terrible threatening, and the next three
strophes, ii. 12—iii. 15, starting from this elevation, to which
the discourse has so suddenly soared, picture with somewhat
more calmness, but all along in high-running waves of language, this judgment-day thus alarmingly announced, the
second showing *that* it is coming, the third, *how* it comes, the
fourth indicating *wherefore* it comes, entering somewhat more
circumstantially into its causes; these three strophes are more
closely connected with each other as the amplification of the
leading thought, and all begin with the amplifying particle
כִּי, *for*. Then, after the fifth, iii. 16—iv. 1, has directed a
similar threat against the haughty women especially, the ora-

tion closes with the sixth iv. 2-6, which recurs to the opening
thought, that the blessed time will come with its full glory
after such a general and severe judgment.

II.   1.

2   " And then at the end of the days the mountain
       of the house of Yahvé will be placed upon the
       top of the mountains, and be exalted before hills |

peoples   that all the Heathen may flow into it; || and many
       nations will go and say ' Come! let us ascend to
       the mountain of Yahvé, to the house of the God of
       Yaqob, | that he may teach us of his ways, and we
       may walk in his paths!' | for from Ssion will go forth
       the doctrine, and Yahvé's word from Jerusalem. ||
       Then he judgeth between the Heathen, and giveth
       decision to many nations: | and they will forge
       their swords into hoes, and their spears into
       pruning-knives, | nation against nation will not
       raise the sword, and not learn war any more." ||

5   House of Yaqob! | come and let us walk in the
       light of Yahvé! || — But thou hast cast off thy
       people the house of Yaqob, because they are full
       of soothsaying and augury like the Philistines, |
       and like the children of strangers conjure, || and
       his land was filled with silver and gold, so that
       there is no end to his treasures, | and his land was
       filled with horses, so that there is no end to his
       chariots, || and his land was filled with idols, | to
       the work of their hands they do homage, to that
       their fingers have made! || — Then men sink and

the man falleth down, | and forgive them not! || —

10 Enter into the rock and hide thee in the dust |
before Yahvé's terror fleeing and the splendour of
his majesty! || The haughty eyes of mankind are
cast down, and men's pride sinketh, | and Yahvé
alone is exalted on that day! ||

2.

For a day hath Yahvé of hosts upon everything
proud and high, | and upon everything exalted that
it should bow down, || and upon all cedars of
Libanon the high and the exalted, | and upon all
the oaks of Bashan,|| and upon all the high moun-

15 tains | and upon all the exalted hills, || and upon
every prominent tower | and upon every defenced
wall, || and upon all the Tarshish-ships, | and upon
all watch-towers of delight; || so that man's
haughtiness sinketh and men's pride boweth, |
and Yahvé is exalted alone on that day. || —But
the idols they will wholly abandon; || and
[people] will enter into rock-caverns and dust-holes
fleeing before Yahvé's terrors | and before the splen-
dour of his majesty, when he ariseth to shake the

20 earth. || —On that day men will cast their silver
idols and their golden idols, which they made
them to do homage to, to the moles and to the
bats, || in order to enter into the clefts of the
rocks and into the rents of the chasms | before
Yahvé's terrors fleeing and before the splendour of
his majesty, when he ariseth to shake the earth. ||
O cease ye from man in whose nostrils is a breath: |
for in what is he to be considered? ||

III.　　　　　　3.

1　　　For behold the Lord Yahvé of Hosts removeth
from Jerusalem and from Yuda staff and stay, |
every staff of bread and every staff of water, ||
hero and man-of-war, | judge and prophet, sooth-
sayer aud elder, || the captain of fifty and the man of
repute, | and counsellor and wizard and magician, ||
and I make children to be their princes | and baby-
5　　boys shall rule over them. || Then the nation is
in strife man against man and neighbour against
neighbour, | they are in confusion—the boy against
the old-man and the base against the honourable : ||
when one taketh hold of the other in his father's
house: "a garment hast thou, chief shalt thou be
to us | and these ruins shall be under thy hand !" ||
—he will begin on that day thus: "I will be no
binder-up, since in my house is no bread and no
garment, | ye shall not appoint me a chief of the
people !" ||

4.

For Jerusalem stumbleth and Yuda falleth, |
because their tongue and their deeds are against
Yahvé, to provoke the eyes of his majesty; || the
hardness of their countenance witnessed against
them, and their sin they revealed like Sodóm un-
disguisedly : | woe to their soul, for to themselves
10　　they did evil ! || Say of the righteous to him it is
well, | for the fruit of their deeds they will enjoy; ||
woe, to the unrighteous it is evil, | for the device of
his hands will be repaid him ! || —My people's com-

manders are a child, and women rule over it; | my people—thy guides are misleaders, and the way of thy paths they have spoilt. || There standeth Yahvé to contend | and ariseth to judge nations! || Yahvé will enter into judgment with his people's elders and princes | "and ye have fed off the vineyard, the sufferers' spoil is in your houses?" ||

-15 "For what do ye tread upon my people, and grind the sufferers' face?" | saith the Lord Yahvé of Hosts. ||

5.

And Yahvé said :

Because the daughters of Ssion have become haughty and walk with necks held up and rolling eyes, | tripping tripping they walk and tinkle with their anklets: || so the Lord maketh scabby the crown of the daughters of Ssion, | and Yahvé will make bare their shame. || On that day the Lord will remove the adornment of the anklets and of the little suns and moons, || of the ear-drops and of

20 the necklaces and of the fine veils, || of the coronets and of the bracelets and of the girdles, and of the smelling-bottles and of the amulets, || and of the finger- and nose-rings, || of the holiday-garments and of the fine robes, and of the fine mantles and of the pockets, || of the gauzes and of the shifts, and of the head-bands and of the great veils ; || and then—instead of sweet-smell there will be putre-faction, and instead of the girdle a cord, | and instead of artificial curling baldness, and instead of

the breadth of a mantle girding of sackcloth | a
brand instead of beauty ! ‖—Thy men (Ssion!) will
fall by the sword, | and thy troops by the war : ‖
25 and—her gates sigh and moan, | and emptied she
IV. will sit on the ground. ‖ Then seven women lay hold
1 of one man on that day saying " Our own bread
we will eat and clothe ourselves with our own
clothing : | only let thy name be called over us,
take away our disgrace !" ‖

6.

On that day Yahvé's shoot will be for adornment
and honour | and the land's fruit for pride and for
ornament | to the remnant of Israel. ‖ And then—
whoever is left in Ssion and remaineth in Jerusalem
will be called holy, | every one who is written down
to have life in Jerusalem. ‖ —When the Lord will
wash away the filth of the daughters of Ssion and
purify Jerusalem's blood-guiltiness out of its midst |
5 by the spirit of right and the spirit of fire, ‖ then
Yahvé createth over the whole space of the moun-
tain of Ssion and over its festive assembly | cloud
by day and smoke, and the gleam of flaming fire
by night : | for over every majesty is a canopy ; ‖
and it will be a tabernacle for shade by day from
heat, ‖ and for refuge and for protection from tempest and from rain.‖

1. The detached passage, ~~vv. 2-4~~, ^{2:2-4} must have been borrowed
from the close of an ancient oracle. When the true religion
and doctrine (that of Ssion) shall be recognised and desired by
all nations, which must at length be the case (at the end of the

days), and which is here, ver. 3 *b*, merely introduced in a parenthesis as a well-established truth, then Ssion, which is at present
so small, will as it were be pre-eminent above all mountains,
and be visible from afar as the holy mountain of all nations
(comp. on Ps. xlviii. 3 ; lxviii. 17), so that the most distant
Heathen make pilgrimages to it, that they also there may receive
from the true God teaching and guidance in life ; and he who
can best teach and judge will also actually establish amongst
them reconciliation and peace, so that then there comes the
beautiful age when universal peace prevails, as is more fully
amplified in the passage, Mic. iv. 5, to its close.—Yesaya then,
ver. 5, makes a rapid transition to his own words, with the
appeal to Israel to walk with him in the light of Yahvé, to submit itself to the enlightening and teaching of Yahvé, who has
given them such great promises, and to listen further to his
voice as the prophet will explain to them, Ps. xxxvi. 10.

But when Yesaya would prefer immediately to connect his
own cheering promises with those, he is overcome by the painful feeling of how far he is from being able to do this at once,
since the nation has precisely at this moment departed so far
from Yahvé ; and turning his face with inexpressible pain from
the people to whom he had just intended to speak face to face,
and turning to Yahvé, he exclaims : but thou hast rejected thy
people Yaqob, because it is full of quite other things than thy
fear, and appears to be wholly unable in its pride to get enough
of godless things ! vv. 6-8. It is full of foreign, un-Mosaic
superstitions, customs, and usages, such as magicians, idol-
priests, and adventurers teach, comp. below, iii. 3, sq. : viii.
19 ; full of treasures gained by wealthy trade, but, alas, only
urged by an immoderate desire for wealth, like Tyre for instance, and has become luxurious thereby, Zakh. ix. 3, sq. ; full
of horses and chariots for war, whereby it imagines it has made
itself secure, comp. above on Hos. xiv. 4 ; full, lastly, of what is
most disgraceful for Israel—of idols ! But by such means, by
proud pursuit of all these ungodly things, and again by such

homage to idols, man lowers himself, becomes unworthy to appear before Yahvé, and to belong to his people; but as if this with wonderful rapidity had suddenly dawned with overwhelming force upon the prophet's mind (and this judgment must come necessarily suddenly, and is already as good as certain), there is an involuntary transition in the prophet's language, ver. 9, and he exclaims aloud, how certainly men will fall under the divine judgment and need hope for no forgiveness! vv. 11, 17; v. 15, sq.—But now the prophet, who had just turned his face in the deepest grief from the people and had spoken only to God, turns his face immediately to the people again, as it were under the irresistible power of divine certainty which he had just received, and as in a voice of thunder, ver. 10, sq., calls, as if seized not so much by the consuming fire of the most righteous indignation as by compassion, to *men* and the human element in Israel which has gone so much astray, and which has nevertheless so blindly lifted itself up against the divine will : Away with thee! creep into rocks and dust before Yahvé, who is coming to judgment in his terrible majesty! Human pride must bow, divine truth alone avail at the day of judgment.

This very first strophe is an exceedingly good illustration of the marvellous power and overwhelming force of Yesaya's style. No oration can begin more calmly than this and give fewer indications at the commencement of the storm with which it will close. The prophet appears before an assembly of the people, perhaps on a Sabbath, with the book of Yôél's prophecies, which at that early period was certainly generally held in high estimation; he reads from it an attractive passage, flattering to the inhabitants of Jerusalem, and wishes to be allowed to speak further upon this passage which concerns the glorification of Israel and Jerusalem. But he is scarcely beginning actually to speak to the assembled people, his eye has hardly wandered over the Israel which stands before him, this people which claims to be Yahvé's people, when he can see nothing before him but a multitude of conjurers, of gold and silver, of horses, of idols; the mouth which was on the point of speaking of the Messianic prosperity is closed, and turning his face and his words to God he is able only with stifled sobs to complain over this nation which is now necessarily rejected before Him, vv. 6-8. But just at this moment he is suddenly overpowered by a vision of the divine irrecoverableness of this nation; an irrecoverableness necessarily growing out of such a condition as he beholds the people in, and by the dreadful power over the people of the curse which he cannot restrain, ver. 9: so that, as if the spirit still more strongly impelled him between these two fires of the most terrible contraries to ward off from the nation the horrible thing which threatens it, he turns his face towards it again, and, like one who will address a final monitory word to a condemned criminal, he calls to the nation which is threatened by the rage of the last divine judgment, and yet proudly turned against God, only quickly to deliver itself, to bow down in the dust before the glory which approaches to punish! ver. 10. How entirely different from the beginning is the close of this strophe, and what rapid transitions of experience and feeling occur during its course! A whole life-drama lies here between the beginning and the end; the change cannot be more marked and rapid, and at the same time more necessary than it is here. But Yesaya has seized the mind of the people with irresistible power and carried it to the point he desired: they are astonished, they tremble, but he is able the more quietly to begin the discussion and proof of what he has to say.—In this way we must rediscover the entire sense of everything in this strophe, even the smallest detail, to be able correctly to appreciate not only it but also all that follows.

2. There is no doubt but *that* the judgment-day of Yahvé will come, as little as that then the haughtiness of all those men who confide in idols will be brought low : thus the last words of the previous strophe, which were almost too rapid and

alarming, are here further and more calmly explained, the discourse ending three times in a re-echo of the former strophe,
that then their pride will be laid low and their confidence in
the idols miserably creep away, as if, notwithstanding the
greater calmness, the thunder of the ending of the first strophe
was still heard reverberating in gradually diminishing waves of
sound. (1.) vv. 12-17, Yahvé has a day upon every high and
proud thing on the earth so that it may bow, nothing on earth
being too high for him and his day of judgment: and if the
storm of Yahvé, as he comes to judgment in tempest and earthquake, drives destructively over all the giant trees of Lebanon
and Bashan, mountains and hills, towers and high fortress-
walls, over the tall ships sailing to Tarshîsh, Ps. xlviii. 8, and
the lofty watch-towers of pleasures, how can weak, puny man
then continue in his defiance and pride?—(2.) ver. 18, sq.: But
the idols, which were mentioned just before, will then be all
abandoned, inasmuch as they whom the idols ought but will be
unable to assist run to hide themselves; for—(3.) vv. 20-22,
at first indeed their worshippers, in their flight from the judge
who is coming in the earthquake, wish to take these beautiful
images with them, but soon in their hurry and alarm cast them
away in the first corner that offers, where filthy, disgusting
animals may creep over and house among them, so that getting
rid of their gods they may only save themselves ('Amôs iv. 3;
Hos. x. 8). When it is seen how easily even the proudest man
falls, how, after all, the life of even the most powerful and most
defiant of men hangs only upon a weak puff of air, a breath,
over which he himself has no power, how can confidence be
placed in him! ver. 22.

3. It was not for no purpose that the exclamation was made
at the end of the previous strophe, that it was time to cease to
trust in mortal men instead of in Yahvé alone; for those men
whom the misguided nation at present follows, may indeed be
the rulers of the existing kingdom, but if an enquiry is made
as to the manner, the *how*, of the approach of the judgment,

it will appear that this forms one chief element of it, that precisely the existing rulers of every class, all the various supports
of the kingdom and its government, must especially fall under
the approaching judgment (a powerful conqueror leading them
away captive, v. 26, sq.) so that then, when the most necessary
upholders of government have been removed, the most
dreadful disorder and corruption, society reduced to an interne-
cine battle, the end of the existing order of things, will be produced amidst the ruins of the nation and the state, as is
described very graphically, vv. 4-7, probably in accordance
with the experience of the Northern kingdom, which was
present to the mind of the prophet.   All the various supports
of the kingdom and government (the authorities as many prefer
now to call them,) will be removed, military and civil, the
counsellors of the prince and those of the people, the officers
and those otherwise most looked up to, the genuine and the false
prophets; but it must be allowed that the latter are much the
more numerous and varied, and it is precisely they whom the
misled people trust, the idol-prophets (soothsayers) and
magicians, with magic arts or magic words; as is significantly
expressly mentioned just at the end of the enumerations, ver. 2,
sq., comp. viii. 19.   And yet this staff and this stay, *i.e.* all
these supports of various kinds, although to a certain extent
they were very bad, are the *necessary* supports of the kingdom,
without which the kingdom and its citizens cannot *live*, its bread
and its water, ver. 1, Ez. iv. 16; v. 16: when therefore they
have been removed, *e.g.* by being taken into captivity, the
most terrible anarchy must commence, when in incessant
internal feuds, oppression, and uproar, only the most reckless
and daring for a moment obtain power, ver. 4, sq., and when a
well intentioned citizen in vain (privately in the house of his
father, for publicly it could no longer be done) asks a man
whose outward appearance has still some promise of uprightness, to take the command of this falling, ruined house, the
kingdom.   *Binder-up*, uniter, ver. 7, one who will hold

together what has fallen into ruins, adjuster, subduer, Job xxxiv. 17.

4. The kingdom falls into ruins, as was just said, *because* it suffers inequality and unrighteousness in the nation, ver. 14, sq., to grow, and always so wickedly repulsed the prophets which rebuked it : but then it was not so much these men who were mocked as God, and his judgment comes notwithstanding, although men make no secret of their perverse speech and action, revolting with a brazen face against Yahvé and the truth, as if it were their purpose to vex the majesty of the Allwise and Allseeing ! In the consideration of such perversity, which must necessarily bring its own punishment ultimately, the prophet's discourse is seized by a grief hard to control, and proclaiming the simple laws of eternal righteousness and retri-bution, it resolves itself into mourning over those who are thus blinded, who in their unrighteousness only injure themselves, vv. 9 *b*—11. But after a brief pause the prophet collects him-self and rises from this sympathetic sorrow with irrepressible force against the chief originators of such mournful perversity, the leaders and rulers themselves, presenting, ver. 12, an over-whelming threat and a description of the true judge, how He is at hand to contend with them as well as with the whole world (*nations,* ver. 13, like Ps. vii. 9 ; lvii. 6, 12), how He in anger accuses them in broken almost uncontrolled language (Ps. ii. 6) of having destroyed the beautiful vineyard they were appointed to keep, v. 1-7, and calls them to a strict ac-count, *wherefore* they trod down *his* people (this vineyard) and even repulsed and ground the face of the sufferers seeking help, vv. 13-15 ? In this strophe which thus alternates between contemplation, mourning and threatening, there is manifest, just as at the end of all these three more closely connected ones, an uncommon power of language, and the progressive threat, irresistible to a degree, of the last verse most effectively ends the strophe. The further delineation of the sins of the mag-nates is deferred to the second main section. What, however,

5. has to be said with respect to the wives of these magnates, who are in their way so luxurious, is immediately briefly summarized, ver. 16, sq. Their luxurious haughtiness must be punished by a corresponding humiliation, losing their husbands in the war, they will sink into the lowest misery, or even be violated by their barbarous conquerors.—This is then delineated in detail, how, robbed of all the objects of their pride by the plundering enemy, vv. 18-23, they will sink into the most pitiable outward condition, ver. 24; how when the young men of the city shall have fallen in disastrous battle, and the whole of the city shall be prostrate with grief, old men and women and children will publicly lament and wail at the gates, *i. e.* in the market-places, ver. 25, sq. (Job ii. 13), these women, who were once in such luxury, will then in vain seek a husband as protection and in outward honour of the marriage state, iv. 1 (1 Cor. vii. 36). How voluptuous these women are is shown by this long catalogue of the articles of their toilet, vv. 18-23, although we need not suppose that they were all, as they are here enumerated, worn at the same time by one woman. However, in this long list of all possible trinkets, the order is observed that their anklets are first mentioned because they had been already referred to in the general description, ver. 16; costly foot-clasps and little foot-chains are intended, with which they trip along in short steps, liking to make a jingling sound to attract attention (Ibn-Khacan, p. 36. 3; 47. 4, comp. p. 122, 162, Journ. as. 1842, I. p. 449, Urvaci dram., p. 48. 8). This description of the adornment of the feet is followed by that of the fine ornaments of the head and the other parts of the body, the transition being made, ver. 22, sq., to the larger materials and coverings of the body. But instead of sweet scents which float around them, there will then be the smell of putrefaction from the multitude of corpses; instead of the beautiful girdle a cord round the body for leading them away as slaves (comp. xxiii. 10); further, instead of beautifully frizzled hair, baldness; instead of the breadth of a costly mantle, the confined girding of sack-

cloth about the naked body, both the baldness and the sackcloth
being the signs of mourning for the death of their husbands
and other brave men in the war; finally, a brand, as it is im-
printed on slaves, instead of their beautifully preserved faces.

6. When therefore, concludes the last strophe briefly, and as
if gladly reverting to the blessed end in view, such a judgment
has come, or as is said, ver. 4, supplying an omission, when
Yáhvé shall have washed away the moral impurity of those
sinfully adorned women, and shall have removed the blood-
drops of those unjustly murdered, whose blood, acc. iii. 14, sq.,
cleaves to the magnates of Jerusalem, effecting both by a spirit
which is at the same time righteously judicial and irresistibly
powerful, destroying all that is evil with purifying fire (i. 25;
vi. 13; Matt. iii. 11)—when this has taken place, and not till
then, the promised blessed age will come, of which that ancient
prophet speaks, ii. 2-4, which no one can long to see more than
Yesaya, and which he now describes in a few exalted pictures
after his own manner.   But it is only gradually that his thought
and language rise again to that height of prophetic vision with
which he began, ii. 2-4: accordingly he says the Messianic age
will come—(1) iv. 2, when, in the estimation of the purified and
reformed Israel, which has not been carried off by the judgment, not foreign people and things as at present, ii. 6, sq. ;
iii. 2, sq., 18, sq., but the marvellous wealth and fruitfulness of
their own land, which Yahvé then causes to sprout forth, will
constitute their adornment and pride (comp. v. 6, 10; xxviii.
5; xxx. 23, sq.; Joel iv. 18; Amos ix. 13; Hos. ii. 23, sq.;
xiv. 8 ;—(2) ver. 3, when every individual of that remnant, that
is, as many of them as have been previously called by the
eternal divine grace to life in the new Jerusalem (for it lies in
the idea of this grace that if not all yet some actually attain
to that life, Joel iii. 5; Ez. xxxii. 32; Apoc. iii. 5; xx. 12),
will be holy, and acknowledged and extolled as such.—But if
the divine prosperity is thus in beautiful harmony both out-
wardly, ver. 2, and inwardly, ver. 3, then comes—(3), vv. 4-6,

3 *

naturally the external exaltation also, inasmuch as at last the place, which is thus august and glorious on account of the true holiness dwelling within it, is also a place distinguished for the protection and peace which it affords its inhabitants, as if the Mosaic ark of covenant were placed there for ever, with its pillar of cloud and fire (acc. Num. ix. 15-23 ; Ex. xxxiii. 7-11 ; xl. 34, sq.) ; as indeed always, even in modern and humbler things, it is the case, that wherever there is true spiritual exaltation and majesty, should it be only that of a king, *e.g.* of the present day, then there is around it a covering and a protection, a nimbus, which keeps the world away from it. But at the very commencement of the description of the third and highest stage, the prophet cannot sufficiently emphasize, ver. 4, the main condition under which the Messianic consummation is alone possible, as it was explained above.

How little the words ii. 2-4, whether in Yesaya or in Mikha, are original, may also be seen from the fact, that each passage presents about an equal number of readings which are scarcely original. In Mikha we have the better reading עמים instead of כל הגוים, v. 2, as agreeing better with vv. 3 and 4 ; in ver. 4 also the first two small members, especially when we consider the beautiful structure of the members in Yôél, are more correct in Mikha, and it is likewise certainly better to read ישאו instead of ישא comp. iii. 5. On the other hand, the addition *afar off* after *numerous nations* in Mikh. ver. 3, (here ver. 4,) is redundant, and rather spoils the structure of the verse.

It cannot be doubted that כִּי, ii. 6, in a connexion of this kind can express an antithesis, acc. § 354 *a*. At first sight the first words, ver. 6, may appear to mean, *thou hast cast off thy nation,* = *thy nationality, O house of Israel !* But further consideration shows that this gives no sense here. That God is addressed, appears also from ver. 9 ; and the change of person addressed in ver. 5 and ver. 6, is not more surprising than that in ver. 9 and ver. 10.—The following words only make any

real difficulty.   If the reading were correct, we should have to
understand them thus : *they are full from the East and practise
magic like the Philistines*, as if עֹנְנִים were a participle, and it
was intended that the Philistines dwelling in the south-west
should form the antithesis to the Easterns, and both clauses
should only say, that conjurers of all kinds had poured in upon
Israel *from all quarters of the world*.   But the sentence, *they
are full from the East*, would be too indefinite ; in that case we
should at least have to suppose that קֶסֶם or לְקֶסֶם, acc. to iii. 2,
had dropped out before מִקֶּדֶם : *they are full of soothsaying from
the East*.   But since עֹנְנִים, acc. § 179 *a*, can denote *augury*, the
sense of the first part of the verse is most easily recovered by
reading מִקְסָם, Ez. xii. 24 ; xxiii. 7, instead of מִקֶּדֶם.   The last
words might be understood as, *and of children of strangers they
have abundance*, comp. סָפַק *to flow*, Job xx. 22, with ספה *to
pour*, and with reference to בְּ Ps. lxxxviii. 4 : in which case a
corresponding idea would be found for that of *fulness* in the
first member, and the foreigners would be specially such men
as those who are intended, viii. 19 ; xxii. 16.   But since two
kinds of superstition are mentioned, it is more probable the
pouring in signifies the superstition of being able to prophesy
by means of a cup consecrated by an idol priest, pouring water
and wine into it, and observing the mixture, an art which,
acc. Gen. xliv. 5, was once highly esteemed in Egypt and
considered as a privilege of priests and kings, and may have
spread at this time into Palestine, amongst the populace even.
If we further read with many MSS. בִּילְדֵי instead of בְּיַלְדֵי,
this member amply corresponds with the first, and three kinds
of superstition are here distinguished, just as in iii. 2, sq., both
passages placing *soothsaying* at the head.

Similarly the words, ii. 9, are in themselves difficult : but if
an accurate comparison is made with the corresponding passages
it appears nothing is here referred to but the righteous humiliation of the haughtiness, and that the words are so brief only
because the whole language is here strained to the highest

pitch. *Men* (Germ. *Mensch*) and *man* (Germ. *Mann*) denote
here, as Ps. xlix. 3, as antithesis the entire race of mankind,
the low and the high.   The verb וַיִּשַּׁח is accordingly in its
prophetic force clear, § 342 *c*.

On ii. 16.   In this connexion the obscure combination
שְׂכִיּוֹת הַחֶמְדָּה manifestly denotes something comparable with
the highest ships in height ; and we may compare the Chald.
סָכוּתָא, *watch-tower*, properly *specula*, from שׂכה, *to look*, and
then suppose places of outlook, or towers, built in gardens for
pleasure, for which meaning exactly similar passages may be
quoted, xxiii. 13; xxxii. 12 and 14; Ez. xxvi. 12. A less
probable conjecture is idols, (מַשְׂכִּית Lev. xxvi. 1 ; Num.
xxxiii. 52,) of wicked pleasure, i. 29 ; xliv. 9, namely, high
statues, obelisks and the like, to which the wicked passions of
the people were then attached ; so that yet another idolatrous
object would be named here at the close.

If יחלף ii. 18, means *to pass away*, the sentence must be
constructed according to the rare manner, § 308 : *the idols—
everything* of them *will pass away*. But neither is this construction here quite clear, nor is the sense it yields quite suitable in
this connexion. It is much better to take חלף after the analogy
of Arab. *khalf* as *to leave behind*, abandon, in flight to leave
them lying ; the change from the singular to the plural, vv. 18
and 19, in general discourse is not surprising, and כָּלִיל is thus
easily understood. If this signification *to leave behind* is
established, we may with greatest certainty understand בְּנֵי חֲלוֹף
Prov. xxxi. 8, as people *abandoned* of their elders and all other
men, and as in that sense miserable.—On לַחְפֹּר פֵּרוֹת, ver. 20, see
§ 157 *c ;* comp. also Layard's *Discoveries*, p. 307, sq.

The double gender of *staff and stay*, iii. 1, is only intended
to make the thought more general, acc. § 172 *c* : the addition
every staff of bread and every staff of water, generalizes it in a
similar way in the midst of its nearer definition, this addition
including all the supports without which that which is here
alone intended, the kingdom, cannot live or last. If the meaning

of the words, ver. 1, was up to this point doubtful, it is made
sufficiently clear by the long enumeration of the individuals;
and in this enumeration nothing is more remarkable than that
the long list twice ends, as if intentionally, with the promoters
of superstition, just as Yesaya had from the first, ii. 6, mentioned
these principally as the promoters of the national misery : the
prophet, who might be a true one, is immediately followed by
the *soothsayer,* and at the end bringing up the train appear *the
magician with enchantments* and *the magician with spells.*
The two latter betray their Syrian origin by their names, just as
לֶחֶם does, whilst Syr. *luchosho* (Lag. *anal.* p. 47, 6), occurs in
the simple meaning *whispering,* the *master* of the חֲרָשִׁים *arts* (in
the sense of magical arts) answers exactly to Syr. *charōshō* (Knös.
chrest. p. 39. 6; 50, 5) ; and originally the distinction between
the two must have been that the latter endeavoured to accomplish everything by manual enchantments and the former by
verbal.　But we cannot help seeing that the enumeration of
these eleven kinds of national supports does not form a very
perfect series, especially as the *Elder* stands too isolated at the
end of ver. 2 ; and since the LXX. begin with γίγαντα καὶ
ἰσχύοντα a better series is recovered if we, (1) introduce such
a word as וְעִזּוּז according to Is. xliii. 17, after גִּבּוֹר, so that three
kinds of warriors come before all the rest : *Gibbors* first, as in
ancient times (*Hist. of Israel,* iii. p. 139, (iii. p. 189, sq.), next
Mighty-men, by whom probably *horsemen* are intended, acc.
ii. 6. and other *soldiers ;* then we have, (2) *judge and prophet
and soothsayer,* a trias similarly ; thereupon, (3) the *Elders, i.e.*
representatives of the people, (see *Alterth.* p. 328, sq. (284, sq.),
and *Hist. of Israel,* iii. p. 11, (iii. p. 17,) *captains* and other *men
of repute* not in office ; finally, (4) appear royal *counsellors,
magicians,* and *enchanters.*　The LXX. in their time read also
וְיָשָׁר.—But it is equally remarkable that Yesaya should again
rank all these twelve classes together, ver. 14, as *Elders and
Princes, i.e.* representatives of the people and officials, not sparing
the former in the least.—As to תַּעֲלוּלִים iii. 4, comp. 167 *b.*

הַהָבָרַת iii. 9, with this punctuation is most likely derived from הכיר with the meaning *their partiality*. But this sense does not harmonise with ver. 8, sq., where the open insolence of their words and deeds is described in general as a witness against them; accordingly הכר, Job xix. 3, should be compared.—*The way of thy paths*, iii. 12, the way in which thou must move and act, the course of thy life.—At iii. 13, as at ii. 9, a divine vision comes upon the prophet : the meaning of which he expounds more calmly, ver. 14.

The possibility of *And Yahve said*, iii. 16, is explained, Vol. I. p. 77.

The word מְשַׂקְּרוֹת iii. 16, which occurs here only, at first sight might be derived from the Aramaic *sekar*, which with *shĕkar* is related to the Hebrew שֶׁקֶר *a lie* and means *fucus*, it would then have to be taken with the Targum as the favourite black colouring for the eyes. But this comparatively innocent adorning or painting of the eyes is represented quite differently Ez. xxiii. 40 ; 2 Kings ix. 30 ; Jer. iv. 30 ; the primary meaning of Arab. *shukra* (Abulf. *ann*. ii. p. 70. 1) rather points to the sense *redden ;* and in this place it is only the ostentatious, insolent and lascivious walking and bearing of these women which is described. It is better therefore to take this word as meaning *to make the eyes spring*, leap, causing them to roll wantonly, from the Aramaic סְקַר as the same as זָקַר ; comp. the *Jahrbb. der Bibl. Wiss.* vii. p. 33.

On iii. 18-23. The correct understanding of several of the difficult names of these articles of attire is greatly aided by observing the order in which they follow, and the whole meaning of the context. Thus at the commencement שביסים cannot mean *hair-braids*, LXX. ἐμπλόκια, 1 Pet. iii. 3, although such artificial hair-dressing is mentioned, ver. 24 ; for that is not an adornment which belongs to this series and which the enemy could plunder ; the word, probably borrowed from Arabian tribes, is therefore, like the following, a diminutive for שמים, acc. § 167 *a*, and the small, *i.e.* golden suns and crescents, (comp. John

Wilson's *Lands of the Bible*, ii. p. 337,) might be fastened to the hair or hang from the breast, while the scent bottles and amulets were probably half hid in the bosom. פְּאֵר ver. 20, comp. Isa. lxi. 10, must be a handsome, probably golden, head-dress, a kind of diadem, quite different from the high and wide head-wrap of some kind of cloth, צָנִיף ver. 23. And that גָּלְיוֹן is not a hand-mirror, as the Vulgate has it, is shown by its position; it is therefore a fine transparent material, Arab. *jalwa*, according to the LXX. Further, the long series of things is here as little as above, iii. 2, sq., without an evident arrangement: and it is easy to see that at first three objects are always taken together, until in the fourth set they are fittingly extended to four, whilst in the case of the large ornaments, ver. 22, sq., two fours follow. The accents must be corrected accordingly.

iii. 24, the word חֲגוֹרָה is used instead of קִשּׁוּר ver. 20, since the same word is not repeated without reason.—On מַעֲשֶׂה מִקְשֶׁה see § 287 *h*.—פְּתִיגִיל must necessarily (since no word of such a formation exists) be written as two words, as is also shown by the analogy of the two corresponding words, *the breadth of a mantle*, inasmuch as גִיל like Syr. *gallō* and *gullětho* from the same root גלל (to roll, to wrap) can denote a *broad mantle*, answering to the garments named, ver. 22.

The fresh and more powerful re-commencement, iii. 25, in the midst of the strophe is made very suitably with the appeal to Ssion; but the level of ordinary discourse is immediately resumed, ver. 26, inasmuch as the future after all is the great object of attention.

הֵדִיחַ iv. 4, has nothing to do with דָּחָה to *cast forth*, but interchanges in the root with לוּחַ and accordingly answers to the German *klären*, and English *purify*; comp. *Lehrbuch der Heb. Sprache*, p. 132 of the 7th ed.

iv. 6, תִּהְיֶה is most correctly referred to Ssion, ver. 5. And since *daily* cannot here form an antithesis to night, it equals *any day* like Ps. xiii. 3; as the Turkish *gün-de*.

2. *The self-condemnation, figuratively and literally*, v. 1-24.

But in this manner the first discourse has presented the
stern judge and threatening God merely in all his righteous
burning indignation; and in the rapid course of the threatening
oration the causes of the punishments threatened were rather
rapidly indicated than particularly recounted, iii. 8-16. Is not
all this a too violent and inconsiderate judgment? But just
as a supposed truth, if it is in reality one, can be proved from
the most various points of view, so in this case the whole
manner of the discourse suddenly changes, and a new note is
struck to show that it is not only Yahvé who condemns the
community, but that it condemns itself equally. And just as a
higher truth confident of the justice of its cause, may assume
another form for a moment, so even the God and judge here
puts on another character; he becomes a simple tender and
owner of a vineyard, who can sing a lamentation over the unfruitfulness and ingratitude of his vineyard which had received
such peculiar attention, a lamentation which his younger friend
and relative, the prophet, had heard from him and now repeats
as he had heard it to the community, in order that the community may be judge as to what a vine-dresser who had been
thus deceived ought to do to his vineyard. The answer cannot
be doubtful; but the judges have scarcely condemned in thought
the unthankful vineyard, when they must see that they have
condemned themselves thereby; for as was already indicated,
iii. 14, the community, the community which for a long time
had been laboriously cultivated by Yahvé, is in reality this
vineyard, so carefully tended by its owner, with which he is so
righteously angry. Thus the illustration of the self-condemna-
tion of the criminal passes very quickly into a literal description, He appearing in his majesty who had just laid aside
his character of judge and God; just as the judge when the
sentence has been briefly pronounced then goes into particulars
in an intricate case, so this judge has only too many details to

enumerate; and without suffering a single suspicion of the
unrighteousness of his judgment and his punishment to arise,
he enumerates all their manifold transgressions and the particular punishments which necessarily correspond to them with
sufficient circumstantiality. He has to complain, (1) of their
unrighteousness and covetousness, (2) of their giddy luxurious-
ness and rioting, (3) of their indifference to the good and true,
which is over and above all these transgressions; whence arise
three strophes, the bantering illustration having been prefixed
as an introduction to this seriousness. But since the transgressions of the community for so long a period have become
increasingly various and serious, insomuch that if they were to
be enumerated in detail, the flood of them would grow in volume
with the progress of the discourse, their condemnation does here
in fact pour itself forth with growing breadth in three strophes,
each successive strophe becoming thus involuntarily longer than
the former one, increasing from four to six, and from six to seven
verses, or from a half gradually to a whole strophe. This however is on the supposition that ver. 17 is restored to its original
position after ver. 10, where from all indications it belongs
in point of meaning.

V.

1   Let me now sing of my dear friend,* as my
     friend singeth of his vineyard!

     A vineyard had my dear friend
        upon a richly fruitful height,
     And he digged it over and picked it clean,
        and planted it with best vines,
     and built a tower in its midst,

---

* The German is : *von meinem lieben vetter singen wie mein oheim singt.* In
English this is less permissible : *vetter* and *oheim* having a narrower meaning
in our language than in the German.—Trs.

hewed out also a wine-press in it,
and waited that it should bear grapes—
but it bore sour grapes!

And now, inhabitant of Jerusalem and man of
Yuda! | judge then between me and between my
vineyard! ‖ what is to be done more to my vine-
yard and I have not done it in it? | wherefore did I
wait that it should bear grapes—yet it bore sour
grapes ? ‖—Therefore let me show you what I will
5   do to my vineyard : | remove its hedge so that it
serveth for grazing, tear down its wall so that it
serveth for trampling! ‖ and I will make a desolation
of it, so that it shall not be pruned and not hoed, and
groweth up into thorn and thistle, | and upon the
clouds I will lay command not to rain upon it one
rain! ‖ — —For the vineyard of Yahvé of Hosts is
the house of Israel, the man of Yuda his darling
planting, | and he waited for right—but behold
might, for exactness—but behold exaction! ‖

1.

O those who join house to house, and connect
field to field, | until there is no more room and ye
alone must dwell in the midst of the land! ‖ —in
mine ears Yahvé of Hosts whispereth: | Verily
many houses will become a desolation, grand and
10   fair without an inhabitant! ‖ for ten yoke of vine-
yard will yield one bucket, | and a quarter's seed will
yield a bushel; ‖ and lambs feed then where they
are led, | and the fat-ones' ruins kids will devour. ‖

2.

O those who rise early in the morning to follow
the wassail, | late into the twilight are heated by
wine, ‖ so that guitar and harp tambourine and
flute and wine is their revel, | without considering
the operation of Yahvé, or at all seeing the work of
his hands ! ‖ —Therefore my people wandereth
forth unawares, | whilst its nobility is spent with
hunger, its revel-rout dried up with thirst. ‖ Therefore hell enlargeth her greed, and openeth her
mouth beyond measure, | so that there descendeth
her [Ssion's] splendour and her revel-rout, and
15   her uproar and what is merry in her. ‖ Then man
sinketh down and the man is humbled, | and the eyes
of the proud are bent down; ‖ and then Yahvé of
Hosts will be exalted by the judgment, | and the
holy God hallowed by righteousness. ‖

3.

O they who draw guilt near with cords of vanity |
and sin as with cart-ropes, ‖ they who say " let his
work hasten let it speed that we may see it, | and
let the counsel of the Holy One of Israel draw near
20   and come that we may know it!" ‖ O they who call
evil good, and good evil, | taking darkness for light
and light for darkness, taking bitter for sweet and
sweet for bitter ! ‖ O they who are wise in their
own eyes, | and intelligent before their own faces! ‖
O they who are heroes—to drink wine, | and men
of might—to mix wassail, ‖ who justify the unjust
for a bribe, | and take away the righteousness of

the righteous from them! || —therefore as the fire's
tongue devoureth stubble, and blazing hay sinketh
down, | so their root will be like rottenness, and
their blossom ascend like dust, || because they
despised the doctrine of Yahvé of Hosts, and
rejected the word of the Holy One of Israel. ||

v. 1-7.   In the structure of the Parable it should be specially
noted, how insensibly and easily the matter itself is unfolded
from the figure, while the point aimed at would have been
reached too circuitously and slowly if both had been kept
separate from beginning to end.   The whole discourse observes
the method of gradually bringing into light what was at first
concealed under the figure, until at last the matter itself stands
alone before the surprised hearer.   (1) Ver. 1, sq.   The discourse commences apparently with something quite foreign to
the prophet's aim, taken from common life, and accordingly
also assumes an entirely different tone, becoming a ballad, as if
the prophet wished merely to repeat after a friend a lamentation
which he had heard him sing concerning a strange misfortune.
The vineyard was from the first in such a condition that it
could produce noble fruit, it was then so carefully cultivated
and protected by its possessor that with a well-founded expectation of his harvest he had already built a wine-press—and still
it deceived his hope of good fruit and bore bitter grapes!—
(2) Ver. 3, sq.   If the hearers have been moved by this mournful story, they are now unexpectedly surprised by the question
of the owner himself, as to how in their candid judgment he
ought to proceed with this unthankful vineyard.   And since
they are silent, therefore cannot take the defendant under their
protection, the owner immediately proceeds—(3) ver. 5, sq., to
announce the righteous punishments which he will inflict; but
if in doing this he at first names only the usual punishments
which even a human owner might inflict to chastise as it were
an ungrateful vineyard, at last he mentions a means which very

quickly leads the hearers to surmise who this is that is speaking, and who will no longer conceal himself: the stoppage of all rain points to Yahvé! And that all further doubt may cease, the discourse—(4) ver. 7, intentionally breaks through its assumed disguise and with terrible seriousness presents the naked truth intended, the incisiveness of some paronomasiæ strengthening the prodigious effect of the rapid conclusion.

1. After the discourse has thus soared from its humble and gentle commencement to this extreme height and vehemence, it remains during the course of the three following strophes upon this height, but with greater calmness and self-possession, for the purpose of exercising the right, which it has thus vindicated, of sentencing the individual transgressions. The first transgression, and the root of all the rest, which was before mentioned first, ver. 7, is unrighteousness, the forsaking of eternal right, born of selfishness and covetousness. By unrighteous means they seek, wherever it is possible, to get all the houses and fields of the whole land; the fools, who act as if they desired ultimately to dwell alone in the wide depopulated land! But, like a higher voice ringing in his ears, the prophet hears that, as a fitting punishment, the many beautiful houses, on the possession of which they stake their soul's salvation, shall stand desolate, on account of a great barrenness of the land, depicted by the examples, ver. 10, which is the counterpart of the sign of the blessed age first mentioned, iv. 2; so that at last a waste heap of ruins will be found, upon which sheep will be driven at the will of their owners, ver. 17, where now these covetous people revel as fat epicures. The meaning of this description of these people who covetously acquire *latifundia* appears fully only from a knowledge of the ancient Mosaic agrarian constitution, which was then breaking up, comp. *Alterthümer,* p. 236, sq. (202, sq.).

2. For even such covetous people like to live luxuriously and spend the whole day in revels of drunkenness and frivolous trifling, whilst they never observe how Yahvé continues eter-

nally his work, not less when men do not heed him, the work of eternal government and of that righteousness which often develops itself in secret, but manifests itself without fail. at the proper moment, and which punishes the frivolity of these men : ver. 11, sq., comp. Amos v. 23 ; vi. 5, sq. ; and with respect to the *work* of Yahvé, xxviii. 21 ; Ps. xxviii. 5 ; xc. 16 ; Hab. iii. 2. The corresponding punishment for this is, that just as they live from day to day without thought, so the destruction of the kingdom itself and the banishment especially. of the more powerful among them, shall come upon them unawares, when what there is in the nation of nobility and revelry, *i. e.* precisely those of highest repute and the most noisy, who at present riot in shameful uproar, perish in the bitterest want, ver. 13 ; or rather, ver. 14, that hell suddenly opens her jaws to swallow altogether the wild uproar of Ssion, as the ancient legend narrates of similar punishments, Num. xvi. 32, sq.,—a terrible judgment but a necessary one, by which the pride of men will again be bent, and Yahvé clearly acknowledged in his true greatness and sanctity, as is observed at the end of this strophe, ver. 15, sq., with most telling emphasis, the discourse ending once more in exactly the same language as above towards the end of the strophes, ii., 9, 11, 17, 21.

3. A third great transgression consists in their resistance to the good and true, when it approaches them and will force itself upon them, *e. g.* by these very prophets of Yahvé : if the prophets speak, as was indicated in the previous strophe, ver. 12, of the work and counsel of Yahvé, *i. e.* of his judgment, which if it has not been made manifest, nevertheless rests in his eternal counsel to come in its time, these godless hearers exclaim in defiance and mockery, May it come very soon, that we may actually see it ! ver. 19 ; Amos. v. 18 ; vi. 3 ; ix. 10 ; but that is in reality to confound all moral distinctions, ver. 20, to wish to be the only wise people, ver. 21, or, at once to say the severest thing, wickedly to draw near and bring upon themselves guilt and sin with the cords of vanity (of a vain and wanton

mind), as with the most powerful and strongest ropes (for such vain mocking speeches appear to be only like a supercilious joke spoken without thought, and yet they really include all sin, in fact, the unpardonable sin against the Holy Ghost, xxii. 14), ver. 18. And this transgression is indeed only the final consequence of others which have already become so predominant; those who are thus obdurate are, acc. ver. 22, also those frivolous rioters of the second strophe, and, acc. ver. 23, those unjust people of the first, ver. 8. But because this intentional mockery of the distinct divine word is suicide of their own inmost life, the suitable punishment can be no other than that as stubble and hay sink in a moment before blazing fire, so their root and blossom vanish rapidly and immediately when seized by the fire of the divine judgment, the first internally devoured as by putrefaction, the second flying away like dust and ashes, Ex. xv. 7; Hos. ix. 16. And with this dreadful word comes evidently the end of a chief section, just as vv. 22 and 23 gradually resume the two previous strophes, and by that means also everything is rounded off in this complete whole.

The words, v. 1, admit no other meaning than that given above; but since accurate delineation suits a story, the word ידידי and דודי must be understood quite definitely. But the words, ver. 2, are certainly to be looked upon as an actual song; and although as containing a narrative they cannot rise to any great elevation, at least in קֶרֶן בֶּן שָׁמֶן an uncommon form of expression occurs. That *a horn* should signify *a mountain* is at least not common in Hebrew; the supposition lacks support that *the horn of Ben-Shámen* (i.e. *son of fatness*) was intended as a highly figurative name for the mountain, *i. e.* mountainous district, of Israel as dwelling, acc. Deut. xxxii. 13, 14, in fatness, as if it were an imitation of the name of Benjamin; since *horn* as a *mountain* may be masculine, it may be taken more simply as denoting a *fat*, fertile, *height*, and in any case allude to the fruitful Canâan; but in that case the expression is the second one of an unusual and poetic nature.

That מָטָר, v. 6, along with הַמְטִיר, expresses to send *only one rain*, appears from § 281*a*, and this emphasis of the expression must not be overlooked.

מְתֵי, v. 13, which as *people* gives no meaning suitable to the verse-members, is incontestably a corruption of מְזֵה, also acc. to Deut. xxxii. 24, as is shown, *Lehrb. der Heb. Sp.* p. 57, note; how the word comes to have this passive force is explained § 149 *g*.

v. 17, instead of גֵּרִים, *sojourning as strangers*, which would be too feeble here, גְּדָיִם must be read, in accordance with the structure of the members and with the LXX. But that the verse originally stood not here at the end of the second, but at the end of the first strophe, is quite clear. The tremendous utterance of ver. 15, sq., which, as in ch. ii. forms the best close to the strophe, would only be weakened in its effect by the addition of ver. 17 in this place. On the other hand, this description as *fat ones* entirely suits the rich ones of the first strophe; and the words in that case form a suitable transition to the following strophe.

The correct meaning of the sentences, v. 18, depends especially on a knowledge of the fact, that שָׁוְא precisely in Yesaya's usage, i. 13; xxx. 28, retains its original force of what is vain, or vanity and deceit, and so far is by no means equal to *sin* or *guilt*.

---

3. *A wider historical and geographical survey, including Samaria*, CH. v. 25; ix. 7-x. 4; v. 26-30.

The discourse rises again to a more free historical survey, extending into the past and the future, and this time it takes a wider sweep to include the sister kingdom. The past shows that many severe calamities, like strokes of the divine anger, have already been sent for the many transgressions of the nation, and it would not be difficult to enumerate just as many severe strokes as there had been transgressions; especially has Samaria been chastised in very various ways: *but all these strokes have not sufficed,* the measure of the transgressions continues still to grow, and therefore the correcting hand of Yahvé in anger is still stretched out to inflict other strokes, until finally the all-destructive blow will come upon the whole land, namely, the approach of the Assyrians, that final blow which has been briefly referred to, iii. 1, 2, 16—iv. 1; v. 13. After a brief transition to this new subject, v. 25, we have a circular series of four brief strophes, ix. 7—x. 4, each of which begins by mentioning one of many great transgressions, and most of which proceed to mention a punishment due to the transgression as already experienced, while all of them without exception end with the ever-recurring sentence, that the punishment has not been therewith concluded; the greater and final punishment which has yet to follow, to which the recurring sentence points with such solemn significance, is then presented with marvellous power of language in the last strophe, vv. 26-30, which fittingly closes the series. Each of these four strophes has from 4—5 verses, and the first three are so much occupied with the transgressions and fortunes of Samaria that the transition thereto is prepared for by a specially marked form of language, ix. 7. Thus the three strophes, ix. 7-20, in reality form a small oracle concerning Samaria which cannot be divided, although in a higher sense it is in itself quite incomplete, and by its concluding words constantly points to something which has yet to follow.

What is known to us as to the calamities and defeats of the kingdom of the Ten Tribes which are mentioned here, is treated of *Hist. of Israel,* iv. p. 156, sq. (iii. p. 646, sq.). That the words, ix. 13-16, are intended to refer to the invasions of the Assyrians under Piglath-Pilésar, is not evident from the context.

V.

25   Therefore Yahvé's wrath burned against his
people, | and he stretched forth his hand over it
and smote it so that the mountains trembled, and
corpses were like off-scouring in the midst of the
streets : ‖ —*with all this his anger turned not, and
still his hand is outstretched!* ‖

IX.   1.

7   A word the Lord sent into Yaqob, | and it will
fall in Israel, ‖ that the whole nation may feel it,
Ephráim and the inhabitant of Samaria, | in pride
and in bravado, saying : ‖ "bricks fell down, yet we
build with freestone! | sycomores were felled, yet
10   we cause cedars to spring up instead!" ‖ So then
Yahvé strengthened Ressîn's princes against it, |
and its enemies he maileth : ‖ Arám in front and
Philistines behind—who devoured Israel with a full
mouth— : | *with all this his anger turned not, and
still his hand is outstretched!* ‖

2.

And the nation turned not to him who smote it, |
and Yahvé of Hosts they sought not. ‖ So then
Yahvé destroyed from Israel head and tail, | palm
15   and rush in one day*; ‖ and the leaders of this
nation became misleaders, | and those of it who were
led destroyed-ones. ‖ Therefore over his youths the
Lord rejoiceth not, | and his orphans and his widows
he doth not compassionate, | because every one is
unholy and of evil, and every mouth is speaking

godlessness—: ‖ *with all this his anger turned not, and still his hand is outstretched!* ‖

 * [*Old-man and man-of-repute is the head, | and falsely teaching prophet is the tail.*]

3.

For long since wrong burneth like fire, devouring thorn and thistle, | and kindling the thickets of the forest, so that they curl up in columns of smoke. ‖ By the wrath of Yahvé of Hosts the land was scorched up, | and the nation becometh like food of fire, they spare not one the other; ‖ and they devoured on the right and were hungry, and ate on the left and were not satisfied, | they eat—each one 20 the flesh of his arm, ‖ Manasse, Ephráim and— Ephráim, Manasse, the two together against Yuda: ‖ —*with all this his anger turned not, and still his hand is outstretched!* ‖

X.   4.

1 O they who decide vain decisions, | and are always penning down mischief, ‖ to thrust away the weak from judgment, and to rob the rights of the sufferers of my people, | that widows may be their prey, and they may spoil the orphans! ‖ (But what will ye do at the day of visitation, and when over-throw cometh from afar? | unto whom will ye flee for help, and whither hide your glory? ‖ —nothing but one cringeth as a prisoner, and as those to be slain they fall!): | —*with all this his anger turned not, and still his hand is outstretched!* ‖

V.

26   So then he lifteth up a signal to the Heathen
from afar, and hisseth to them from the end of the
earth, | —and lo quickly hastily he cometh; || no
weary one and no stumbler therein, he slumbereth
not and sleepeth not, | and the girdle of his loins is
never loosed, the thong of his shoes never torn off;
|| he whose arrows are sharpened, and all his bows
bent, | the hoofs of his horses deemed like flint, and
his wheels like the hurricane; || he hath a roar like
the lioness, | he roareth like young lions and
rageth and catcheth the prey and secureth it

30   without a deliverer. || And it rageth over them on
that day like the sea's raging; | though they look to
the earth, lo there is thick darkness, | and the
light hath become dark in its fogs. ||

v. 25 makes plainly the important transition to what follows.
Once (during the present generation) Yahvé manifested himself
also in Jerusalem as the God who inflicts rigorous chastisement
when his anger is provoked by such transgressions, and the
blow he inflicted was such that the mountains trembled and
many men became corpses in a moment, for whom none
troubled themselves : but that was only a first stroke ; he
threatens to strike still further. In the last words we have the
fundamental utterance, which as a continual echo forms the basis
and the life of the four following larger strophes, in which the
discourse takes new starts in order to follow out this thought.
What historical fact in the kingdom of Yuda is referred to, is
made somewhat problematic by the brevity of the words ; the
great earthquake under 'Uzzia, Am. i. 1; "Zech." xiv. 5, in
which many people perished, may be thought of, *e. g. ;* a
pestilence is not clearly described,

1. A threatening word (namely, that same fundamental utterance), thus the discourse makes a new start with added energy, has Yahvé sent from heaven into the nation like a heavily falling burden ("Zech." ix. 1), that the whole nation, but especially the Northern kingdom, may be made to recognise and feel it: and feel it just in the midst of its infatuated pride, notwithstanding that it has already been made tributary to the Assyrians, which leads it to imagine that it will more than recover its former power by means of injustice and depredatory raids, ver. 8, sq. Accordingly Yahvé recently put into defensive armour, as if to punish the nation for its sins, all its smaller enemies, so that the Syrians (the princes of Ressîn from Damascus) and Philistines, the first from the North-east, the latter from the South-west (1 Kings xv. 27) committed depredations in its territory: but because the afore-named pride is not broken down and this punishment has not attained its end, another and severer punishment must follow! Thus the fundamental utterance recurs here in sufficiently close connexion with the whole strophe, although the figure in which it is clothed has its original place, v. 25 only. The two phrases, ver. 9, are figurative: bricks, sycomores are commoner than hewn-stones and cedars. Ver. 10, sq., must refer to small conflicts with the surrounding nations with the exception of the Assyrians, in which the reduced kingdom became involved, comp. "Zech." xi. 10; just as vv. 13, 15, sq., refer to a somewhat more important battle, which the kingdom lost in these struggles probably against the Syrians, and as a distant result of which probably the alliance, vii. 1, was formed.

2. A second transgression of the Northern kingdom is its impenitence, which was never displayed more plainly than just now, when Yahvé has sought to bring it to attend and reflect by the chastisement which it has just felt so painfully. Accordingly a calamitous day of battle followed, when the nation, misled by its leaders and not seeking the right leader, was overthrown together with its heads, vv. 13, 15, comp. iii. 12;

yea, ver. 16 proceeds with reference to this recent severe overthrow, on this very account Yahvé permits the warriors of
Israel to perish, as if he had no pleasure in them, and as if he
felt no compassion at seeing a multitude of widows and orphans
made thereby, because within the nation everything is perpetually corrupt — therefore again the necessity of still
severer punishment.—Since in this connexion the figures, ver.
13, head and tail, palm and rush, (xix. 15), can only denote
officers and privates in the army, the explanation, ver. 14,
which is also very unpoetical, cannot have originated with
Yesaya, but from a very early reader who compared iii. 2, sq.,
and made the passages refer to each other; comp. x. 16-19,
33, sq.

3. For there is added, as the third transgression of this
kingdom, ver. 17, an unrighteousness which like burning fire
seizes upon and destroys everything, both high and low, in the
nation, the thorns and thistles as well as the thickets of the
high forest-trees, so that they are dissipated and pass away in
a column of smoke, ver. 17, comp. x. 16-18. But unrighteousness which commits ravages upon its own nation from the first
carries its own divine punishment within itself, as is immediately added, vv. 18-20a, with similar imagery: indeed nothing
short of the wrath of Yahvé itself, the fruit of unrighteousness,
appears to have blazed through the land to its very centre, so
that already it is unable to get free from a fire which is feeding
upon its vitals—all the horrors of anarchy; a condition of
anarchy, where there are no laws and no rulers, when once,
like unmanageable fire it gets the upper hand, is like *bulimus
(heisshunger)* which is never satisfied, a man destroys everything, devours right and left ("Zech." xi. 6), and yet is not
satisfied, until every one begins to devour the flesh of his
own arm, his own members (Job xviii. 13), one inseparable
brother-tribe the other; or, by way of variety, both some day
unite against Yuda, the distant brother-tribe! With all this

there is therefore again no rest : a final punishment must follow! comp. "Zech." xi. 6, 14.

4. The special, refined character of the unrighteousness of the covetous judges and authorities which is condemned, x. 1, 2, points of itself to Yuda and to what was said above, iii. 14, sq.; v. 7, sq., 23; but the transition to this kingdom had already been prepared at the end of the previous strophe, ix. 20, by that form of sudden transition in which Yesaya is a master. Since, however, no special calamity, no suitable punishment, except that mentioned at the commencement, v. 25, and here again pre-supposed, had befallen these magnates, the prophet is unable to compare the past in this as he had done in the previous strophes : he can only point them in a parenthesis to the future approach of the judgment and overthrow, and enquire what they will do to meet it when their destruction is announced by a distant noise, to *whose* castle they will flee (as if a castle and fortification would then avail!), and *whither* they will bring into security and there *leave* their glory and power which they have won unrighteously?   O then there is nothing left for the magnates but that they should cringe in fetters like the basest captives, or that they should sink down amongst others who are to be slain, and dead like them! that is, treated thus by the Assyrians; which already gives an inkling of what immediately follows, v. 26-30; but this strophe also is first closed with the fundamental thought, that for such transgressions a final punishment must yet come.

v. 26-30.   What therefore is the final blow which must necessarily come?   Far distant barbarians, whom they have never seen, must come upon the whole land, to finish the punishment as Yahvé's instruments and to reach every sinner; the Assyrian especially, whom Yesaya does not name here but intends and plainly enough describes, so that the discourse from ver. 26 *b* suddenly falls into the singular and keeps it up. Yahvé need only plant a signal of alarm upon a high mountain (xi. 12; xiii. 2), or, according to another figure which is

equally natural here, need only hiss, as men call a swarm of
bees (vii. 18; "Zech." x. 8), to bring the swarms of the most
distant nations quickly into the holy land, ver. 26, and how
marvellously rapid and unimpeded is their march, ver. 27, how
unrivalled their equipment when they are seen approaching,
ver. 28, how irresistible their dreadful attack at the decisive
moment, ver. 29! There is then heard, ver. 30, not merely the
terrible battle-cry, the thunder of the victorious and destructive
enemy; what is much worse, and constitutes the consummation
of the judgment divine, it then thunders over him who is
attacked and is crying to heaven for help, terribly raging in
the heavens like the raging of the sea; from below and from
above no deliverance or comfort, and if the eye, which had
been turned away from heaven by terror of the thunder, turns
to the earth again, lo, there it sees all light darkened into close
(thick) darkness! comp. viii. 21, sq.; Qôran ii. 18, sq. The
image taken from an earthquake, Plin. Epist. vi.; xx. 16;
xvi. 17. Harris' *Æthiopia*, i. p. 319, sq.

It is incontestable that the four small strophes with the
recurring verse originally belonged here, and are intelligible
here only. The very first strophe of these four is intelligible
by means of v. 25 only, and the last is plainly intended to
bring the discourse back to the point where it was broken off.
The recurring word, which prepares for the final judgment, is
repeated *five times*, this being an ancient sacred number.

ix. 10, it is necessary to read with many MSS. שָׂרֵי instead
of צָרֵי, which only apparently corresponds to the following
אֹיְבָיו. One of these powerful princes of Syria, or rather
Damascus, was at that time that Tâbeél of vii. 6.

The words, ix. 14, which have a reference to iii. 2, sq., are
such a bold and telling satire that we may safely conclude that
they originated during the period that the prophets were still
very active in public affairs, as was the case as late as Yéremyá's

time. Some younger prophet combining the words, ix. 13, with those iii. 2, sq., may have hit upon this satire, put it into the poetical garb of two members, and written it in the margin opposite this passage: but that the words are from Yesaya, and that this is their original place, cannot be said. The prophets at that time, like so many ecclesiastics of our day, had come to that, that they were quite content if they were only suffered to come in as the tail in public affairs; and it may be very acceptable to us to meet in the Bible a telling utterance upon their conduct in this respect: but it does not follow that it owes its origin in this passage to Yesaya. If the two members are excluded, the strophe has still twelve members, only one less than the first, whilst, it is true, the other two have fourteen each.

It should be observed how compressed the words become in the members of ix. 20: the measure allowed for the strophe must speedily come to an end.

x. 4, בִּלְתִּי to be taken acc. § 356 *b*, and תַּחַת *instead of* means *as good as,* or *not better than,* in the same way as בְּעַד, xxxii. 14, means no more than *as;* the change from the singular to the plural, which is elsewhere so common when the language is general, in this case follows the change of members, and is one of its ornaments. So far as the meaning is concerned, we have nothing more analogous than the words of the poet, Ps. lxxxii. 7.

On the repetition of the simple *imperf.* with the equally simple וְ v. 29, sq., see § 343 *b*.—If we follow the accents, v. 30, we must translate: *then behold there is darkness; straitness and light; it has become dark in* the earth's *fogs;* then the rapid change from light to darkness in the last moments, and the vain, and therefore more terrible, darting of flashes of lightning into even the deep darkness, appears to be more vividly described, so that we might feel inclined to choose this collocation of the words. But in reality the description is not then by any means clear and simple enough; the similar concluding words, viii. 21, sq., also lead us to a better meaning. The combination, צַר חֹשֶׁךְ, *narrow,* close, *i.e.* thick, horrible *darkness,* only gives an image like that of Job xv. 23, sq.; xviii. 6, sq.; xx. 16.

II. Yesaya's Second Book, ch. vi. 1—ix. 6; xvii. 1—11.

While Yesaya's first book belonged to the commencement of the reign of Ahaz, 740, this second, according to all indications, belongs to the commencement of the reign of Hizqia, 724, when the prophet during the sixteen years of the reign of the former frivolous and capricious king had passed through the most painful personal experiences and had also seen the power of Yuda fall very low. Incontestably he considered this juncture, when in Hizqia there arose a new king justifying revived hopes, as again well fitted for extending his labours by means of writing also, and to fix more firmly the memory of many of his most memorable actions and fortunes. He had already laboured thirty-three years under three very different kings: the wealth of his prophetic experiences impelled him, and now the kingdom again stood before the unknown beginning of a new period, which as far as the king was concerned permitted better hopes, but, as the result of long confusions and serious errors in the past, was threatening new calamities, especially since in the interval between this and the former book the Assyrian power had become oppressive to Yuda as well as to Israel. But however varied the fortunes of the kingdom and those of the prophet himself had been during these thirty-three years, when he reviewed the whole period of his labours, and realised to himself with what divine forebodings and thoughts he had laboured from the very first, he discovered in all that he himself and especially in what the kingdom had gone through nothing that had not already passed before him clearly in its divine necessity in the first moments of the excitation of his prophetic spirit. Accordingly, he resolved to describe now more in the form of a prophetic survey of his entire past prophetic career both the profound defects of the kingdom, the consequences of which had continually become more and more manifest during his life, and his own enduring hope, and to describe them both as they had been most vividly present to his mind from the first, and had since, amidst all the changing circumstances, been constantly more clearly and convincingly expounded by him.

The main portion of this book had, therefore, necessarily an entirely different plan and execution from the foregoing. Its style is historical : and although very long orations are brought within this frame-work, it remains essentially narration, from which everything proceeds and which everywhere recurs at the proper place. Pieces of another kind might be attached, but they do not form the substance of this book. The book fell clearly into three parts : (1) the splendid introduction in the narrative of the call of the prophet, ch. vi ; (2) the continued narrative of his prophetic labours, ch. vii.-ix. 6 ; (3) more loosely appended pieces, of which at present we have preserved at least the piece, xvii. 1-11. We are no longer in a position to know what the commencement of this third part originally was : the second part, as a closer examination clearly enough shows, has come to us unfortunately incomplete : and since the pieces which compose it must have originally stood in a close connexion, it is more easy to recognize this in its case.

From viii. 16, it appears that the prophet availed himself in the composition of this book of the help of disciples. Long ago a circle of more intimate friends and disciples had gathered around him. It is all the more easy to understand how in places he can here be spoken of in the first person, ch. vi. and ch. viii. and in the third ch. vii. The immediate present is alluded to at most incidentally in such words as ix. 3.

1. Introduction.

Yesaya's Consecration, ch. vi.

When Yesaya, after so many years of prophetic activity, looked back to its first commencement, full of the experiences of the intervening years, he could recall various feelings which had flooded his mind in the strength and consecration of that moment. For there can be no doubt that the prophet as a fact once passed through such an elevating moment of consecration, when he became conscious both of the full glory of Yahvé and of his own mission, a moment the immeasurable power of which, determining his whole life, continued to influence him, unchanged and undecaying, and impelled him to everything which he undertook : it is entirely consistent to suppose that the prophet in such a moment, before which stands a whole life like a crowded picture, clearly foresaw at the same time the uncommon difficulties with which he would have to contend, and the picture of which nevertheless did not terrify him !* It is necessary to suppose such a historical basis. But of all the feelings which then overwhelmed him there is one especially which had so often been confirmed during his whole prophetic career, and which he now recalls most vividly, because it most accorded with the tone of mind in which he then was. This is the feeling of the unfruitfulness of his past labours, at least in general. For Yesaya does not merely describe historically what he once saw and felt in the spirit, nor merely with a historical purpose. But what he had then seen in vision had now become in his mind by the experience of many years an abiding idea and a certain conviction of a higher necessity, and he now writes for the readers of a time which is far distant from that sacred moment of his consecration. In this reminiscence, which was thus conditioned, it seems to him

---

* Like Christ from the first commencement of his Messianic labours, he thought of the end, nor did he shrink from the image of death, so that the subsequent fact as it approached nearer, only confirmed what had not seemed strange to him from the commencement.

as if He, before whom all connexion and all development is clearly open from first to last, had consigned to him from that very first moment the mournful commission to be a prophet of evil. Thus he sketches in this introductory piece, first, indeed, vv. 1-4, the picture of the infinite glory which he once saw, since no one can become a prophet who has not at some time first so beheld the glory and greatness of Yahvé that he can never lose the picture of it again; he then describes, vv. 5-8, how the divine commission and strengthening for the prophetic office follow the clearness and certainty of these previous intuitions after all fear of man has been overcome; but the most important thing follows at the end, vv. 9-13, the state-ment of the commission which he who was thus called, the prophet thus prepared for everything, receives, namely, the mournful commission to speak and to labour in vain, as if a curse were laid upon his labours which were designed for the national weal; neither for the future is there any other hope than that mixed with wormwood, that the salvation of the true community, which is indeed eternally secure, can come only after the entire ruin of the existing order of things and the most unsparing purification of the nation and the state. Thus fruitless the prophet had for a long time found his labours; with hopes thus cast down by dark forebodings, he was then looking into the future: that which he will subsequently expand in many discourses is here in this sublime introduction to the whole book comprised within a few strong words, eluci-dated from the highest stand-point and introduced with reference to its eternal necessity, in order that from the very first it may be evident for what purpose this prophet was called, what his leading truths are, and what fortunes of his this book will describe. In this way the piece becomes a suitable introduction to the whole book: and in the way in which the far-off future is touched upon with a rapid glance, this preparation accomplishes its end: the attention is kept sufficiently alive. But just as the third part, vv. 9-13 is the most important both as regards this piece and the whole book, so the second part constitutes the true centre, the first explaining upon what insight and knowledge the call to the prophetic office rested, and the third what the nature of this office would be, while the second describes the genuine prophetic courage which will be alarmed by nothing when once it has received the higher consecration.

But in order to form a perfectly correct estimate of this sublime introduction, which remained ever afterwards as a preeminently glorious picture before the eyes of the later prophets, we must not overlook the fact that this portion in its entirety receives its true meaning only when viewed as an introduction, while with respect to its close it would be entirely unsatisfactory if its express design were not that of an introductory piece, the business of which is to draw the attention to something which is to follow. If Yesaya had in reality had nothing beyond the fruitlessness of his prophetic labours to which to look, nothing could have been more dreadful : but the eternal Messianic hope is here indicated, although but barely indicated, and with a single word at the end, ver. 13, and below the place will occur when it will appear more prominently and reveal itself with all its blessed consolations. Hence, only the one great truth remains here at the beginning, that the genuine prophet may not suffer himself to be frightened from his duty, when once he has found this in God, but must be emboldened by the clearly foreseen and divinely necessary fruitlessness of his pains, although the fruitlessness may continue for a long time, indeed, may be increased by the course of his very labours in proportion as they come into collision with the resisting world. A final prospect of better times is nevertheless opened at last, ver. 13.

VI.

1   1. In the death-year of the king ' Uzziya saw I the Lord sitting upon a high and exalted throne,| his train filling the temple ; || Saraphs stood high

around him, six wings had each: | with twain he
covered his face, with twain he covered his feet,
and with twain he flew; || and one called to the
other and said:

> Holy, holy, holy is Yahvé of Hosts!
> the fulness of the whole earth is his glory! ||

Then the ˉprojections of the thresholds shook at
the sound of him that called, | and the house
filleth ʻwith smoke. ||

5.   2. Then said I: "woe is me, for I am undone, |
because a man of unclean lips am I, and in the
midst of a people of unclean lips I dwell, | that
the king Yahvé of Hosts mine eyes saw!" || Yet
there flew to me one of the Saraphs, holding a
chipstone | which with tongs he had taken from
the altar; || and touched my mouth and said: lo
this hath touched thy lips: | and so will thy guilt
depart, and thy sin may be atoned for. || Then
heard I the voice of the Lord saying: whom shall
I send? and who will go for us? | and I said:
" here am I, send me!" ||

      3. Then said heɤ go, so that thou sayest to this
people:

> " hear on and understand not!
> see on and perceive not!" ||

10   make slothful the heart of this people, and its ears
heavy and its eyes closed up; | lest it see with its
eyes, or hear with its ears | or its heart understand
and it return, that one may heal it! || — Then
said I: how long, O Lord? | and he said: until

2   5

the cities are waste without inhabitant and the
houses without men, and the ground shall be
wasted to desolation, ‖ and Yahvé removeth the
men | and great is the emptiness in the midst of
the land! ‖ and is there then still therein a tenth,
yet that also must go again into the fire : | like the
terebinth and like the oak to which at the felling
remaineth a root-trunk, 'tis a holy seed—its trunk! ‖

1. vv. 1-4. The unhindered glance into true glory and
holiness, which must precede the call and labours of every
true prophet. In the present instance, when a prophet is
about to be called whose mission it is to originate a new and
decisive epoch in the history of the divine kingdom, the glory
of Yahvé cannot be conceived and described under a more
suitable image than that of a ruler, who, in the midst of a
solemn gathering of counsellors, the magnates of the empire
doing him homage, is seated upon his exalted throne, as for
the purpose of delivering a highly important resolution with
regard to the necessities of the kingdom. For it cannot be
denied that the appearance of a great prophet deeply concerns
the inmost nature and true prosperity of the divine kingdom ;
and inasmuch as he can appear, at the moment he is wanted,
only for the purpose of meeting a requirement of this kingdom, his appearance is preceded, as it were, by a divine council with regard to this requirement and his mission. All the
great and sublime things which the imagination can picture in
connexion with monarchs enthroned in the midst of grave and
awful counsellors, may, therefore, be pictured here in a far
loftier form where Yahvé is concerned. Possibly such actual
pictures as those supplied in Rosellini's *Monum. Stor. pl.* cxiv.
may be present to the prophet's mind. But inasmuch as it is
contrary to the primitive Mosaic feeling to actually conceive
and describe the Highest in material images and pictures, the

imagination does not venture to behold and to delineate the
face or the heart of the Almighty himself. At that moment
when He himself is beheld, it is merely the more external and
lower parts of Him, such as reach down to the sphere of visi-
bility, which are more particularly described, ver. 1. The
infinitely awful, holy and astonishing characteristics of this
picture can be fully brought forward only in the description of
the highest servants of this kingdom, of their *salutation* at the
appearance and at the commencement of the transaction, and,
therefore, of their doxology and its effect, vv. 2-4. One proof
that the Saraphs were originally conceived as animal figures is
supplied by the way in which they are here represented as
turned in homage towards the throne, covering their feet with
wings : for this supposes that they were conceived as naked, like
animals. As has been before explained in my *History of Israel*
I. 322 (I. 462), they are primarily *Dragon-like* creatures, whose
distinctive characteristic, in antithesis to the Kerûbs, is their
sharp, flaming eyes, a characteristic which qualifies them to be
the guards of the Throne and the guardians of the commands
which proceed from it. However, in proportion as the Mosaic
religion was of a spiritual nature do these creatures appear
here in a more spiritual form, as the highest servants of Yahvé,
in profound reverence, surrounding his throne, and emulously
singing his praise, as priests in the heavenly temple. When,
however, these servants have presented to him in their doxology
that offering which is to him the only acceptable one, there is
heard from the Throne also a cry so powerful that the thres-
hold, where the prophet stands listening in the distance, shakes
at the mighty voice. The cry in this instance has another
meaning than that in Amos vii. 4 : it is intended to convey the
declaration that something is *well-pleasing*, as is immediately
made known by the fact that *the house, i.e.* the inner temple,
begins to fill with smoke, as from the acceptable incense of
this offering (Rev. viii. 3) ; and therewith the end of this
ceremony, which opens the divine service, is indicated. In this

way scenes taken from the proceedings around the throne of
a king holding a solemn council, are mixed with those from
the temple service, inasmuch as no ordinary king is here described. Every word of the description is well chosen, not
one too many, and even the wings of the Saraphs are
specially described, ver. 2, only to make clear what follows,
ver. 5.

2. vv. 5-8. The man that has thus gazed into perfect glory
and is electrified by it, is capable of becoming a prophet. At
the first moment, it is true, doubt and fear may fall upon him
in the presence of the glory of Yahvé, which he now for the
first time clearly perceives, ver. 5, inasmuch as the conscious-
ness of human weakness, both personal and general, becomes
oppressive and consuming in proportion as the true glory is
beheld and felt. Hence the ancient legends beautifully narrate
how so many perish, or are in danger of perishing, at the sudden
sight and the piercing nearness of the Infinite (Gen. xviii. 23,
sq.; Ex. xxxiii. 20; Judges xiii. 22): for he is always *higher
still* than men think. At the same time, this human fear, in
the case of him in whose heart a true foundation has been previously laid, is felt only in order that it may be overcome for
ever by the stronger impulses of the spirit. Whilst the
prophet is in dread of perishing, a Saraph has already flown to
his side to purify his still unprophetic lips as with a hotstone
from that altar upon which the purest offerings, those pure
words of the Saraph's, burn, the fire of which, therefore,
purifies the human lips, and by consecration renders them
Saraphic, vv. 6, 7. As therefore now the cry from the Throne
is heard inquiring who will undertake the divine mission, which
has just been considered as needed in the divine kingdom;
just as this cry falls kindly and sympathisingly upon the ear of
Yesaya, as if he belonged already to this heavenly circle, and
is clearly understood by him in this sense, he offers himself
confidently as prophet, having become already strong and
courageous in Yahvé. Thus free, and at the same time thus

determined by higher instigation, is the happy resolution to undertake the pure service of the spirit.

3. vv. 9-13. Yesaya is to become a prophet, a prophet of *this people* (contemptuously spoken, a people which Yahvé is not willing to call *his people*) : but he must utter as it were a curse over the nation which is perpetually hardened against the words and deeds of Yahvé, ver. 9 : this prophet receives the hard commission by his labours to make the nation only more hardened and less open to receive the prosperity which his efforts were intended to promote, ver. 10. For it must be allowed, that when a prophet of this eminence labours, no one can remain indifferent and undecided with regard to him : either men follow him to their well-being, or they resist the truth of his words to their destruction, so that it may be said, with severity and enigmatically yet truthfully, at a time when this mournful effect generally prevails, that the prophet brings hardening and calamity instead of conversion and prosperity. On the other hand, this mournful effect cannot be conceived as final, otherwise the prophets would despair of their own mission. Nor can Yesaya rest content with this curse upon the immediate future. He ventures, therefore, in pain to ask how long the perversity will last. Indeed, the truth, as a final prospect surrounded with clouds, is made known, that there must first take place a complete destruction of the existing kingdom and a purification of the whole community, penetrating to its very centre ; that a trial of fire, which repeatedly coming spares nothing, must first destroy all existing external things, even unto the mysterious hidden foundation. This basis is, indeed, indestructible, and will remain as the sacred germ of the new improved community, just as the trunk of terebinths and oaks, which is deeply and ineradicably sunk into the earth, bears constantly new shoots, an image of eternity and immortality springing from an inward rejuvenating power, comp. Job xiv. 7, sq. The emphasis of the whole sentence, ver. 13, thus rests upon the last word, *its* (that of the earth and community)

root-trunk.   *Holy, i.e.* inviolable, indestructible seed and germ
of a new improved community is alone the root-trunk, hidden in
the earth, of the existing community, its life-root, the *remnant* as
Yesaya elsewhere so often calls it.   In these few words lie both
the mournful seriousness as well as the indestructible hope of
those times, all the apprehensions and joyous surmisings of the
prophets compressed into one picture.

On vi. 2.   The *Saraphs,* which only accidentally occur in
this connexion, will never be properly understood, unless it is
borne in mind that as the Kerûbs and Griffins are primarily
even verbably and historically the same, so also the Saraphs
and *Dragons.*   Both go back, therefore, into those primitive
ages, which explain how it is that even in China from that
earliest time to the present the residence of the Dragon is
synonymous with the residence of the Emperor (see Prémare
on Gaubil's *Shuking*).   In fact the Arabic word *sharafa* as
related to הִשְׁקִיף and שָׁזַף and, on the other hand, also
to the Arabic word *tarafa* points in many derivatives to a
kind of *looking ;* and the further departure from the letters of
the word δέρκω is explained by the great distance of time since
the two families of language separated.   However, the primary
meaning of the word has been preserved precisely in Hebrew
both in Yesaya's own writings, xiv. 29 ; xxx. 6, in the case of
the mythical *flying dragons* occurring only in poetry, and in
the name of the *Saraph-Serpents* as a special kind of serpent
even still in use in the narrative Num. xxi. 8 ; and the only
thing that is remarkable is that the short word *Saraph* bears the
above exalted meaning.   At the same time, in this simplicity it
is only a parallel case to that of *Kerûb.*   Comp. on the *Saraphs*
the picture from Umm-el 'Avâ-mid in Renan's *Mission de
Phénicie* I. p. liii. [See also the Author's *Die Lehre der Bibel*
§ 219.]

The song of the Saraphs, vi. 3, is the salutation of homage
with which the nearest servants of the king approach their

sovereign on a solemn occasion, and with which the whole
solemnity opens. But how entirely different is the homage
which must be paid to Him from that rendered to even the
most mighty earthly sovereign ! No wish can be expressed on
his behalf, since he has everything; only truly to know and
praise Him is the proper homage, at least for those who know
Him as his immediate servants do. The true knowledge of
Him, however, consists in perceiving how there is corresponding
to his *infinite holiness* or exaltation beyond everything evil,
which is his inmost nature, his equally *infinite glory* of revelation externally, *i.e.*, in the world : or that his glory is itself the
fulness of the world, and there is nothing in the world in which
that is not revealed. The verse, in accordance with these two
comprehensive sentences of the Saraphs' hymn, falls into two
members, and as they sing antiphonally, the one half of them
the one part and the other half the other part of the hymn,
their hymn becomes an antiphone (in choirs Ps. xxvi. 12).
This is expressly said ver. 3, and must be supposed from the
nature of the temple-music of the priests. When it is considered with what sublimity and how worthily they sing it, the
shortest doxology must be deemed sufficient ; and how im-
perishably must it be fixed in the memory of that mortal who
may have once distinctly heard it !

Nevertheless, the thought would be quite unsuitable at this
place, that this hymn was so powerful that its sound had made
the projections of the thresholds tremble : it is intended to
vibrate through hearts, Yesaya's, for instance, not thresholds. There is but one loud cry which can be heard above
this hymn and make everything tremble : that is the voice of
God himself, who is certainly meant by *him that crieth*, ver. 3,
as in the similar case Amos vii. 4, see vol. I. p. 197. Neither
can it be proved from ver. 3 that *he who crieth* is the same as
they who cry. On the contrary, it appears immediately by the
smoke which soars lightly from the altar what the meaning of
this cry is. The word קַם bears the same relation to שָׁפָה as

labrum to *labium,* and probably came as an architectural term
from the Phœnicians; אֲמוֹת denotes, in accordance with the
meaning of its root, the *foreparts* or projections, exactly like
the Arab. *imām;* comp. also Tanhûm on Judges xix. 27.

From the mention of a *chipped stone (stückstein),* or a *bond-
stone (legstein),* רִצְפָּה ver. 6, which could be easily detached
from the rest with tongs, it follows that the genuine altars even
in the temple of Israel still continued to copy the primitive
simplicity of the true Hebrew altars, especially in the construction of the hearth. (Comp. *Alterthümer* p. 162 sq. (137)).

Ver. 9: *hear* the divine truths, which are preached by the
prophets, which is what is primarily intended; and *see* the
divine wonders which are still always appearing in history. But
it is as if they were destined never to *understand* those nor
to *perceive* these.

מַצֶּבֶת vi. 13, precisely like *stipes* from *stare,* is our *stump,*
(Germ. *stumpf, strunk*) trunk. With a marvellously incisive
brevity the whole thought to which the sentence points is
thrown into the last word.

---

2. The main portion of the book.

Ch. vii. 1—ix. 6.

This entire chief section of the book could only have
supplied, by its narratives and discourses, the confirmation of the twofold truth with which the introductory
narrative so emphatically closed. As far as we can now see
from evidence that has been preserved, it consisted of the
following pieces:

(1). *(lost.)*

In all probability there stood here at the commencement a
piece the contents and objects of which may be surmised from
the words of viii. 18. We see from this verse that the
prophet's own name had been made an object of prophetic

significance to his own mind. Whether he had received the
name *Yesaya*, i.e., *God's salvation*, from his parents before he
became a prophet or not, in either case it could symbolize the
genuine prophetic truth, that eternal salvation is to be sought
in Yahvé only, but in him is certainly to be found. And just
as his entire family, as we shall soon see, became in our
prophet's mind lofty symbols of his divine convictions and
hopes, so was this the case especially with his own name. It
must have once appeared to him in his prophetic ecstacy as if
Yahvé said to him: as certainly as he had been called *God's
salvation*, and must continue to be so called, does salvation
dwell only in the true God, but certainly, in spite of all the
existing gloom, exists in Him for all those who desire not to
keep far from Him ; the prophet must, therefore, continue to
live as an unmistakable witness to this twofold truth, and to
walk openly before all men in its bright light. And from that
time he could neither hear his own name nor remember who he
was without having this fundamental hope brought afresh to
his mind : his bare name, when it had once been explained in
this sense, might also serve as an admonition to the world
around him. It is not difficult to comprehend what a number
of the profoundest and most glorious truths could be connected with the simple event of this solemn consecration of
the prophet's name. In his description of this event, he had
but to give vent to the thoughts which flowed from the immediate stream of divine thought and speech of that occasion.
It may be certainly gathered from what Yesaya says towards
the end of the book viii. 18, with a brief backward reference,
that somewhere in the book such words of God were poured
forth in connexion with a narrative. And·it is quite allowable
to suppose that this piece stood at the opening of this chief
section of the book, and also in close connexion with ch. vi.
How gloomily the piece ch. vi. closes ! And shall he who has
just received the divine call, who has just been brought into
the presence of God, remain content with his first faint, inter-

cessory utterance, vi. 11, and the immediate answer to it, vv.
11-13 ? Must he not at least, as at other times is his habit,
wrestle at the conclusion for a divine sign and pledge with
regard to the promise which lies concealed in the words, vi.
11-13 ? Well, thou thyself with thy name *God's-salvation* shalt
live and move as this sign ! This might be the response of the
divine oracle. At this time the prophet was still quite alone,
a mere man and a name ! But if he henceforth only constantly lives and labours in the true divine idea of all that
lies in his name, to how great an extent can he labour, suffer,
and overcome in the divine spirit !

The above supposition can, however, be made probable from
another consideration. Both Yéremyá and Hézeqiêl in the
commencement of their books have the introduction of our
book before their minds, and sketch similar descriptions. But
when Yéremyá, i. 11-19, and Hézeqiel, ii. 9—iii. 21, attach to
the description of the call, with which Yesaya ch. vi. corresponds, some additional ones of a like character, it looks exactly
as if they had read in their book of Yesaya something further
after ch. vi. which was closely connected in point of meaning
with the description of the call and consecration.

(2). *(lost.)*

For similar reasons it is clear that a piece immediately
followed, in which was narrated how Yesaya, when his first
son was born, came by divine instigation to give him the name
Sheár-yashûb, i.e. the remnant will be converted. This is presupposed by the words which follow vii. 3-viii. 18, and corresponds
to the following instance, viii. 3 sq. The matter itself had also
its solemn import in the mind of Yesaya. The prophets Yôel, iii.
8, 'Amôs ix. 7, sq., and Hoséa had, it is true, already substantially proclaimed the bitter, and yet in another aspect, cheering
anticipation, that an entirely new and really Messianic Israel
must be formed,—that of the existing nation only a *remnant*,
proved and purified by the profound sufferings, which had

been sent as a divine punishment upon the present incorrigible Israel, would remain as the indestructible germ of a new and truly reformed nation. But this view came upon Yesaya, acc. vi. 13, from the very first with much greater force. As early in his life as the birth of his first son, it appeared to him as if he were impelled by the divine spirit to name him, in accordance with this view, as a divine image and pledge of a future nobler Israel, in order that this child might grow up as a divine sign of the conviction, that there might be a nobler Israel, and that this was confidently to be looked for, at all events in the future. This prophetic conception with its blessed certainty was thus compressed as briefly as possible into this entirely new name. He subsequently refers at every opportunity to the comfort which had been given him in the short name and its idea, vii. 3 ; viii. 3 ; but not less to the humbling truth which was included in it for Israel as it then was, x. 20-22. Indeed, it is noteworthy how familiar this short word *Sheár* gradually became to him everywhere in quite other connexions.*

It cannot be concluded from the example of the following case, viii. 3, sq. that this piece was very short. In the case of the birth of his second son, Yesaya might naturally make his narrative more concise. Besides, the meaning of the name of the second son had been already to a certain extent prefigured by what had been said with regard to the name of the first. But in the case of the first son he would desire to expound at some length the thought which was to be conveyed in the new name both for its own sake and because the case was quite a new one.

If this event as Yesaya narrated it, took place during the

---

* One may say he was himself the first to form this very short word שְׁאָר acc. § 153 *a* : the earlier word is שְׁאֵרִית or פְּלֵיטָה, which he himself employed in the previous book, iv. 2 ; it is from this time that he also uses frequently שְׁאָר xvii. 3 ; xxi. 17 ; xxviii. 5; x. 19 ; xi. 11, 16; beside in Yesaya it is used afterwards only Sseph. i. 4, and still later authors. This instance clearly shows in what way a new word is originated, and how it gains currency.

reign of Yotham, it is easy to explain the transition to the events which occurred under Ahaz, which is made in the first words of the next piece.

(3). vii. 1-17.

We here learn that under this king the kingdoms of Damascus and Ephráim had, from fear of the Assyrians, formed an alliance with the view of making a more energetic attack upon the kingdom of Yuda. Under Ahaz this kingdom had sunk very low, and the two allied powers hoped to strengthen themselves against the Assyrians by its complete subjugation. The inroads of the two powers into the territory of the bordering nations which were subject to Yuda had commenced during the reign of Yotham, and were continued successfully under Ahaz, 2 Kings xv. 37 ; xvi. 5, but the powers now concluded a close alliance for the purpose of making an advance upon Jerusalem with their combined armies. They intended to take this strong city, and to place there a king of their own choice as their vassal, of the name of Ben-Tâbeél, vii. 6, probably one of the Syrian magnates mentioned ix. 10. Accordingly as soon as the report reached Jerusalem, that an army with this object in view was collected in the north, in the ancient territory of the tribe of Ephráim, all the inhabitants were thrown into the greatest alarm. The king Ahaz, with the rest of the royal family, suddenly lost all self-possession and courage : it was evident that he was in danger of adopting the most disastrous measures from base fear ; and at last in his alarm he did really resort to the exceedingly doubtful and humiliating expedient of calling to his rescue by submissive requests and homage the Assyrian king, who then, we know, destroyed Damascus with one blow and made Yuda tributary, 2 Kings xvi. 10-20. The people of Yuda, to a great extent, without doubt, tired of the weak and unjust rule of this Davîdic king, was glad of some change, but had such little knowledge of the sources of true help, that it beheld with a certain satisfaction the progress of the combined enemies, viii. 6, 12. This unhappy state of things was made worse by the false prophets and magicians of all kinds who enjoyed the favour of the king, viii. 19. Yesaya, with his more intimate friends, alone preserved in this dark time of trial his manliness and presence of mind, maintaining and expounding, everywhere and against everyone, the true view of the situation and its divine lesson; and as his fellow-citizens refused for a time to understand him, he repeated unweariedly in the most varied forms the same fundamental truths. The following very important pieces supply a compressed abridgment of the very various prophetic discourses and labours of this period. The first piece narrates only Yesaya's transactions directly with the king.

vii. 1-9.

The eternal, unchanging, fundamental principles which Yesaya held could not leave him in doubt with regard to his message to the king in the first moment of his surprise and despondency. The first advice of the prophet would be, before all things, circumspection, calmness and trust in Yahvé are needed here, that no precipitate step may be taken. Nor, when the resources and purposes of the enemy were quietly thought over, could it escape any but a superficial glance, that this desperate resolve of the combined nations, who were already not only greatly weakened by internal commotions but also threatened by the Assyrians, would not succeed. To the prophetic mind which without difficulty sees clearly through everything that is vain and weak, it very quickly became a certainty, that Yahvé would wholly overthrow the plans which had been projected with equal insolence and weakness against Jerusalem and the Davîdic kingdom. For, notwithstanding the first confusion, there was at that time too much inward strength remaining in Jerusalem to permit it to be taken by a *coup de main,* and the Davîdic kingdom to be so easily destroyed; and a confident and hopeful mind in this prophet

and his friends was the best guarantee of this. Without being
invited by the king, Yesaya goes boldly to him for the purpose
of explaining this exhortation to be calm and the divine promise, that the enemy will not attain their object. This his first
utterance is purely one of encouragement, scarcely a syllable of
a slightly threatening tone creeping in at the end in reference
to the king's tendency to unbelief, vv. 1-9.

VII.

1   And it came to pass in the days of Ahaz the
son of Yotham the son of 'Uzzia, the king of
Yuda, that Ressîn the king of Arâm and Péqach
the son of Remalyáhu the king of Israel, marched
against Jerusalem to attack it, (but he was not
able to attack it). Then it was told to the house
of Davîd "Arâm encampeth in Ephráim," and his
heart shook and his people's heart as forest-trees
shake before the wind; but Yahvé said to Yesaya,
"go forth now to meet Ahaz thou with Sheâr-
Yashûb thy son at the end of the conduit of the
upper reservoir, upon the path to the fullers' field,
and say to him: Take heed and be quiet, fear not
and be not faint-hearted | at these two stumps of
smoking firebrands, | because the wrath of Ressîn
and of Arâm and of the son of Remalyáhu burneth. ||
5   Therefore because Arâm purposeth against thee
evil, | Ephráim and the son of Remalyáhu saying, ||
"let us march against Yuda and alarm it and take
it for ourselves, | and make as king in its midst the
son of Tâbeél!" || thus saith the Lord Yahvé: |
It will not stand and not come to pass! || For
Arâm's head is Damascus, and Damascus' head

Ressîn, *and Ephráim's head Samaria, and Samaria's head the son of Remalyáhu: [but Yuda's
head is Jerusalem, and Jerusalem's head is
Yahvé]. | If ye confide not, verily ye shall not
abide. || *

 * *and within sixty-five years Ephráim is broken,
no longer a nation.* ||

The observation, ver. 1, that the intention of these kings was
not as a matter of fact carried out, is here merely by the way,
since it really interrupts the thread of the narrative (comp.
something similar xx. 1). It appears also as if the intention of
the remark was to give prominence at the outset to the folly of
the fear which prevailed in Jerusalem; for the addition is clearly
made because subsequently the event fully confirmed Yesaya's
announcement. In the continued use of the singular number of
the verbs, ver. 1, is implied that the Syrian king was generally
considered to be the more powerful of the two, and the king of
Samaria as not much more than his vassal. The reason why
Yesaya was directed to go to the place indicated outside a gate
on the north of Jerusalem, is probably no other than that
Ahaz was generally unwilling to appear in public, but now
probably desired to examine the walls of the weakest side of
the city and make preparations against a siege, induced to do
so by blind fear (comp. xxii. 8-11); but as appears from ver.
13 sq., he had gone out with many other like-minded servants
of his royal house. The fact that Yesaya had to take with him
his son, whom (as must have been fully explained in the piece
which has perished) he had named *the remnant will be converted*,
had manifestly the object, that the presence of the boy should
again call to remembrance the divine and comforting thought
which was implied in his presence and life—the thought,
that there was a sure hope for Israel at least in the future,

 * Germ. *Glaubet ihr nicht, ja so bleibet ihr nicht.*

comp. x. 21.—Circumspection and calmness is so much the
easier, it is said ver. 4, inasmuch as the enemies do indeed burn
with anger, but not like a new brand which may burn for a long
time and consume a great deal, they, on the contrary, are no
more than two ends of burnt-out smoking brands. Rather
because they have formed plans which are as wicked as they
are vain, nothing that they purpose shall according to the will
of Yahvé in anywise come to pass ; otherwise the world of
these three kingdoms, which have been thus brought into comparison, would have to be revolutionised, and those two would
not have their well-known capitals and kings, and Yuda would
have neither Jerusalem for its capital nor Yahvé himself for its
king ! But in order that all this may come to pass according
to the will of God, there is needed on the part of the threatened
inhabitants of Jerusalem *confidence,* firm trust in Yahvé, faith
in his word ; and sad will it be if there is no firm *confidence !*
in that case, it is certain there would be no firm *continuance,*
no deliverance ; a play on the thought and the word (see Vol.
I. p. 69).

Vv. 2 and 19 נוּחַ is exactly like the Arabic *anākha* with
bi—, Hamâsa, p. 536, 10 sq.

Ver. 8, the last member is in this connexion clearly out of
place, and disturbing to the thought ; it destroys the pregnant
brevity and the uniformity of the sentences ; in any case it
must come after the first member of ver. 9, inasmuch as the
mention of Ephraim first occurs there ; and the thought itself,
is both incongruous in this connexion and contradicts the subsequent words ver. 16, by specifying the long period of 65
years. At the same time, the sentence has the genuine early
Hebrew and early prophetic ring ; and the period of 65 years,
i.e., a little less than a a life-time,* before the end of a man's

---

* Just as 1005 in the narrative, 1 Kings v. 12, is clearly intended to denote as a
round number simply *something more than* 1000.

existence, may be conceived as proposed by a prophet as a round number, equally as well as the well-known 70 years of Yéremyá, comp. also Ez. iv. 5. The most natural supposition, therefore, is that these words were found in an early oracle of some prophet, and were originally, on account of the similarity of their meaning, placed simply in the margin ; comp. further on this passage, Vol. I. p. 304.

On the other hand we have every reason to suppose that the bracketed words, ver. 9, have accidentally slipped out of the text, and must be restored for the sake of the sense. We should otherwise have to take the כִּי, ver. 8, with the LXX, as meaning *but*, and interpret the word as saying, In reference to the great change which the two kings purpose to make, everything shall, on the contrary, remain as it is, Jerusalem shall not be their capital and they shall not be its heads ! But even this meaning, which would be moreover somewhat insipid, could only with difficulty be found in the words. It is therefore, better to separate the sentences with כִּי and supply the above words : the words which would be suitable here must be few and forcible !

vii. 10—17.

Since Ahaz hesitates to give his answer, Yesaya, impressed with the importance of the matter, goes further and does his utmost to inspire him with faith and confidence : he offers to give him any external sign which he may wish of the truth of the promise from Yahvé, however difficult and far off the sign may be, whether in hell or in heaven. For it would indeed be desirable that the pure divine word, where it is manifest, should at once suffice for every emergency, and should have inherent power to produce faith and confidence. But in actual life it is only too often the case that the mind of men is too much confused and their courage too weak to permit them to yield up themselves to the pure force of the word : it is then that the sign comes in with its palpable meaning to aid

human weakness. The sign is a sign, or token, of the truth
which has been uttered, a prelude and beginning of the promised matter, a likeness in lower and sensible things which
points to corresponding higher things that have not yet
entered the world of sense ; it is at the same time a proof that
that Spirit who grants this prefigurement and prelude will also
bring to pass at the right time that which has been only
guaranteed or promised by him. If therefore, for instance,
some one who had expressed his desire to assist a country, should
meet the unbelief of his hearers by proving before their eyes
upon some individual of their number his power to help, he
would be able to appeal to this as a sign, and he would attract
the attention of all. Just as a person who has long been inwardly prepared for a great event, nevertheless often gladly looks
for some external indication, or preliminary instigation, corresponding to the matter and seeming to him to supply a pledge of
success (Judges ch. vi.). It is true enough that there is no real
inward connexion between an external sign and the truth ; and
as the sign does not necessarily produce belief in the truth, the
whole attention may easily be absorbed upon the mere external,
remarkable, and wonderful aspects of the sign. The desire to
supply a sign may become in the case of the prophet jugglery,
and to see one, in the case of the people, simple curiosity.
Indeed, in the latter case, it may become obduracy against the
truth itself, when the people, who might perceive the truth
without a sign, reject it by demanding as the condition of its
acceptance, a sign, and perhaps one of the strangest which has
no connexion with the matter itself. Hence even in the Old
Testament the principle is laid down, that men may not tempt
God, *i.e.* may not demand from him in an improper way things
or signs with reference to which they either doubt, or ought to
doubt, whether he will grant them in the form in which they
were demanded, ver. 12 ; Exodus xvii. 2, 7 ; Deut. vi. 16.
Nevertheless, notwithstanding these imminent dangers and
very early abuses, primitive antiquity was especially the time

when an assistance of this kind could hardly be dispensed
with. Insight into higher spiritual things was at that time too
uncommon, faith in truths at a distance from the common life
of man was too weak, and the great prophets stood so much
alone that they were probably often compelled to stoop to
supply signs and tokens, in order first to arouse the faith and
to prepare the minds of their hearers to enable them to perceive
higher things. In the case of some prophets this might easily
grow into a custom; and it is precisely Yesaya, the prophet
who both illuminates and illustrates by examples any subject
with such impressive force and also carries the weak and
resisting along with him, that loves, both at or without his
hearers' request, to supply such signs, and to connect this
special exertion with his proper prophetic work, xxxvii. 30;
xxxviii. 7, 22. There is no doubt but this was an exertion, for
in those cases in which the sign is not promised as one which
will appear in the future, in the natural course of things, as,
for instance, vii. 14, sq.; xxxvii. 30, it must have cost no little
effort to supply this external supplement and show-piece on the
spot. And the more Ahaz was led astray by his false prophets,
evidently the more Yesaya made vigorous efforts in this direction also to bring him to a better faith (see on vii. 11).

In the present instance therefore, Yesaya endeavoured to put
forth all his energies and make use of the most extreme measures to overcome the serious unbelief of Ahaz. The king is
asked to request a sign from Yahvé, of some kind or other,
inasmuch as the prophet fully hopes that that God who impels
him to proclaim the urgent truth, will also give him power to
grant the sign which Ahaz may call for. In all cases a sign, a
supplied proof, lays a moral obligation upon him that requests
it: when, however, a tried and acknowledged prophet offers to
supply a proof, when in reality it is not necessary, and puts
forth his utmost energies, it is certainly, to say the least,
nothing more than reasonable that he to whom this offer is
made should not reject the proffered method by which he may

6 *

discover the truth. If he were to decline it, it could only be
because he entertained a secret dread of the truth, and on that
account spurned the way to it which had been very mercifully
proposed. In that case he would really fall into a double
error, and by his hopelessly invincible unbelief would excite
the prophet's displeasure, and, without doubt, plunge himself
into still greater errors and misery. It appears very soon that
Ahaz is really in this deplorable condition: because from the
very first he is too weak to possess pure faith and divine
courage, he declines, with a miserable excuse, to request a sign,
thereby displaying nothing but the true and irremediable
condition of his soul.

And the prophet cannot hold his peace nor withdraw, because Ahaz, from a cowardly unbelief, withdraws. Divine
truth cannot be mistaken, and asserts itself with the greater
energy precisely when men intentionally decline to receive it:
Yahvé must unsolicited give a sign which Ahaz is unwilling to
see. The sign, however, will now be of a different kind from
what it would have been had he evinced faith and fidelity at
this decisive moment: this sign confirms what had been previously promised, and proclaims a happy event which the king
had not looked for, and which shall nevertheless come against
his will; but it also proclaims a calamity which he by faith
and fidelity might have averted, and which now becomes the
necessary punishment of his unbelief and resistance. The sign
becomes in more than one respect a marvellous symbol of the
true unfolding of the future, which no resistance on the part of
Ahaz can withstand.

For the Messianic views and hopes, which in the case of
Yesaya especially are the important stays and supports of all
his conceptions of the future, of themselves contain by their
very nature much that is wonderful, which may easily assume
the form of a more definite conception of particular important
signs and divine tokens of the future. It is indeed true that
the great changes and forms of the future must properly arise

according to their own inner necessity, without respect, therefore, to a Messiah. Without him, it is still certain, that the
eternal, divine work will be carried on. It no less appears from
the condition of affairs at the time through what vicissitudes
and in what stages the prophet must have thought the attain-
ment of the final divine end would be effected. If (1) the
future blessedness and perfection of the divine kingdom is to
be hoped for, a perfection which Yesaya, like all the prophets
of those centuries, conceived as not very distant, which their
prophetic aspirations probably delighted to discern on the
fringe of the horizon of their lives ; if then (2) Yesaya everywhere insists upon the truth that this very consummation can
never come in the midst of the serious transgressions of that
age, but that a grand destruction of the prevailing wickedness
must precede it, in order that a perfect state of things might
spring out of the existing untenable condition,—a destruction
which the prophet could then imagine only as brought about
by the Assyrians, and not by Damascus and Ephráim :—if
these two points were fixed, Yesaya must (3) have further supposed, that this great destruction would not take place at once
in the immediate future, but that instead of it there would be
deliverance from the danger which was threatening from
Damascus and Ephráim. These are, therefore, the three stages
in which the course of the future must have appeared to his mind,
and his last experience of the conduct of the king could only
make his conception of them still more vivid : first, deliverance
from the present danger, a wonderful, divine salvation, in
spite of all the fear and unbelief of Ahaz ; then subsequently
the great Assyrian conquest and destruction, rendered all the
more necessary as a chastisement of the whole land and especially of the royal house by the fact that both have become
entirely perverse and estranged from the true faith ; finally, the
great long-promised prosperity of the nation after it has been
tried and regenerated by the great affliction. At the same
time, although all this is true without a Messiah, it is not

Yesaya's habit to conceive it taking place without him. This
prophet always conceives of the Messiah as a chief member of
the blessed age, and precisely at this moment of most intense
excitement the thought of the certain existence and of the
appearance of this king, the diametrical opposite of the weak
and unworthy king before him, flashes through his soul, and
in a moment there stands before his mind the bright picture
showing how the coming of the Messiah, whose coming cannot
be doubted, although no one has visibly seen him, will be
related to these stages of the veiled future, and how he will
impress upon his age the divine signs and indications of his
appearance even before the great time of the consummation of
prosperity. At this moment all this appears suddenly to
Yesaya to be quite natural, although it is really a tremendous
stride, or rather leap, of the prophetic imagination, that it
should conceive the gradual rise of the Messiah, his birth, his
youth, and his coming to maturity, in the closest connexion
with the above three stages of the future; for the Messiah is
the representative of the nation in all its highest relations.
Accordingly (1) the birth of the Messiah falls in the not very
distant period of deliverance from the present peril, as if this
minor deliverance were a prelude, and as it were, the first
glimmerings of the great general deliverance to be looked for
in the third stage; and it is indeed fitting that at the birth of
the Messiah, who is to appear fully at the time of the great
deliverance, the first beams of the great light should flash
through the world, since the light must subsequently return in
his manhood, and, having become perfect, remain for ever.
The fact that a child who is to be the Messiah comes into the
world, is of itself the commencement and possibility of complete perfection, the first dawn of the bright day: accordingly
on his very entrance into the world he must announce himself
as an uncommon child; and, born under wonderful conditions,
inasmuch as a light of divine deliverance then flashes upon
men, he must become by his birth and the name he receives a

pledge of his future high destination. On the other hand, he cannot come earlier, and until this period no child can bear the name *God-with-us*. (2) As it is proper that the child which is destined to such high prosperity should also share the sufferings which the whole nation through its own fault suffers under, his youth falls in the time of the great destruction and degeneracy of the land, and he suffers like all his fellow countrymen, in this time of trial and transition. But of course (3) his manhood falls in the time of the great prosperity, of which he is the real stay and protection. And thus his own and his nation's happiness and prosperity spring forth and grow in inseparable connexion through all vicissitudes.

Now, just as the flash of this prophetic glimpse darts through the prophet's mind, the marvellous signs which Yahvé will give to the present king on precisely this mysterious history of the *Coming One*, the man and king of the future, also present themselves clearly to his vision; certain strange tokens, occurring with reference to a child which will soon be born, shall at the right time be given to Ahaz, whether he wishes to see them or not. These are the attesting marks of the birth and the youth of that wonderful child. They are given that the king may perceive how certainly deliverance is at hand in the immediate future, and how vain is his present fear, but that he may at the same time perceive how great the distant calamity is which he will bring upon his land by his present resistance of Yahvé and what is good, and how certainly Yahvé will punish him in the future. A sign or a description from the third stage of the whole future and of the life of the child, has no place in this connexion, where rather the calamity and the punishment which he will bring upon himself and his land, together with the deliverance from the immediate danger, must be shown to Ahaz; and though the punishment of his unbelief may be delayed, it is all the more certain that it will come in the somewhat distant future. The description of the manhood of the boy and of the blessed age is supplied subsequently, viii. 23—ix. 6.

Yesaya knows that he cannot hold long discourses, at all
events in the presence of this king; his words must be shorter
in this case than they were before even, vv. 4-9. But he
neither can nor will do more than point to signs which God
himself will give to him, although he is unwilling to see them.
It thus follows naturally that the signs which the prophet declares against the will of Ahaz must be presented in as brief,
abrupt, and pointed a form as is possible: the more briefly and
pointedly they can be framed the better; they must take the
obtuse hearer by surprise, and arouse him from his insensibility;
only a few words can be spared having immediate reference to
Ahaz himself, for the purpose of necessary explanation, ver.
17 sq.

10   And Yahvé spoke further to Ahaz thus : ∥ " Ask
for thee a sign from Yahvé thy God, going deep
down to hell or high into heaven!" ∥ But Ahaz
said "I will not ask nor tempt Yahvé!" ∥ Then
said he: hear now ye of Davîd's house! | is it too
little to you to weary men, that ye also weary my
God? ∥ Therefore will the Lord himself give you
a sign : | lo the young-woman will conceive and
bear a son, and then calleth his name *With-us-
God.* ∥ Cream and honey will he eat | when he
will know to refuse the evil and to choose the
good. ∥ — For before the boy knoweth to refuse
the evil and to choose the good, | the land will
be desolated before whose two kings thou art
alarmed. ∥ — Yahvé will bring upon thee and
upon thy people and thy father's house days which
have not come since Ephráim revolted from
Yuda, | the king of Assyria! ∥

To desire not to tempt God, ver. 12, is certainly laudable,
when it is prompted by an effort of self-control, but in the

present case, when it serves, for want of a better, as a pure
excuse for unbelief, it includes a two-fold transgression, as the
prophet immediately explains, ver. 13, namely, contempt of the
human endeavour of the prophet, of his care and earnest zeal,
and, which is much more important, contempt and grieving of
the divine spirit itself, of the God of the prophet, who was
just about to put forth all his power at this moment through
the prophet for the purpose of helping the king. For it was
evident, and the prophet himself felt it, that in offering a sign
he exerted his spiritual powers to the utmost, and determined
with all his force to let the God work through him. Nothing
could cause him greater pain than that Ahaz then desired with
his hollow, and, indeed, Pharisaical, excuses, to retreat from
the Divine when it summoned up its utmost forces to lead him
into the right way. But Yahvé cannot be thwarted: if men
will not receive what he mercifully offers to them, he still
presents it, only in the form in which the rebellious deserve it;
a sign will be given by him without solicitation, which brings
the good that Ahaz would not accept by his free choice, ver.
14, but also a great evil, which he now doubly deserves, ver.
15. When she, who is now a young woman, *i.e.* marriageable,
shall conceive and bear a son, which may very well take place
within the space of a year, she will call the new-born child by
the name *With-us-God,* we feel marvellously Yahvé's help (and
the new-born child, born at the time of such an unexpected
manifestation of divine deliverance, as upon the first stage of
the new reformed era, bears in himself the eternal hope of the
kingdom, is the young Messiah at the first stage of his development, viii. 8, 10; ix. 5). But in an equally strange manner
he will eat cream and honey as he approaches the period of his
youth, when he enters upon the time of maturer growth (Manu
2. 212), when he is some 10 to 20 years old. Dost thou know
what that signifies? I will briefly indicate it. Before the boy
enters upon this riper age, a few years from the present time,
therefore, the allied Damascus and Ephráim will be already

desolated, so little are these two kings able to conquer Jerusalem, and so certainly is a divine deliverance immediately in prospect for this land, ver. 16 in explanation of ver. 14, only that the same image is preserved to a certain extent. But, which especially belongs here to be dealt with further, Yahvé will bring subsequently a great punishment upon thee and the whole land, days of calamity such as have not been experienced for centuries, namely, the Assyrian king, who when he has finished the destruction of the northern countries, will come to Yuda, ver. 17 in explanation of ver. 15. Accordingly nothing is in reality said, ver. 14, as to the nature of the mother of the Messiah, since the young-woman is mentioned only in antithesis to the immature girl, in order to indicate the time ; indeed, there is nothing said as to who the young-woman was, whose wife, of what family, because it has nothing to do with the connexion, and we can only conclude from xi. 1, that the prophet, like Mikha, conceived of the Messiah as coming from the stock of Davîd. But every interpretation is equally false which does not perceive that the prophet is here speaking of the developing Messiah, of him, therefore, to whom the land and the kingdom properly belongs, and with the thought of whom the heart of the prophet leaps in blessed hope, viii. 8 ; ix. 5 sq.

Ver. 11, הַעֲמֵק and הַגְבֵּהַּ are infinitive absolutes, acc. § 280, and for that reason alone the Massôrites cannot have considered שְׁאָלָה as the imperative instead of שְׁאַל, which would besides destroy the structure of the verse members. Neither can it stand for שְׁאָלָה, simply on account of the pause, as appears from § 93 *a* ; but mainly on account of the harmony of sound with לְמָעְלָה the *ô* is changed into an *â*. It is moreover unmistakable that when Yesaya mentions, and, indeed, in the first place, a sign from Hell, it is done only because he well knew, acc. viii. 19, how greatly Ahaz preferred his necromancers and other false prophets of the same kind, and, as it were, for the purpose of rivalling them, whose arts he did not fear. Thus was repeated the ancient contest between Moses and the Egyptian magicians! Comp. Sur. vi. 35. But in what way Yesaya would have waged the contest had the king accepted the challenge, it is now impossible to say.

In ver. 13 sq. it is obvious that the prophet is perfectly able to moderate his words, although it is the very moment when his righteous anger is burning hotly: instead of addressing the king exclusively, he turns intentionally to the *house of Davîd*, or the court which attended the king, and which was in a certain sense the same as what is now called the government. Yet ver. 16 sq. the *thou* recurs with equal propriety.

In ver. 14 it must be especially remembered that הָעַלְמָה, *the young-woman*, forms the antithesis of both the *girl*, as the not yet marriageable child, and the *old woman*; but at least in such a serious and accurate discourse as this, the married woman, although she may be young, cannot be intended; however, the use of the article, *the* young-woman, follows naturally in this connexion, acc. § 277 *a*, from these antitheses, and it would be absurd to think it was used to point out some particular, and in so far definite, young women who might be standing near. It is, therefore, the indication of the time of this birth which the prophet primarily aims at; and it is only from the entire sense of the two members of the sentence that the thoughtful hearer can discover that the Messiah is intended. In fact, it would not have been easy to discover the reference to the Messiah from the words alone, unless his coming had long since been foretold, with sufficient clearness and publicity, by Yesaya and other prophets. It is the special manner and certainty of his coming from the first conceivable moment of his entrance into the world, that is the new element in this passage. Nothing can be more preposterous than to imagine that the prophet intended by the young-woman a wife of the king's, or even his own. Comp. further, *Jahrbücher der Bibl. Wiss.* I. p. 43 sq., VI. p. 102. On לדעתו ver. 15, as indicating the time of the action, see § 217 *d*. As, however, the language

is here everywhere remarkably pliant and apt, a new definition
of time is immediately connected with it, ver. 16. But since the
rapid language at the close hastens especially to the threatening portion of the discourse, which is still kept back and yet
must necessarily be uttered, this is at length, ver. 17, introduced with great abruptness. It might be supposed that the
words את מלך אשור both here and ver. 20; viii. 7, are an
ancient gloss : but the occurrence of the same words three
times is of itself remarkable, and the addition ואת כל כבדו viii.
7, is quite Yesayanic ; in addition, the explanation is in point of
meaning correct, for in ver. 18 Egypt is mentioned with
Assyria merely because it might be surmised that Egypt would
not quietly suffer the Assyrian to occupy Yuda, whilst it was
equally easy to foresee that the Assyrians would nevertheless
ultimately alone prevail, comp. ver. 20; viii. 7 sq., and all the
other oracles of Yesaya's. And if such an explanatory addition
or parenthesis would not be allowable in poetry, no one can
object to it when used by a prophet as a speaker. The discourse is here evidently unusually abrupt at the close, because
the prophet hastens to bring even it to a conclusion, knowing
well what and to whom he is speaking, and is already at the
point of leaving the king in haste.

(4.) ——— Ch. vii. 18—viii. 4.

Thou wilt not hope or expect anything divine, although the
time itself is of so unusual a nature ? Well, then, hear something which is incomparably more marvellous than thou wilt
now believe, and which will take place in spite of thy unbelief
both for thy unexpected deliverance as well as for thy distress !
Yesaya had thus spoken to Ahaz, who was so deaf to every
earnest word ; in brief impressive terms the prophet had even
proclaimed, as far as this could be done to such an unwilling
hearer, the truth which was most fitted to be of immediate use.
But when this was done his stay could not be prolonged : and

Ahaz would scarcely have suffered him to remain longer in his presence. It is of itself inconceivable that the following words, vv. 18-25, were a continuation of his address to the king, and they do not show a single trace of having been uttered in his presence.

We must therefore suppose that between ver. 17 and ver. 18 something has been lost. We ought to have here an announcement that Yesaya left the king; probably also that he then went quietly home with his boy, and that from that time he commenced at every opportunity to set forth and to prove more fully, to a circle who would better understand him, the same surmisings and truths which Ahaz would not hear. It is probable that several particulars were recorded here in a form which may be gathered from such passages as viii. 19. But the prophet must especially have seized an opportunity to explain more particularly the name 'Immanûel, vii. 14, and to give prominence to the certain coming of the Messiah. This follows from viii. 8-10, where there is such an emphatic retrospective reference to 'Immanûel that the expression there used in such a rapid manner is by no means explained, simply from the almost enigmatical words, vii. 14. It follows also from Mikha, v. 2, where the Messiah's mother and his relation to a greater part of his brothers, *i.e.* fellow-countrymen, are mentioned in such a manner that we must suppose a reference to a detailed description by an earlier prophet, who could have been no other than Yesaya, inasmuch as he first spoke of a mother of the Messiah. It follows, finally, from the passage which has been preserved as

vii. 18-25.

For this fragment has all the appearance of being the last strophe of a longer piece on the Messiah, which is amply descriptive and serves as a further explanation of the words, vv. 15, 17. But we may say with truth, that if Yesaya thus deemed the second of the two signs, mentioned in this order,

vv. 14, 15, needed more particular elucidation, he must with still greater certainty have further explained in a similar piece the first sign concerning 'Immanûel and his mother, and precisely here before ver. 18.

For on that day will Yahvé hiss hither the flies which are on the uttermost streams of Egypt,| and the bees which are in the land of Assyria; || they come and encamp all of them in the valleys of the mountain-walls and in the clefts of the rocks, | and in all thorn-hedges and in all pastures. ||
20 On that day will the Lord shave with the razor of the one hired beyond the river, by the king of Assyria, the head and the hair of the feet; | and also the beard it taketh away. || — And on that day will a man keep a young cow and two sheep; || and because they give much milk he will eat cream, | for cream and honey will every one eat that remaineth in the land. || And on that day will every place where are a thousand vines for a thousand silverlings, | — it will be for the thorns and the thistles; || with arrows and bow will men come thither, | for thorn and thistle will the whole land
25 be. || And all the mountains which are hoed with a hoe, thither will the fear of thorns and thistles not come, || but it will be a free pasture of the ox, and a place to be trodden of the sheep. ||

Vv. 18-25. Inasmuch as the rapid and brief explanation, ver. 17, could not embrace the unusual figure of eating cream and honey, ver. 15, because this requires a more circumstantial elucidation; and since the second half of the sign, the half announcing the punishment, no less needed further expansion;

the detailed explanation of these things follows, with freer
treatment, in a special strophe. As easily and quickly as a
bee-master calls his bees with hisses (v. 26) will Yahvé, ver.
18, call up into Yuda to battle the armies of the two great
countries which are so jealous of each other — all the most
injurious, stinging and tormenting creatures, the flies, or rather
gadflies, the symbol of Egypt, in which such creatures abound,
the Egyptian soldier, therefore, even from the extreme limits
of the land, and the troops of Assyria (Deut. i. 44; vii. 20.
Ps. cxviii. 12). They will not be slow to come, and then
quickly settle down in the land in vast multitudes, just as the
swarms of flying insects, these gadflies and wasps, at certain
times cover all the damp and lower portions of the country,
ver. 19. Then the entire land will be devastated, as if it were
eaten off, or rather shaved quite bald, and lose its ornament
and adornment, just as when every hair has been shaved off a
man, from top to toe, also the ornament of the beard, as if
Yahvé had for this purpose hired the razor beyond the
Euphrates, as an earthly king hires soldiers from foreigners to
use them for his own purposes, the razor being in this case, the
merciless king of Assyria, ver. 20.—When the land of Yuda is
thus totally devastated, it must again become uncultivated and
waste, full of thorns and thistles instead of its present
valuable vineyards and cornfields, v. 6; xxxii. 13 sq.; the few
persons who are then left in the land need keep only a few
milch animals, since in such a country the wild pasturage will
be everywhere free, and, in conformity with this wild condition,
they will be able to live upon cream and honey alone, perhaps
also to a small extent from the chase, which will then be everywhere free, ver. 24; husbandry is not to be thought of, there
is not even *the fear of thorns and thistles* in those places which
are now most carefully by hoeing preserved from them, thorns
and thistles are allowed anywhere to grow up undisturbed.
And in this way therefore the young Messiah, who has not yet
appeared but will not fail to come, will also share as one of this

few the mournful lot of his land, will eat cream and honey as
he grows to manhood, and the marvellous sign will be fulfilled
in his own person.

In ver. 20 one might be led to suppose that הַשְּׂכִירָה, as a
simple passive participle, formed acc. § 149*e,* and construed
acc. § 335*a,* was a *razor which is hired beyond the Euphrates.*
But the flow of the words is smoother, if the word, newly
formed acc. § 166*a,* denotes *the hired army* itself, so that its
razor, as it is here called instead of *sword* merely on account of
the prevailing figure, is the king himself, as the further explanation itself adds.

With regard to ver. 23 comp. *Dichter des A.B.* ii. p. 414,
2nd ed.; and on ver, 25, comp. v. 2, 6, it may be again
remarked that the words יראת ——— לא תבוא cannot be understood in any other sense.

Other signs, viii. 1-4.

Whilst the prophet had in vain endeavoured to inspire the
king with faith and a good courage he lost (as we said) no
opportunity of otherwise illustrating and establishing in every
possible way the same great truths. He endeavoured, especially
to present and impress upon every one in the clearest way by
means of new signs the truth most needed at that time, namely,
that there was nothing to fear from the two allied kings, but
that they would themselves soon see their own capitals conquered. Two opportunities of this kind which then presented
themselves are here briefly subjoined. In the first place, a
prophet, when his contemporaries will not at once understand
him, consigns with confidence the truth of his words to the
future to be thereby attested. A natural method of doing this
is, that he exhibits them in writing at the market-place, having
first reduced them into a brief and expressive sentence. Every
one may read this sentence, and lay to heart its meaning, and
in the end the fulfilment of his words may give to them

additional force, comp. xxx. 8 ; Hab. ii. 2. At that time nothing was of such importance as to hold fast the truth, that
Damascus and Samaria would soon be themselves taken, and
that there was already one at hand who was not in the habit of
waiting long to fetch the prey assigned to him, this is, the
Assyrian. Accordingly Yesaya sets up in the presence of
witnesses a public monumental tablet to *Quick-robbery, Hasty-
booty*, or (as may be equally well said) *Robbery-quick, Booty-
hasty*, the meaning of which every one should lay to heart, and
look for the early fulfilment of the prophecy which was thus
clearly given. Proper names formed in this way from entire
sentences take readily a double meaning : *Quickrobbery* may
declare that something will be quickly robbed, or may indicate
the person who is quick in robbing. In the latter sense the
name may therefore point to the Assyrian : but inasmuch as
the first thing in the prophet's mind is the deliverance of
Jerusalem by the sacking of the two cities of the enemy, he
forms two names of a similar signification in allusion to the
two kingdoms. In the second place, he gave this same newly
coined name of the age to a son who was born at that time, in
order that the divine certainty that Jerusalem, *i.e.* the community of true religion, enjoyed secure protection, might also be
perpetuated in the life of this son of his, and be constantly
brought up again into the memory by his name. These two
facts concerning this new name with its two applications are
so briefly narrated that its signification is not explained before
the end of both narratives, ver. 4. The significant name of
the prophet's older son was referred to, p. 74.

VIII.

1   And Yahvé said to me: " take thee a large
tablet | and write thereon in popular characters
Bootyquick's Spoilspeedy's, ‖ and I will take me as
faithful witnesses the priest Uria and Zakharya

2   7

son of Yebérekhyáhu." ‖ And I approached the
prophetess and she conceived and bare a son;
then said Yahvé to me: "call his name *Bootyquick Spoilspeedy;*" ‖ for before the boy will have
knowledge to say my father! my mother! | they
shall carry away Damascus's wealth and Samaria's
booty before the Assyrian king. ‖

The new name, vv. 1, 3, denotes properly *he of the speedy
booty of the quick robbery*, construed acc. § 288c, the greatest
brevity combined with the greatest clearness being desired in
names; on מַהֵר see § 240 e. To this name is further prefixed,
ver. 1, the ־לְ, as in all inscriptions, acc. § 292 a, properly monument *of the (des)* .... comp. Ez. xxxvii. 16. Yesaya must also
write the few letters upon a great tablet in *popular characters*
(*leuteschrift*), *i.e.* large and plain, that every one may read the
inscription easily; the name חרט אנוש indicates most likely
the opposite of the literary character, which the learned only
could read, and which probably by that time was already distinguished from the general popular character by its brevity
and smallness. Lastly, witnesses are used at the erection of a
monument, in order that it may be subsequently known by
whom and when it was erected; and Yesaya could not choose
two better historical witnesses than Uria, who acc. 2 Kings
xvi. 10 sq. was then High Priest, and Zakharya, who, to judge
from his being associated here with Uria, was probably at that
time the mayor of Jerusalem (that he was a prophet is the
baseless supposition of some moderns). That Yesaya carried
out all these directions is too much a matter of course to need
to be mentioned.

The manner of narration, ver. 3, would be interpreted too
rigidly, if it should be supposed that וָאֶקְרַב describes an
action which occurred immediately after ver. 2: but vv. 3, 4, as
regards their facts, are distinct from the foregoing verses, and

it seemed to the later time when all this was written unnecessary to supply the special dates of the different actions mentioned here; it was enough that conception, birth, and naming
occurred generally at that time, and nothing more definite is
conveyed by the indications of time chosen. The definition
of time in ver. 4 agrees in a general way with that of vii. 14;
and both of Yesaya's sons, the one mentioned here, and the
elder one, vii. 7, with their significant names are intended,
ver. 18.

5.   Conclusion.   viii. 5—ix. 6.

What the prophet has further to say, partly new and partly by
way of conclusion to what has gone before, he finally collects
into three strophes, which are in the form of a discourse rather
concerning than to the mass of the people. Unhappily the
people, putting out of view their seducers, the false prophets,
are not at this time of trial without blame; and yet not only
is deliverance from the immediate danger certain, but the great
final Messianic deliverance is equally so; indeed, it is guaranteed by a multitude of signs and precious pledges. Thus
this closing discourse continues to sway hither and thither with
the ebb and flow of the most varied emotions, till at last all
the storms of agitated feeling are laid to rest in exclusive remembrance of the divine certainty of eternal blessedness. Because
the people cherished a secret satisfaction at the progress of the
two allied kings (see p. 76 sq.), they must suffer in the future a
severe and deserved punishment from the Assyrian conquest,
but there is nothing to fear from the present dangers, since in
general, as Yesaya has again on this occasion himself most
vividly experienced within his own soul, there is in Israel an inexhaustible salvation the moment they yield not to the common,
but to the true and higher fear, the fear of Yahvé, lest they fall
in the time of trial, vv. 6-15. With trust in all these truths
and signs and pledges of the eternal salvation, the prophet is
able to calmly look into the future; but they who now build

upon vain things and false prophets, will one day, when the great destruction comes upon the land, in vain wish that they had followed these truths, vv. 16-22. Nevertheless, in spite of all the present darkness, which is to some extent already at hand and partly still threatening, the final approach of the blessed time with all its glory is certain, and even now the longing heart beats joyfully a welcome to it, ver. 23—ix. 6.

VIII.

5   And Yahvé spoke further unto me thus:

1

Because this people scorneth the softly flowing waters of Silóah | and with joy followeth Ressîn and the son of Remalyáhu: ‖ therefore then will the Lord bring over them the great and mighty waters of the Euphrates—the Assyrian king and all his glory; | which mounteth then over all its channels, and passeth over all its banks, ‖ striketh into Yuda overflowing and rolling, reaching to the neck, | and the outstretchings of its wings will fill the breadth of thy land *O With-us-God!* ‖ — Be enraged nations and—despair, and give heed all ye far-off lands! | equip you and—despair, equip you and despair! ‖ form a plan—then it it will be broken, | speak a word—then it will not stand! for *with us* is *God.* ‖ — For thus said Yahvé unto me in the ecstacy | and warned me not to walk in the way of this people: ‖ Ye shall not call everything rebellion which this people calleth rebellion, | and what it feareth neither fear nor dread: ‖ Yahvé of Hosts—him shall ye hallow, | and *he* shall be your fear and he your dread! ‖

He will indeed be both for a sanctuary | and for a stone of offence and for a rock of stumbling to the two houses of Israel, | for a gin and for a snare to the inhabitants of Jerusalem; || and many among them will stumble | and fall and break their limbs, and be snared and taken. ||

15

2.

" Roll up the oracle, | seal the doctrine by my disciples!" || Thus will I wait for Yahvé who hideth his face from Yaqob's House, | and hope in him; || I myself and the children which Yahvé hath given me are for signs and for omens in Israel | on the part of Yahvé of Hosts, who dwelleth on the Ssion-mount. || — And when they say unto you " Apply to the ghosts and to the soothsayers, that chirp and that mutter:" | (do not the people apply to their gods, instead of the living to the dead?) ||—" for doctrine and for oracle!" | yes thus will he say who hath no daybreak; || then he runneth through bowed down and hungry, | yet when he hungereth and fretteth himself, he curseth his king and God and gazeth upwards; || and to the earth he looketh : | yet there is distress and darkness, the gloomiest trouble—and into the blackness is he driven. ||

3.

Yet the land cannot be darkened which is distressed : | as the former time brought shame to Zabulon and to Naphtali, the latter also bringeth

IX. honour—towards the Sea, beyond the Yordan,

1   towards the Heathen-march; ‖ the people that walketh in darkness seeth a great light, | they who dwell in the land of gloom—light shineth upon them; ‖ thou multipliest the generation, to it increasest the joy, | they rejoice before thee as men rejoice in the harvest, as they exult at the division of spoil. ‖ For the yoke of his burden and the staff of his shoulder, | the rod of his driver thou breakest

5   as in Midian's days. ‖ — Yea every boot of him that marcheth with noise, and the garment rolled in blood— | that will be for burning, for fuel of fire. ‖ For a child is born to us, a son is given unto us, | and the government cometh upon his shoulder, | and they call his name *Wonderful-Counsellor Hero-God, Everlasting-Father Prince-of-Peace*: ‖ for the increase of the government and for endless weal, | on behalf of Davîd's throne and on behalf of his kingdom, | to sustain it and to support it by justice and by righteousness henceforth and for ever; | the zeal of Yahvé of Hosts will do this ! ‖

1. The softly-flowing brook Silôah near Jerusalem is an image of the rule of the ancient Davîdic house, which, however small it might be, was in comparison with other kingdoms of the time, very mild and gentle, Ps. xlvi. 5 ; as, on the contrary, the Nile, with its monstrous animals, was the image of the cruel Egyptian rule ; and the great Euphrates, with its frequent and widely-devastating overflowings, the image of the dangerous Assyrian power and its rapid extension, comp. xxvii. 1. Because, therefore, the multitude in Jerusalem now foolishly despises the gentle native rule, and takes pleasure in the progress of the two allied kings, Yahve will punish them

by causing the mighty, roaring and overwhelming Euphrates to come over the land, so that the water reaches to the neck of every one without any deliverance, xxx. 28, this flood being really the Assyrian king with all his dreadful, splendid army, whose widely extended wings cover the entire land, however wide it may be, yea, thy sacred land, thou surely expected, passionately longed-for, With-us-God! vv. 6-8.—But at this name (originally explained before according to p. 93), and the elevated thought which it conveys, the discourse, with a sudden spasmodic emotion, starts up with the overwhelming force of divine threatening to direct itself against all the heathen nations, including the Assyrians just mentioned. To you nations, not only of Damascus and Samaria, but to all Heathen however far off they may dwell, I say from God, and pay good heed to what concerns you : wax angry, prepare yourselves in your wrath for battle, lay plans and make great harangues as much as you like—ye shall nevertheless despair and see all your plans frustrated ! as had already been said, vii. 5-7 : for in Jerusalem is still an eternal, indestructible power and hope, with us is God, and soon that exalted man of the eternal hope, the Messiah, will be born under this name *With-us-God* whilst ye perish ! vv. 9, 10. Thus the true meaning of the name 'Immanûel still keeps up its vibrations here, although the signification of the man's name as far as it denotes the Messiah as a child must have been previously given above.—If it is desired to know whence Yesaya derived confidence and assurance of such a lofty nature, he must reply that but recently in an hour of sacred ecstasy his spirit became again deeply alive in Yahvé to the true fear and strength, and, in opposition to the present conduct of the multitude, had heard for himself and his friends in this dangerous time the following divine warnings : (1) not to consider everything which the multitude called sedition and treason as really such, in general not to share that base fear which springs from pusillanimity and want of divine trust, ver. 12.

When the multitude, who are so easily led astray at the first appearance of confusion, discerns revolution and revolt, it is often, when considered calmly and closely, nothing of the sort, as now, *e.g.*, at the approach of the armies of Damascus and Samaria. (2) On the contrary, so much the more to hallow and fear Yahvé alone in every way, and to take serious care with reference to him and his will and his light, ver. 13, comp. xxix. 23. Indeed, it is He who on his part will be a sanctuary, an inviolable, always protecting asylum, if in this approaching time of severest temptations he is hallowed by his servants, ver. 14*a*, comp. Ez. xi. 16; 1 Kings ii. 28-30; but as they who in blind fear flee to an altar, which may serve as an asylum, may easily stumble and fall at its base, so the same Yahvé will be equally a touch-stone, a stone of offence and stumbling for the two kingdoms of Israel, and especially for the people of Jerusalem. And it may be surmised that many, who are moved by blind fear and not by the true fear of God, will in the approaching time of trial stumble upon this rock and irremediably injure themselves, or if they do not immediately fall in battle, will yet be caught as it were in fetters and led away captive, vv. 14*b*, 15; comp. further xxviii. 13, 16 sq. In fact, divine justice is something which is either observed, desired and attained, and is then men's weal; or, on the other hand, is overlooked, rejected, or sought after in a wild, unintelligent spirit and only in the hour of need, and is then their lasting ruin.

2. But enough of this; it is time to make an end. What the good have to do in this time has been explained sufficiently, and it seems to the Prophet that he hears the divine voice urging him to bring the whole matter to a conclusion, having written down, rolled up, and sealed the divinely imparted warning and doctrine, to preserve it carefully, that in the future it may serve as a witness to the truth at its fulfilment, ver. 16, comp. xxx. 8, Hosea xiii. 12. And at least the prophet will calmly hope in Yahvé in the threatening time of calamity :

indeed, he possesses from him external pledges also for the truth of the hopes and promises which sustain his soul, for he himself lives and moves, and the children which Yahvé has given to him live and move as living signs and prefigurations of the better future and the eternal hopes, which are also embodied in all their names, as was previously explained, ver. 17 (comp. *ante* p. 72 sq.). It may be seen from this that the name of the prophet must also have been explained in connexion with some weighty thought in a foregoing chapter, which has been lost.—But no help is to be looked for from the false prophets, magicians, and misleaders of the people of every kind (although the king and his courtiers at present believe in them); it is therefore said by way of addition : If you are exhorted instead of listening to the true divine word to apply to the oracle of the ghosts and necromancers, those deceivers who imitate by a chirping, sighing voice the tones of spirits, iii. 3; xxix. 4, do not pay attention to such people : for, first, it is not to be wondered at if such people, who are themselves spiritually dead and insensible to the truth, apply to dead gods instead of to the living God, in accordance with the universal law, that the gods are like the men and nations that worship them ; and then—how greatly will they who now desire to know nothing of the true oracle wish to return to it when the dark horrible judgment-day takes from them the daybreak and all hope (xlvii. 11 ; Job xi. 17) ! (a mass of thoughts very closely packed together, vv. 19, 20). But, alas, the wish is then too late : in extreme distress and afflicted with the pangs of starvation the man rushes as a maniac through the land, in the moment of his terrible anguish and exasperation curses indeed his god and lord whom he slavishly and yet vainly served, and directs his eyes upwards to the true God ; but when he then looks down to the earth again because he had discerned no light above, he sees there the most dreadful darkness and distress, equally without any ray of light, without any hope, breaking through it, and thus he is again hunted forth into the darkness, to perish therein! vv. 21, 22; v. 30; comp. especially Job xv. 22 sq.; xviii. 5-13.

3. But no, much higher than all present or future threatening dangers and distresses stands the certainty of the eternal Messianic prosperity, in the intuition of the glory of which the discourse now stops, and dwells upon it with such a deep and happy composure that the language even bears the clearest marks of it. As if he were describing something which he had long ago seen in his spirit as certain, the prophet presents every thing here, even in the unusual peculiarities of the language with the greatest composure, and only in one instance makes scarcely an exception from this at the new start in the middle, ix. 4. Thus the discourse first breaks out in contrast to the above impenetrable darkness of those who have turned away from Yahvé, with the thought, that nevertheless a light, and indeed a great light, will come: *no* (ii. 6) *darkening is not to the* (land ver. 21) *to which there is distress,* the sacred land can be distressed but not for ever darkened! on the contrary, even the northern and eastern portions of the kingdom of Ephráim, 2 Kings xv. 29, which have been already rent away by the Assyrians, shall be again restored, and its future honour shall be as great as its shame from this Assyrian conquest, ver. 23. The poor people perishing in spiritual darkness and physical distress sees suddenly a great light, a wonderful deliverance ver. 1: happily prospering under Yahvé they exult with joy in the holy place (comp. Cant. vii. 3; Ps. lxviii. 13), that the Assyrian yoke has been broken by Yahvé, and that there has been a defeat of the Assyrians as great as that which once overtook Midian, vv. 2, 3, comp. x. 26; Judges vii. sq.—But in reality some day every trace of savage war and barbarity must be destroyed, every boot of the foreign soldier, striding in the noise of war proudly upon his boots, every red battle garment, as is said v. 4 in allusion to the ancient Mosaic custom at a victory over the Heathen (see *Alterthümer* p. 102 sq. (87 sq.) :

for the everlasting peace must come, a pledge of which has been given us in the sure promise of a child, which, when he has grown up to take upon his shoulders the burden of government, then receives, instead of the short name of his childhood, 'Immanûel, the new double names, which convey the complete idea of his boundless greatness and glory : *Wonderful-Counsellor* (strictly wonder of Counsellor) *Herogod* (who as an invincible God fights and conquers x. 21), *everlasting Father* (maintainer of his subjects) *Prince-of-Peace* (who nevertheless never desires war and eternally established peace) ver. 5. It is a somewhat long name, but beautifully rounded and pleasant. It consists of two members, each member containing two names, while again each name is a compound. Thus as the ruler's name it forms a fitting antithesis to the child's name—'Immanûel. Inasmuch as the Egyptian and Assyrian kings had long been in the habit of placing the longest names upon their banners and elsewhere, as the Cæsars did subsequently, Yesaya might very well gather up the whole idea of this highest conceivable king into an artistic group of names of this kind ; and since even the kings at Jerusalem had long observed the custom of taking a new name at their ascension (see *History of Israel,* iii. 271 (iii. p. 371), Yesaya could foretell a similar act on the part of the Messiah.—This is all to take place in order that the true, eternal Divine kingdom with its prosperity may grow, a kingdom which appeared to the prophet capable of being combined with the Davîdic rule, if only it thoroughly recovered itself from its present decline by means of complete righteousness : but as this is included in the promotion of the eternal divine kingdom the true object of the entire work of God, it follows also that the zeal of Yahvé will do this and his promise may be confidently trusted, ver. 6.

---

viii. 6 מְשׂוֹשׂ אֶת cannot possibly mean the people *trembles at* the two kings, as if מֵשֵׁשׁ were the same root as מָסַס *to melt,*

and this were the same as *to fear :* in any case the word must
come from שׁוּשׁ or שִׁישׁ, and its formation and construction
must be explained from §. 240 *d* and §. 351 *c.* Inasmuch as
the sudden fear of the people is represented as the same as
that of the king, vii. 2, and its fear is here also severely condemned, viii. 12, the question might arise, whether שִׁישׁ does
not like גִּיל denote the violent agitation of both joy and alarm,
so that in that case the word might here be construed with the
sign of the accusative אֵת: still the idea of a *leaping,* i.e., unrestrained joy predominates here too plainly. We must therefore consider that ver. 12 there is ascribed to the people the
thought of the possibility of dethroning the Davîdic house,
that in such a condition of affairs excessive fear is already
verging upon treason to the royal house, and that Ahaz might
very well have a powerful populace in the capital who would
take pleasure in his discomfiture, which, quite regardless of the
distant future, desired to use the present opportunity, with a
scarcely veiled satisfaction at the progress of the Allies: שִׁישׁ
with אֵת is then similar to רָצָה with עַם, Ps. l. 18. In fact, the
antithesis conveyed by the paronomasia between מַאַם and מָשׂוֹשׂ
is thereby completely brought out; the LXX. also represent it
in a loose way.

In viii. 9, 10, it should be carefully noted that Yesaya
intends a reference to the Assyrians also, as he himself more
distinctly indicates at the end of the piece, ix. 1-5; thus
correctly did he glance even then into the more immediate as
well as the more distant future. וְהָיָה ver. 14 must be taken
acc. §. 353 *a,* as the entire context requires.

viii. 19. Evidently two kinds of necromancers are distinguished, which their visitors were also necessitated to apply
to in different houses and institutions: first such as imitated
the voices of children or women, and second such as made
dead men and old people speak. Yesaya with just satire de-
nominates the first the *chirpers,* the second the *mutterers*
(which הגה may very well mean in the *Hiph.,* which occurs

here only). We then see that אבות was the technical name
for the first, and יִדְעֹנִי for the latter.

As to מוּעָף viii. 23 and מְעוּף ver. 22, which clearly are
intended to correspond, comp. §. 215 a; we may accordingly
derive מְצוּקֵי 1 Sam. ii. 8 from מוצק which occurs elsewhere,
as its meaning favours this. The combination מְעוּף צוּקָה is
acc. §. 313 c. The most remarkable thing in this verse is the
wholly different manner of the discourse, which is perceivable
at the very beginning of this last strophe: we find the certainty
of the future expressed from the first in the *perf.*, as in ii. 9. 11
and the corresponding places. The וְ before אַחֲרוֹן has
therefore the force of *also*: but it is better to read גְּלִילָה גּ'
instead of גְּלִיל הגּ' acc. §. 216 b, to give prominence to the
mere local direction in agreement with the context; after this
a the article is less necessary.—The particle לֹא ix. 2 b, which
must here equal לֹו must at the commencement of the
sentence receive a certain emphasis.

The more closely one looks at the new and elevated name of
the Messiah, ver. 5, the more convinced one must become that
Yesaya has constructed it with great artistic skill. We must
look upon it as the name which a new king assumed to be
placed upon his shield, banners, or arms: it could not be
allowed more than a limited space upon the shield, as one sees,
for instance, from the figures on the shields of the early
Egyptian kings. Much had to be expressed by it with the
greatest brevity, and a great deal would depend upon the right
combination and position of the component parts of the name.
At that time the principle upon which names were constructed
was the neat combination of two simple nouns, acc. §. 273 d;
and these four as well as the earlier name Immanuel are composed of two words to each. If we then suppose this great
fourfold name with its four members arranged so as to form a
beautiful group thus—

Wonderful-Counsellor   Herogod   1.—2.
                                                    | × |
Everlasting-Father   Prince of Peace 3.—4.

it is evident that in whatever direction, one may combine them
in pairs, beginning with the first, a new and magnificent meaning
is obtained.   If they are connected in pairs (1) in the straight-
forward order, 1—2, 3—4, the first two describe what the
nature of the Messiah must be subjectively considered, the
second pair what it must be with regard to the world:
personally the Messiah must possess the greatest measure both
of counsel and decision and of power; with regard to the
world, he must have an equal fulness of both inexhaustible
provident paternal love (comp. xxii. 20; Gen. xlv. 8) and victorious pacificatory power.   If (2) they are connected laterally
1—3, 2—4, the first describe the spirit accordingly to which he
in thought always comes to the right conclusion, and the feeling according to which he suffers himself to be guided eternally
purely by love, while the latter describe the power which he
must have to give effect to his love, and the lofty work of
founding and maintaining peace to perform which this power
will be given him.   Lastly, if they are connected diagonally,
1—4, 2—3, they prescribe, that peace alone may be the end
and aim of the counsel and all spiritual endeavour, and that
love alone may be the power.   The unfailing stream of true
counsel and decision must form the commencement, and peace
as the true end, the conclusion of the whole, as Yesaya immediately again says, ver. 6.   Characteristics which ought to be
found combined in all kings, must be found in Him in the
highest, *i.e.*, the divine, measure; and if an everlasting reign
is desired for even the ordinary king (see on Ps. cx. 4), how
much more must the idea of eternity be applicable to Him !
And this is the final word, ver. 6.   At this place at least, because
it was most suitable according to the plan of this book, Yesaya
determined only in great lapidary characters to pourtray Him
whom the deepest feeling of his heart and life ran to meet,
with wonderful desire and longing : and that he is a great
master in this kind of style also, is evident enough.

In conclusion, it may also be remarked that the animation of

the language of ix. 3, which had its origin in the oppression of
the Assyrians, points to the fact that this book did not receive
its final shape before the commencement of the reign of Hizqia.
It was not earlier than the end of the reign of Ahaz and the
beginning of that of Hizqia that the Assyrian rule was felt as
immediately oppressive by Yuda ; its insupportably heavy yoke
is here described almost in the same language as in the later
book, xxx. 31 sq., comp. x. 5 sq. It also appears from the
historical narration of vii. 1, that Ahaz was not then alive. On
the other hand, it is absolutely inadmissible to take a later
date than quite the commencement of the next king's reign :
which will also appear from the next book.

---

3. A new Oracle concerning Samaria.　xvii. 1-11.

As Yesaya concluded his first book with an oracle concerning
Samaria also (see p. 50 sq.), he wished to attach to the second
book a similar piece, which would serve at the same time in
the form of a more general review to explain further what had
been said with regard to the two kingdoms of Damascus and
Samaria, ch. vii. and viii. although it was probably originally
written earlier. It is true, this piece, xvii. 1-11, which has
been inserted here, shows not only that the Assyrian conquest of
the north-eastern portions of the kingdom of Samaria, 2 Kings
xv. 19, was already past, comp. ver. 3, but also that the early
fall of the Syrian kingdom of Damascus already presented
itself to the mind of the prophet as certain. Now, according
to 2 Kings xvi. 9, Tiglath Pileser took Damascus at the wish
of Ahaz when he was in distress from the Syrians ; the alliance
of Ahaz with the Assyrians, referred to in ch. vii. may have
finally decided the attack of Damascus : yet the prophet was
able much earlier to foresee the necessity of the fall of Damascus, and as a fact this discourse shows no trace of the combined
march of the Syrians and Ephrámites against Yuda, ch. vii.-

ix. 6. On the contrary, acc. to ver. 3, the remnant of the
kingdom of Ephráim had then from fear of the Assyrians
already formed an alliance with the Syrians, in the belief that
they possessed in the strong fortification of Damascus a secure
barrier against new inroads of the Assyrians : and the hostilities
mentioned, ix. 10 sq. had found an end.   But, in contrast with
these expectations, Yesaya foresaw that the impending fall of
Damascus would bring after it as a further consequence disaster
to the Northern kingdom, in order that, (1) precisely this vain
reliance upon Damascus as a strong rampart, (2) pride, (3)
idolatry, and (4) false trust in external help generally, these
four fundamental faults from which that kingdom, notwithstanding all the heavy losses and calamities of the last years,
still continued to suffer, might finally be thoroughly removed.
Thus this piece, which should much rather be called an oracle
concerning the Northern kingdom than concerning Damascus,
falls into four short strophes, the first of which indeed treats of
Damascus, but in such a way that even in it the discourse finds
a transition to the fate of the Northern kingdom, which is exclusively dealt with in the following strophes.   The third is
somewhat mutilated at the end.

1.

[*High-oracle concerning Damascus.*]

XVII.

1   Behold Damascus will cease as a city | and
become a seat of falling ruins; || forsaken are
'Aro'ër's cities, a portion for flocks: | which settle
there by no one frightened. || Thus is the defence
taken from Ephráim, and the kingdom from Da-
mascus, | and the remnant of Arám will be like
the glory of the sons of Israel, | — saith Yahvé of
Hosts. ||

2.

And then on that day will Yaqob's glory be humbled, | and the fulness of his flesh wasted. ||
5   And when the harvest-time carrieth off the standing-corn, and his arm harvesteth the ears, | then he will be like him that leaseth ears in the valley Rephaîm; || and there surviveth in it a gleaning as at the beating of olives, two three berries above on the top, | four five in the fruit-tree's boughs— saith Yahvé Israel's God. ||

3.

On that day the man will look up to his maker, and his eyes will have regard to the Holy One of Israel, || and he will not look to the altars the work of his hands, | and what his fingers have made he will not regard, | together with the idol-groves and the sun-cones. ||

4.

On that day his fortified cities will be like the desertion of bush and summit which were deserted before the sons of Israel: | and it will become a
10   waste. || Because thou forgottest the God of thy weal, and the rock of thy fortification didst not remember, | therefore thou mayest plant plants of tenderness, and crop it with vines of the foreigner: || on the day when thou plantest them thou cherishest them, and in the morning thou bringest thy seed to blossom— | but the harvest is flown on the day of sickness and incurable pain. ||

2   8

1. Vv. 1-3. Both the capital, ver. 1, and the smaller cities
of the Syrian kingdom, ver. 2, will be demolished and made
desolate stretches of pasture, v. 17; of the smaller cities
Yesaya singles out those belonging to the district of ʻAroʻer,
because they had belonged formerly to Israel and must at this
time have been conquered by Damascus.—The result is, ver. 3,
that after the conquest of Damascus, Ephráim loses its
advanced protecting wall and Damascus its independence as a
kingdom and ceases to be a royal city, whilst the remainder of
the Syrian kingdom will be equally pitiable with the wretched
glory of the kingdom of Ephráim, that kingdom which notwithstanding its great losses still, acc. ix. 7 sq., acts so proudly
and overbearingly. There lies in the word *glory*, when the
circumstances of the time are considered, manifest irony, a
bitter sarcasm, which becomes the most serious truth in the
following strophe. For

2., vv. 4-6, precisely this glory, this perpetual arrogancy of
the Northern kingdom, must be humiliated, its superabundant
fulness be brought down, ver. 4, comp. x. 16, and with regard
to the Northern kingdom similarly, ix. 8 sq. When the great
harvest comes, the time of the decision when Yahvé will sit in
judgment upon the whole earth, comp. ver. 11, Amos viii. 1;
Joel iv. 13, when therefore the harvest-time snatches away by
heaps the standing-corn (and the judgment men in crowds)
and Yahvé's arm harvests, cuts off, the ears: then the Northern
kingdom will see but a very few of its citizens remaining; if
it counts its spared members, it is as if some one gleaned ears
in the valley Rephaïm south of Jerusalem (a valley, as appears
from this passage, whither the poor of Jerusalem were most
in the habit of going to glean, and where for that very reason
there was usually but the scantiest gleaning left), finding,
however, but a few, or the gleaning which is left in this
kingdom is even equal only to the wretched gleaning of a few
scattered ripe olives, which the gatherer had forgotten to take

away to the press and the poor people knock down with sticks (xxiv. 13).

3. Vv. 7, 8. And when this final judgment has taken place, it is true enough that these men will at last turn from the service of the numerous false gods and idolatrous objects to the true God who alone is able to help and heal ; as Yesaya, with certainty, had often shown at greater length, comp. ii. 8 sq. ; Mic. v. 13. With regard to the *idol-groves* and sun-cones, see *Alterthümer* p. 301 (260). The reason why the *altars* are specially mentioned, ver. 8, appears from the history of the period of the reign of Ahaz, comp. *History of Israel*, iv. 171 (iii. p. 667).

4. Neither will the fortifications of their own land, in which the kingdom now places such foolish trust, avail them anything. On the contrary, they will then be just as desolated and deserted, comp. vi. 12, as the entire land of Canaan, its thickly populated valleys and its towering heights, was once forsaken of the ancient Canaanites in their flight before the conquering Israelites under Yosúa, ver. 9, which is in this connexion a comparison well adapted to humiliate all national pride. To denominate the valleys and heights, Yesaya correctly and intelligibly makes mention of *bush* (thicket) and summit (tree-top), following the figure of a forest, since the ancient Canaanites divided themselves into inhabitants of mountains and valleys, calling the first *Emorites*, from *Amôr*, *i.e.*, top, tree-top, and the latter *Chittites*, *i.e.*, lowlanders ; and the LXX. have caught this meaning with substantial correctness. Comp. *History of Israel*, i. 234 ; ii. 241 sq. (I. 337 sq. ; II. 339 sq.).——And summing up all this with what has gone before, it is said, finally, vv. 10, 11 : because Ephráim has forsaken the true help and fortress, he may indeed continue to sow and plant his field with lovely plants from abroad (*i.e.*, with flattering heathen worship and customs) ; at the beginning in planting he employs a great deal of pains and care upon the growth and cultivation of these splendid poisonous plants, and in the

8 *

morning he continues to rejoice in their growth ; but the
evening comes after the toilsome day, when the reward of the
toil should be reaped, and then the harvest has suddenly flown
and the joyous morning become a day of incurable sickness.
Thus thoughts and images crowd together at the end, and it is
clearly evident that here is the conclusion.

Ver. 1, מוּסָר must be understood acc. § 295 *b* : Damascus
will be removed so that it is no longer a city ; comp. the similar
construction xxiii. 1.

Ver. 10, נעמנים is most correctly interpreted, acc. § 287 *a*
note, as *Adonisses,* or *tenderlings,* effeminate gods, from the name
of the Syrian god Adonis, who was worshipped also in
Phœnicia ; in that case *the foreigner* of the next verse-member
answers to this name well, and the discourse in the course of
this strophe recurs again to the idolatry referred to in the
previous one.

It would be quite conceivable that Yesaya added to this book
further the pieces concerning foreign nations xiv. 28——xvi ;
xxi. 11-17. These oracles would the more suitably follow
here, inasmuch as they show that in the immediate future the
foreign nations rather than Jerusalem will have to suffer from
the Assyrians ; which would also accord well with the foregoing pieces. The date of xiv. 28 agrees with vi. 1. Since,
however, the following book, to which we subjoin them,
appeared but a little later, this difference is unimportant. In
any case xvii. 1-11 does not belong originally to the same
series as the above.

III.—YESAYA'S THIRD BOOK.

As the great events of the time followed each other in Yuda since the first days of Hizqia's reign with increasing rapidity and decisiveness, and Yesaya's activity was also thereby greatly widened and intensified, his literary publications succeeded each other from this time at shorter intervals. Hizqia favoured true religion and morality once more in his kingdom (comp. xxxvi. 7 sq., and other proofs). One of the first noble fruits of Yesaya's past labours at the centre of the kingdom was about to come to perfection, and a fresh, strong current of the influence of true religion promoted a more harmonious and free co-operation of both king and prophet. But the first endeavour to take up a more independent position with regard to the demands of the Assyrians, which Hizqia ventured upon was immediately followed by their hostility: and although the Assyrian king was at that time occupied in other ways at a great distance from Palestine, he was nevertheless very well able to encourage the petty nations around Yuda to make inroads upon this kingdom. As Yuda had then been weakened by the misrule of Ahaz, it needed but the destructive incursions of the Philistines (comp. xvi. 28 sq.) and similar nations to throw Jerusalem as it then was into unexpected alarm. But while both within and around it everything grew darker, the inhabitants of the capital, who had become habituated to their full-grown vices, and more recently, under Hisqia's rule, to a hypocritical piety, would hear nothing about that true repentance and amendment which Yesaya had so long demanded. Under these circumstances, he resolved to follow up his other labours by a new literary publication. He now for the first time gave to his two earlier books a connected form, and enlarged this edition by such important additions as the necessities of the later date seemed to require. The way in which the two earlier books were connected may be seen from chap. ii. 1—x. 4, which forms the body of this third en-

larged book; but at the commencement Yesaya placed the
piece chap. i., as the most telling introduction to the larger
book; and at the close, in connexion with the entirely new
view which had just opened up to him into the great heathen
world, he added a number of oracles concerning foreign
nations, and thus gave a beautiful completeness to this enlarged book.

----

1. The Great Arraignment.

ch. i.

How long and how often has the prophet, or (as may equally
well be said, and in accordance with the profoundest feeling of
the prophet) the divine spirit itself, whose living presence
within him the prophet so powerfully and constantly feels,
endeavoured in every possible way to bring back the nation,
which is the community of Yahvé, dwelling here at the
ancient sacred centre of the kingdom, to that sincerity and
constancy of the divine life, without which it is impossible for
it to attain to a better condition! But hitherto his profoundest endeavours, looking at the nation generally, had
remained without effect. It was then that the same spirit was
moved from the innermost agitation of the entire life of the
prophet once more to appeal to the community. Once more,
precisely in the sacred city, this spirit, in the most forcible and
at the same time most lucid and calm manner, presents itself
before the community, with the profoundest effort arraigning
and explaining, judging and punishing, to discover whether it
will finally succeed in breaking down the obstinacy of the
nation and in opening its heart to a fresh and powerful ray of
divine light. Never before did such an oration as this burst
from the heart and mouth of the prophet; an oration of such
pure spirituality, handling every detail from the highest stand-
point, with greatest clearness and irresistible force, treating
the most difficult matters from this standpoint with greatest

truth and profundity, and irresistibly carrying away every hearer whose heart was not entirely dead to the divine word. Nor does the human side of the speaker anywhere else fall into the background to the same extent as is here the case with Yesaya, and the purest divine voice come forward with all-radiating floods of light and fulness of power.

It is manifestly the profound result, the spiritual residuum, of the experiences and feelings of a long prophetic life to which the fundamental thought of this piece, with its wonderful elevation and energy, owes its origin: just as the previous book, see p. 60 sq., opened with a similar piece, which, although in another manner, could not rise to a loftier elevation. While the piece just mentioned dealt with the earliest years of the prophet's life, this is clearly meant to refer to the time which was then present, although his language on account of its sublimity appears so general. It is, therefore, the more important to inquire particularly what period it was which his words had reference to. From vv. 7-9 it appears that at that time some enemies were devastating the territory of Yuda, and had scarcely spared the capital. These enemies are called *strangers*, ver 7: but this word denotes (acc. xxix. 5, also) simply foreign enemies, and says nothing with regard to their home. We are not allowed to suppose that the invasion of the Assyrians in the time of Sancherib is intended, because when that event occurred Yesaya used quite different language from that we find here, xxxvii. 21 sq.; comp. xxxiii. 1-24. We might then suppose the Assyrians made an invasion at some earlier time, probably shortly after Hizqia's accession to the throne; and although the historical books do not mention it, there is still a number of indications outside this oration which favour this supposition. An Assyrian inroad of this kind is quite plainly presupposed, xxii. 1-14, which, like the inroad of our oration, was not followed up by an actual siege of the capital. Further, the way in which some time later Mikha, v. 4, and Yesaya, x. 28-32, speak of a future invasion of the Assyrians, points clearly to an unsuccessful invasion which had already taken place, inasmuch as the imagination could borrow pictures of this kind only from such an event. Finally, the position of affairs itself is in favour of the supposition, that after the time of Ahaz a great change must have taken place in the relations of Assyria and Yuda to each other. Under Ahaz, who concluded the alliance with Assyria and without doubt regularly paid his tribute, the Assyrians had no occasion to invade Yuda, and we know of no invasion of this kind during that period. But Hizqia was a man of a totally different character and views from Ahaz; he appears from the very first, as well as later, to have disliked the Assyrian alliance, and to have desired greater independence : and the powerful impulse which was very shortly felt to conclude a counter-alliance with Egypt, chaps. xxviii.-xxxii., is only on this supposition quite intelligible. However, although for these reasons we are compelled to suppose that the Assyrians at no distant date from the accession of Hizqia sent an invading army against Yuda, owing to the different feelings of the new king towards them, and that this army very soon accomplished its object, and also Yuda for the first time saw the Assyrian arms in its neighbourhood, and, in fact, fled before them in a shameful way (as appears from xxii. 3)—it cannot nevertheless be proved from this piece that the enemies mentioned in it were Assyrians. On the contrary, the requirements of this piece are amply met by the supposition that the Philistines and other surrounding nations are here intended, which may also be gathered from the words, xiv. 28-32. But they may have been encouraged by the Assyrians to invade Yuda; a supposition which explains the tone of the oracles concerning them which are found at the end of this third book.

The foreign customs and religions which had been introduced by Ahaz were not favoured under Hizqia, while, on the contrary, the directions of the ancient Yahve-cultus were again more carefully observed by both king and people (vv. 11-14,

comp. xxix. 13 sq.) But Yesaya saw too well through the
hypocrisy of those people who, especially because the new
king favoured it, put on the appearance of religion, and
endeavoured by the most noisy external Yahve-cultus to obtain
by violence the divine and the royal favour at one and the
same time, and who imagined they had done enough before
God, although at the same time they allowed the favourite
popular superstition of those days to exist in perfect peace,
and probably themselves continued to favour it in secret (vv.
29-31; xxx. 22). Thus this most recent phenomenon in the
very centre of the nation is to him only a new proof that the
internal perversities, which have been growing for such a
long time and at the present moment exist in undiminished
numbers, require still greater chastisements from the future,
and how little Jerusalem itself can have any advantage before
Yahvé on account of its deeds. The justice of the complaint
of Yahvé against Israel, the profound meaning of which has
completely filled the prophet's mind, while its irrepressible
tones will now burst forth from him, appears to him to have
therewith reached its most extreme point.

For the tone and life of this oration is exactly as if a great
judicial act were about to be introduced and proceeded with: a
thought which had long before Yesaya been received into the
number of the prophetic thoughts (see Vol. I. p. 147), but is
nowhere else worked out with such sublimity and grandeur
and such completeness and cogency as here. Yahvé appears
as a plaintiff with his witnesses, Israel as the defendant, and
the prophet as the daysman. Inasmuch as a proper trial
(*processus*) implies (1) the production of the charge with an
appeal to the right witnesses, (2) the answer of any objection
which might at the opening be made against the production of
the charge, (3) that full freedom to defend himself be given to
the accused before (4) judgment is passed, this piece accordingly falls of itself into four symmetrical strophes. After the
most solemn accusation has been made by Yahvé against his

people, which is burdened with every sin, and therefore
punished with increasing severity, so that it can scarcely be
further punished, vv. 2-9, the second strophe anticipates the
excuse, that the external Yahvé-cultus together with true
doctrine sufficed in these things, vv. 10-17; and after the guilt
of the nation has been proved even by its own witness, vv.
18-23, the storm of the threat of new punishments can no
longer be repressed, which are nevertheless such divine punishments as will lead back the kingdom to its original destination,
and open to it the glorious time, vv. 24-31. Thus the whole
falls quite properly into these four strophes. Further, comp.
Jahrbb. der Bibl. wiss. I. p. 40 sq.

i.   1.

1   Hear ye heavens and attend O earth ! for Yahvé
speaketh : | sons I reared great and exalted, but
they have become unfaithful to me. || The ox
knoweth his owner, and the ass his master's crib : |
Israel is without knowledge, my people is without
understanding ! ||—O sinful people guilt-burdened
nation, race of evildoers worthless sons | who have
forsaken Yahvé, reviled Israel's Holy One, gone
5   backward : || whereupon will ye still be smitten,
sinning still further ? | the whole head is sickly
and the whole heart is ill ; || from the foot-sole
and unto the head there is nothing sound in it,
wounds and wales and fresh strokes— | not pressed
and not bound up, and not soothed with oil ! ||
Your country is a waste, your cities burnt with
fire, | your soil—before your faces barbarians
devour it, and it is a waste as if Sodóm were over-
thrown ! || and the daughter Ssion is left as a booth

in a vineyard, as a hammock in a cucumber field, |
—as a besieged city. ‖ Had not Yahvé of Hosts
left us a small remnant, |—like Sodóm we should
be, Gomorrha we should resemble. ‖

2.

10   Hear Yahve's word ye chiefs of Sodóm, | attend
to the doctrine of our God ye people of Gomorrha !‖
What is to me the multitude of your sacrifices ?
saith Yahvé, | full am I of the gifts of rams and of
the fat of fed-calves, | and blood of bullocks, lambs
and he-goats I have no pleasure in ! ‖ In case ye
come to appear before me : | who requireth *this*
at your hands, to wear out* my courts ? ‖ Ye shall
not any more bring meat-offerings of vanity :
incense of abomination is that to me ; | new moon
and Sabbath, festal-peals—I cannot bear hypocrisy
and solemn festival ; ‖ your new moons and feast-
days my soul hateth, they are a burden to me, |
15   am weary of bearing them ! ‖ and when ye spread
forth your hands I cover mine eyes from you, also
when ye pray much I do not hear : | your hands
are full of blood ! ‖ Wash ye make you clean,
remove the evil of your deeds from before mine
eyes, | cease to do evil ; ‖ learn to do well, seek
right, reform the destroyer, | judge the orphan,
plead the widow's cause ! ‖

3.

     " Come now and let us argue [the case]" ! saith
Yahvé, | " were your sins as purple, they may
become white as snow, | were they red as scarlet,

---

* Germ. *austreten.*—*Tr.*

they may become as wool !" || —. ... " If ye are
willing and obedient, | the marrow of the land
20   shall ye eat ! || but if ye are unwilling and rebel-
lious, | by the sword ye shall be eaten !" yea,
Yahvé's mouth hath spoken it. ||—

> O how hath become a harlot the faithful
>   city,—
> she that was full of right, in which righte-
>   ousness tarried—
> but now murderers !

Thy silver hath become dross, | thy noble drink
adulterated with water ; || thy rulers are rebels
and thieves' comrades, every one loveth bribery
and runneth after pay, | the orphan they judge
not, and the widow's cause cometh not before
them ! ||

4.

Therefore is the sentence of the Lord Yahvé of
Hosts, the Strong One of Israel : | O I will satisfy
myself of mine adversaries, and will avenge myself
25   of mine enemies, || and will turn back my hand
against thee, most purely melting thy dross, | and
will remove all thy lead-alloy, || will make thy
judges again as aforetime, and thy counsellors as
at the beginning : | afterward thou shalt be called
" centre* of righteousness, faithful city" ;* || Ssion
will be redeemed by right, | and her Converts by
righteousness. ||—But demolition of evildoers and
sinners together ! | and they who have forsaken
Yahvé perish. || For ye will grow pale at the
Terebinths which ye longed for, | and blush at the

---

* Germ. *stätte* and *stadt*.—Tr.

30   gardens which ye preferred ; ‖ yea ye will be as
      the Terebinth whose leaf withereth, | and as a
      garden which lacketh water, ‖ and the powerful
      one will become tow, his work a spark : | thus they
      both burn together quenched by no one. ‖

1. The charge of Yahvé is that of a father who has been
faithlessly forsaken by ungrateful sons. As Hosea had previously taught, Yahvé prevented them in ancient times with his
paternal love and care, and formed them as peculiarly his own
into a great nation. But they who ought to be Yahvé's sons
are more unwise and unthankful than cattle that have no understanding, so that it appears as if they had neither memory
nor intelligence. That is the distressing accusation which
heaven and earth are called upon by Yahvé to hear, because it
is the most serious complaint that can be conceived, to which
scarcely any other than the highest witnesses can be summoned,
those which are ever present as the eternal witnesses of the
universal glory and power of God in creation, and in whose
presence every nation lives and moves as though these witnesses of creation also heard and saw everything which the
nation does or suffers (Mic. vi. 2 ; Deut xxxii. 1 ; Ps. l. 4.)
But, after this introduction, the discourse turns more directly
to the accused themselves, bringing the proof of the charge,
and questions the nation, whose innumerable sins may all run
up into that of unfaithfulness to Yahvé, ver. 4, whether they
will still go on sinning and then continue to be punished, now
that they have been so much punished that there is hardly
anything further left ! therefore, at once to speak more briefly
and pointedly, whereupon, on what other member of the body,
do they intend still to be smitten,—since every spot is already
covered with old and new wounds of all kinds ? and whereupon, based upon what still untried transgression do they
intend to depart further from Yahvé and go on sinning—inasmuch as there is no further transgression left for them to

commit ?   This two-fold question is compressed into the one—whereupon will they still be beaten, will they still further sin ? ver. 5 sq. ❦The immediate reference to that time is particularly explained, vv. 7, 8 : the whole of your cultivated land, in spite of all that the magnates in Jerusalem can do, is laid waste by enemies, who as it were turn the ground upside down, and cause a devastation almost like that of Sodom and Gomorrah in former times, whilst Jerusalem, although hitherto spared, is nevertheless quite isolated and alone in the wide and silent country.   Yea, it is said finally, ver. 9, with a fresh outburst of energy in the discourse, we should already have been completely devastated like Sodóm, if Yahvé had not graciously spared us a small portion of the whole people.   Since Jerusalem was not actually besieged at that time, but as good as besieged, *i.e.* deprived of all connexion with the rest of the country, which was occupied with the enemy's foraging army, Yesaya was able to add, ver. 8, this comparison to a besieged city.

2. It is true, the magnates of Jerusalem imagine that they have discharged their obligations to Yahvé by their numerous temple-sacrifices.   But with regard to this, it must immediately be brought before these people, who may be denominated morally people of Sodóm, that so far from Yahvé taking delight in the multitude of their magnificent sacrifices and of the profane noise with which they bring them, as if they would wear out with their feet the courts of his temple, thinking that by these offerings they are doing God great service, he is, on the contrary, tired of them, and must ask, who it is then that has given to them the power (hand) and the right to enter with such insolence and noise into his presence, inasmuch as they properly came only for the purpose of seeking his face with prayer and supplication ? vv. 11, 12.   No, as they at present are, polluted with unrighteousness and sin, it behoves them to bring no sacrifices, since every one that they bring is in truth but a sacrifice of vanity and sin which they manifest in Yahvé's

presence, and wickedness and holiness, falsehood and sanctity can never accord together ! Sacrifices and feasts of this kind Yahvé cannot any longer endure in any form, and however much they wring their hands and pray when they present them, he will not hear them, vv. 13-15. Accordingly, all possible kinds of sacrifices and solemn days are mentioned, vv. 13, 14, yet in such a way that the names change beautifully with the structure of the verse-members and the sense ; ver. 13 consists of two larger sentences, each of which falls again into a protasis and an apodosis. Since the incense was deemed the portion of the entire sacrifice most acceptable to Heaven, it is said : " Ye shall not bring meat-offerings of sin : abominable incense is that to me ;" and since the solemnities are of innumerable kinds, it is further said : "new-moon and sabbath, keeping feasts—as for all that, I hate the contradiction, wickedness and worship."—But that which ye ought to do and do not, the one thing needful, is that ye first wash your blood-stained hands, that ye first learn to do good and give proof of your amendment by your actions, especially that ye root out in the kingdom the violence and oppressions of the magnates, and help those who are bowed down, vv. 16, 17. Comp. Amos v. 21 sq.

3. When whatever could in any way be urged against this grievous charge and its judicial consideration has been thus by anticipation set aside, both sides must of necessity enter respectively upon the trial of the case, and whatever can be said on behalf of the defendant must be brought forward. What will the result be ? He, the plaintiff, shrinks from no court and no objection that can be raised, he descends for a moment from his elevation as judge, and desires even that the nation may clear itself from its sins, whether they be real or alleged, may wash itself from that blood, in order that its sins, which seem to be deep red, may become white as wool ! ver. 18, comp. xliii. 9. The eternal measure by which the judge measures has indeed been long known, and is here, vv. 19, 20, once more repeated as an introduction to the pending enquiry and deter-

mination of the possible punishment : it is the truth, that a
spirit obedient to Yahvé may expect blessing also in the world
(in the land), while a spirit of rebellion against him in the end
finds everything turned in hostility against it in the world also,
a truth which is at the same time both the eternal divine
promise and threat, and which will in any case find its application in this trial.—But what is the answer of the nation to this
appeal? A long pause occurs, ver. 21, to allow it time to
defend itself : but it is silent, and shows by its silence that it
is unable to defend itself. Accordingly the prophet himself as
the daysman, after the painfully long pause, raises a strain of
lamentation over the city which has so utterly fallen from her
earlier moral elevation and purity, vv. 21-23. The incorruptible
and irrepressible truth from the mouth of the prophet must
witness against the defendant, and this strophe has to conclude
with the bitter declaration, that the just demand of the divine
law, which was made at the end of the previous strophe, has
not been in any way fulfilled. Thus painfully do the last words
of the previous and the present strophes answer to each
other !

4. And the just divine judgment must now break forth in an
overwhelming stream ; spoken by the *strong* God (x. 13) who
has sufficient power to carry it out. Indeed as if the divine
punishment and retribution (vengeance) had already delayed
too long against those who arouse it by their obstinacy, the
stream of threatening breaks forth, v. 24, in sweeping currents
as from suppressed fire, coming gradually to explain itself more
calmly, ver. 25 sq. By a great judgment the dross and the
pieces of lead mixed with the silver, mentioned ver. 22, must
be separated as in a purifying fire, what is good and approved
must be collected to form a new and pure commencement, as it
were a new Davîdic age, vv. 25, 26 : only by means of the
divine power of righteousness, when it once more assumes its
full activity, can the redemption of Ssion and its converts be
effected, but by that it will be effected in its time, ver. 27.

Still, on the other hand, all those who obstinately remain in their rebellion meet their ruin, ver. 28 : for the false gods and idolatries at the Terebinths and in the pleasant gardens (lvii. 5 ; Deut. xii. 2 ; 2 Kings xvi. 4), which are at present so ardently preferred to the true God, will so greatly deceive the worshippers who trust in them that the latter will one day themselves present as mournful an aspect as a withered Terebinth and a garden without water, the fools who ought to have known the perishable nature of the things in which they placed their trust, vv. 29, 30; or rather, both together, man and his handiwork, *i.e.*, the wooden idols (ii. 8) perish without remedy, the man who is the moment before powerful and proud becoming suddenly slack tow, and his idol, the creation of his sin, becoming the spark to enkindle it, just as men are always destroyed by the products of their sin and their idols, xxx. 13.

On i. 5, 6. Since the complete picture of the corporate state appears in this way in the explanatory answer, the *suff. masc. sing.* is used בּוֹ with an implied reference to this. Ezek. xxix. 7 shows that כל ראש may certainly be used in poetic language in the sense of *the whole head*. The word לָחֳלִי means inclined *to* sickness, that is, sickly ; רְפֻכָה refers back to מכה טריה simply.

It is essential to bear in mind with regard to i. 7, that מחפכת, in accordance with its constant usage (comp. *History of Israel*, I. 314, (I. p. 450)), necessarily dates back to Sodóm, which may be alluded to even in this passage, acc. vv. 9, 10. If the following word זָרִים were the true reading, the sentence would have to be understood thus : "as if foreigners (barbarians) overturned *it* (the ground), devastated it after the manner of Sodóm"; for מַהְפֵּכַת is in any case, like Amos iv. 11, an *inf. acc.* § 239 *a*. The emphasis would then not fall upon the idea of the *foreigners*, but upon that of the *overturning of the ground* alone ; yet acc. to *a* it is the thought of the

2 9

foreigners which is meant to be made prominent. On this
account, therefore, as well as on account of the חֶדֶק, it is
probably best to read סְדֹם instead of זֵרִים, since the latter
reading could easily arise in this place by taking the ד for
a ר.

On i. 8. That נָצַר may mean *to keep an eye upon a city,*
i.e., to invest and *begin to besiege it,* is clear from Jer. iv. 16 ;
Ezek. vi. 11: and when it is remembered that Jerusalem was not
actually besieged at that time, although the country was devastated, the meaning of the words in this passage is not
doubtful. It is true that עִיר denotes originally a *citadel* (acc.
History of Israel, IV. 100, (III. p. 572 *note*)), but this signification would not supply a better meaning here, and the LXX.
already give the translation πολιορκουμένη. A besieged city is
as solitary in the midst of a country as a booth for the vine-
dresser in an extensive garden : but the worst part of it is
that Jerusalem at present lies in a great waste and a silenced
country, as if it were besieged, while at the same time this is
not the case.

The severity of the meaning of i. 12 only appears when כִּי
is taken with the following *imperf.* acc. §. 362 *b* : *although ye*
come to appear before me (comp. §. 279 *c*), I do not object to
it while I do not demand it : but *who demandeth this of you*
and hath given you *authority,* that ye deluge and trample off
my courts as profane places with the noise of such offerings ?
This idea of trampling off, wearing out with the feet, the
temple courts is later often adopted from this passage, *e.g.,*
Rev. xi. 2.

As to חָמוֹץ, ver. 17, comp. §. 152 *b* : the meaning is further
made clear by the fact that אִשֵּׁר can only denote putting a
wanderer or sinner upon the right way again.

It appears from the context itself that the sentence vv. 19,
20, is meant as a quotation from some ancient and well-known
sacred book of law : but the language is also peculiar, as the
phrase חֶרֶב תְּאֻכְּלוּ acc. §. 279 *c,* its paronomasia with תֹּאכֵלוּ,

and the words *surely Yahvé's mouth hath spoken it,* which
occurs only in Yôél, comp. Mic. iv. 4, (and repeated in an
artistic way "Is." xl. 5 ; lviii. 14), whilst elsewhere Yesaya
uses the formula יְיָ נאם, explained Vol. I. p. 9, and very
rarely (xxii. 25 ; comp. Obad. ver. 18 ; Joel iv. 8 ; "Is." xxv.
8) the shorter phrase *surely Yahvé hath spoken it* as a concluding sentence. It may also be correctly maintained that the
transition from ver. 17 to vv. 18, 19 is too rapid, and a verse
has been lost which pointed in express words to this ancient
utterance as that which was to form the basis of the pending
judgment. Only on this supposition does this strophe receive
its full number of verses.

On the other hand, Yesaya evidently intentionally chooses,
ver. 21, a more poetic form of language on account of the
lyric, as appears especially in the form מְלֵאֲתִי §. 211 *b ;** comp.
the similar case v. 1. But the language resumes the ordinary
prophetic form with ver. 23.—*Rulers are rebels* ver. 23, as an
attempt to represent the play on the words : more closely, *thy
princes are stubborn, vicious :* but Yesaya in this case follows
Hosea's lead ix. 15.—The word כַּבֹּר may originally have meant
as with soap, but in this connexion can only denote generally
most purely, and in respect of construction is very different
from בְּבוֹר, Job ix. 30.

The construction נֹבֶלֶת עָלֶהָ, ver. 30, may be taken as
stat. constr., according to the similar combinations xxx. 27,
comp. §. 288 *c ;* although it is true that the simpler עָלֶה is all
that is required, and the above punctuation may point to the
reading עָלֶיהָ which is found in several MSS., according to
which עליה is the subject of a relative sentence, and נבלת is
its predicate, *whose leaves wither.*

The stormy, agitated language of ver. 24 is explained by
the ancient procedure of court of justice, in conformity with
which at the close the condemned man, *e.g.,* for murder, was

---

* Elsewhere in Isa. the only instance is הֹזְקִי xxii. 16, but the position is not
quite the same.

delivered to his accuser and prosecutor to execute the punishment in whatever way he might think well : at length
therefore he could have his revenge ! It is as if we still heard
in this passage the words which would be used in such cases in
those times.

---

2. (THE TWO FOREGOING BOOKS),

without doubt as they were before their present transpositions
and hiatuses.

---

3. THE ORACLES CONCERNING FOREIGN NATIONS.

Since the nearest neighbours of Yuda, as was above
remarked, immediately after the death of Ahaz harassed this
kingdom with greater violence on account of its apparent
distress, it was opportune that Yesaya should declare to them
how much more than Yuda they themselves had cause to fear
the Assyrians. Besides, the time was rapidly approaching
when the Assyrians attained the summit of their power, and
threatened to subjugate all the nations around Yuda, even as
far as Africa. It was then Yesaya turned his attention more
closely to all the surrounding petty nations, and in the light of
the religion of Yahvé considered their condition, and their
hopes, their past history and the future which now threatened
them. There was at that time a good degree of intercourse
between all these nations, and it was probably no rare occurrence that an embassy from one of these threatened countries
should come to Jerusalem to get information or to seek aid.
In such cases, the exertions of a great prophet would not in-
frequently be aroused, whether he was expressly applied to for
advice, or whether he felt merely an inward call to make himself heard. Comp. the references xiv. 32 ; xxi. 11 ; xviii. 2,
also xvi. 1-6 and Jer. xxvii. 3, which require the above sup-
positions to make them intelligible. Of this kind of oracle
there have been preserved four examples, for the most part

short, in all of which the Assyrians are represented as the instrument of just punishments, by which Yahvé will make himself felt amongst the heathen also, that they may be led to consider their great moral defects. We may consider that precisely these four were in any case published with this third book: it is possible that it contained others. The first of them, however, is distinguished in many respects from the other three.

---

1. Concerning the Philistines.
xiv. 28—32.

As appears also from its heading, ver. 28, this oracle was on some occasion spoken by Yesaya before the death of Ahaz, but was now for the first time received into this book. The Philistines, from the time of Davîd only partially subdued, had used the weak government and other difficulties of king Ahaz to free themselves completely from the rule of Yuda; indeed, they had made conquests in the territory of this kingdom itself, 2 Chron. xxviii. 18; comp. Isa. ix. 11. But just at that time Yesaya had proclaimed to the Philistines who had become insolent on account of their successes against Yuda, that they should not exult too confidently, since soon a much harder master than even Yuda had been would come upon them bringing total devastation. It is true that Yuda is also greatly depressed and troubled; but there is in it an inexhaustible spring of eternal hope and future weal (as Yesaya had explained definitely and in detail in his earlier orations, especially in the last book, so that here a brief reference to the subject was quite sufficient), and Ssion supplies, precisely in the greatest danger, a higher refuge such as no heathen sanctuary can offer. In its distress, therefore, Philistia will learn to its terror how little cause it has to rejoice at the fact that it has withdrawn itself from the rule and accordingly from the protection of the God of Israel and his sanctuary !—This wealth of ideas is expounded with greatest brevity and precision in two short strophes of two verses each.

XIV.

28   In the death-year of king Ahaz came this high-oracle :

1.

Rejoice not all Philistia, that the staff is broken which smote thee : | for from the root of the serpent will sprout a Cerastus, and its fruit is a flying dragon ! || And the poor feed upon my pasture, and the helpless couch quietly : | but I kill with hunger thy root, and thy remnant will he murder. ||

2.

Wail thou gate, cry thou city, be dismayed all Philistia ! | for from the North cometh smoke, and none separateth himself in his ranks. || And what will one answer the messengers of the people ? | —that Yahvé hath founded Ssion, and upon it the sufferers of my people trust. ||

1. Rejoice not, thou whole land of Philistia with all thy smaller provinces, that thy former superior government, the Yudæan, has been abolished : for allowing that this had been a serpent, or a poisonous tree, yet from the roots, hidden under the earth and ineradicable (vi. 13 ; xi. 1) of the serpent, a much more dangerous one, a Cerastus (xi. 8) would sprout, and its ripe fruit would be even a dreadful flying dragon (xxx. 6 ; Herod. ii. 75) ! without figure : from the abolition of the comparatively mild suzerainty of Yuda will arise the much more

oppressive one of the Assyrians, nay, in the end, from their
rule the complete devastation of the land.   They who are now
the most unfortunate and helpless, the Yudæans, will then lie
down as in a quiet pasture, led by Yahvé, the best shepherd :
whilst Yahvé, by the results of this war, slays thee from the
very foundation, leaving neither root nor remnant (v. 24).

2. Rather instead of exultation at Yuda's misfortune, wail
and despair, gate and city (iii. 26), all Philistia : for from the
North (from Assyria) there already comes, as the prophet sees
in his spirit, that smoke which announces the approach of
great armies (Cant. iii. 6 ; Rev. ix. 2) ; and indeed an army
approaches in whose ranks the most marvellous order and
discipline prevails, in which no one isolates or separates himself, but all remain in closed ranks, v. 27.   If in this extre-
mity ambassadors of the Philistines hasten to the place of their
former protecting government, they will not find in Jerusalem
equally helpless perplexity and the same destruction, but, on
the contrary, a calm trust in Yahvé and his sanctuary, courage
and power to hold out, acc. viii. 13, 14; xxviii. 16.

The reading בְּכוֹרֵי, xiv. 30, would mean *the first-born of
the bowed-down, i.e.,* those bowed-down beyond all others.   A
similar reading is found at least, Job xviii. 13 : but in this
passage the corresponding member, as well as ver. 32, has the
simple word *the helpless,* and the simple meaning is in each
case all that is required.   It is better, therefore, to point the
word בְּכוֹרִי, from כּוֹר, another form of פַּר, which Yesaya
used elsewhere as appears from xxx. 23 : and, in fact, the full
meaning is only then brought out.

The form נָמוֹג, ver. 31, must be considered the *inf. abs.* acc.
§ 240c, 328c ; and at all events the change from the *imper.*
serves to bring greater variety of expression into the two
members.

It is in every way suitable to this connexion that Yesaya

should pass from the Philistines in the south-west to Môab in
the south-east," chaps. xv.-xvi. The circle of foreign nations
concerning which he was intending to speak began thus to be
described. In the same way Yéremyá passes from the Philistines
to Môab, chaps. xlvii., xlviii., while Hézeqiél, ch. xxvi., observes
a different order only because for special reasons he begins with
'Ammôn. But it is equally clear that Yesaya immediately
passed from Môab (if some other oracles of the same kind
were not inserted after this concerning Môab) to the two brief
oracles concerning Arabian peoples, xxi. 11-17, since they as
being farther eastward naturally came after Môab. These
three oracles as they were delivered by Yesaya have further
the greatest similarity to each other. Yesaya used in all alike
oracles of older prophets, and of one older one in particular,
as we shall soon see. He spoke concerning these three nations
not in public as before concerning the Philistines; but he
interwove these three oracles in a written form only into this
book. On the other hand, the pieces which are now placed
between xvii. 1—xxi. 10, cannot, according to all these indications, have had this portion originally. The simple heading,
xv. 1, might be from Yesaya's hand when compared with xiv.
28; but the two others, xxi. 11, 13, are clearly from a later
hand, which renders it doubtful whether the first of the three
is not also from the same source.—The first of these oracles is
of very special importance; its greater length would of itself
give it this.

2. Concerning Môab, ch. xv., xvi.

The people of Môab, nearly related to Israel but remaining
in heathenism and after the Davidic conquest often involved
during those centuries in sanguinary struggles with Israel, was
at that time free, and could not be easily subjugated again by
Israel. Yet inasmuch as it had only cast off the Israelitish
yoke to fall back again completely into a more unrestrained
heathen life, Yesaya had therefore in the case of this related

nation still greater occasion than in the case of the Philistines to anticipate that the threatening Assyrian conquest would bring righteous punishment, and that the proud nation would in vain wish that it had not revolted from Yuda. However, the manner in which Yesaya handles this subject is quite new. He purposely repeated the prophecy of an older prophet, and merely adds a few words of his own, xvi. 13, 14. Closer examination, however, shows that the ancient oracle in the form in which it had been preserved almost entire in ch. xv., xvi. 7-12, had itself been enlarged by an older prophet by the addition xvi. 1-6, when Yesaya received it into his book. We must, therefore, distinguish between these three prophets.

1. At the time of the oldest of these prophets, a devastating invasion, as his words clearly show, had suddenly been made upon Môab; its capital had been stormed and the entire land thrown into a state of extreme confusion and terror. This was probably an inroad and nocturnal sally of Arabian tribes, Môab's northern neighbours, who had made an alliance for this purpose xvi. 8; at all events the evidence for a more definite supposition is wanting.* That the victorious invasion came from the north-east, appears from the flight in a north-west direction, xv. 5-7. Already general lamentation was heard through the land, many hastened to the sacred places, which lay generally upon the high mountain summits of the land, to call upon the national gods in great despair, xv. 2; comp. xvi. 12, whilst many more escaped with their possessions into the south. Yet deeply as the prophet was affected at such great distress, and although he gave free vent to his human sympathy, he could not in the higher divine sense see any true salvation for a nation which had all along been turning to its false gods and

---

* To suppose that the advance of the three kings of Israel, Yuda, and Edóm, against Môab, 2 Kings ch. iii., is intended, is forbidden by the great difference in the locality (comp. *History of Israel*, IV. 88. (III. p. 555 sq.)). With regard to the date, there is nothing in the way of the supposition: but every other appearance is against it.

even now in deepest distress sought protection from them alone.
This sudden calamity, which was also likely soon to pass over,
seemed to him, therefore, but a prelude to future and greater
chastisements of Môab, which he conceived as necessary to
bring back this nation, which had sunk so deeply into
heathenism, to the knowledge of the True One, xv. 9; xvi.
11, 12. The prophecy fell, accordingly, as far as we can now
see, into the exceedingly simple parts of only two long strophes,
sorrow and sympathy with Môab occupying almost the entire
first strophe, ch. xv., the prophetic anticipation of greater sufferings in store for the nation only just appearing at the end; on
that account this anticipation then recurs in the second, xvi.
7-12, with the greater force, and concludes with the prospect,
that only when Môab has fully recognised the helplessness of
its gods will it finally turn to the truth and at the same time
to deliverance.

It is difficult to determine who this older of the three prophets was. The peculiarities of feeling, art, and language
lead to the supposition that he was a very ancient prophet,
from whom nothing further has been preserved. Among the
more ancient prophets there is no one else whose feelings are
like those we find here; the prophet is carried away by his
grief and pity; his tone is rather that of melting tenderness,
of elegiac lamentation, than prophetic sternness. There is much
in the style and tone of the discourses of this prophet which
strongly reminds us of Hosea, although the difference between
them is too great to permit us to suppose that they are the same.
In point of language, the constantly recurring כִּי and עַל כֵּן,
the unusual word הֵידָד xvi. 9, 10, which Yéremyá adopts
from this oracle and again uses more frequently, the equally
uncommon forms יְעֵר xv., 5, §. 121 b, אֲרַיָּוֶךְ xvi. 9, §. 253 a,
and several other peculiarities are such as do not occur elsewhere. The number of paronomasiæ is also remarkable in a
prophet of such evident antiquity; and just as the prophetic
thought retains here its early simplicity, so the art observed in

the structure of the strophes is also of the most ancient type. Each of the two strophes falls into three smaller ones, and the first retains completely the form of a primitive elegy. Now, recent inquiries have shown that it was precisely the poets and prophets of the Ten Tribes who cultivated very early an extremely artistic, tender style, adorned with numerous paronomasiæ. Inasmuch, then, as our prophet evidently had full personal knowledge of the districts of Môab, which he here describes with great accuracy; and also watched everything with such great interest, it may be concluded that like Hosea he was an ancient prophet on the other side of the Yordan, and like Hosea a citizen of the kingdom of the Ten Tribes, for the further reason that Môab belonged originally to this kingdom. And since the only passage in which the authors of the nocturnal attack are distinctly mentioned, xvi. 8, points to allied heathen tribes, probably therefore Arabian neighbours, but Yarob'am II. conquered the land of Môab, acc. 2 Kings xiv. 25, comp. 'Amôs vi. 14 and here likewise xv. 7, it follows that our prophet is older than 'Amôs. On the other hand, this prophet must have written some time after Môab had revolted again from the kingdom of the Ten Tribes (see *History of Israel*, IV. 77, 88, (iii. 541, 555, *sq*.)), *i.e.*, after 897 b.c. Thus everything leads to the conclusion that he lived about the time of Yôél, or, at all events, not much later. That a prophet of the kingdom of the Ten Tribes should at that time follow with very peculiar interest the fortunes of the people of Môab, which had not so very long before revolted, is quite natural.

2. But the words xvi. 1-6, which, as we now find them, have been inserted as a middle strophe between the above-named two, are plainly enough of an entirely different character and complexion. The difference of language and of the tone of the discourse is so great that we might be led to think that Yesaya himself is the writer rather than the previous prophet. Indeed, we might have been inclined to suppose, from the considerable similarity of the words xvi. 4 *d* with xxix. 20, that

Yesaya is the only writer possible, had he not himself too plainly said at the end, xvi. 13, 14, that he here repeated the entire piece concerning Môab as he had received it. Neither does the likeness between the language of the prophet and of Yesaya extend far enough ; and that solitary case of similarity between xvi. 4 and xxix. 20 is explained by supposing that this piece was in Yesaya's mind. The same result is yielded by the historical circumstances which are discernible in this interpolation. For the righteous and prosperous King of Yuda, with whom Môab at that time wished to be connected, acc. xvi. 4, 5, was manifestly 'Uzzia in his better days, some time, therefore, before Yesaya's public appearance. At that time Môab must have been threatened afresh by an alarming enemy : but because the kingdom of the Ten Tribes had already become very weak, it sought aid and protection from Yuda, which our prophet advised Yuda not to grant, because Môab appeared to him to be still far too unprepared to return to the true religion. But this aid must have been lent by 'Uzzia subsequently, sometime after 770 B.C., when without doubt it was sought with greater modesty, and moreover the house of Yehû in the northern kingdom had already fallen, as the course of events shows (comp. *History of Israel*, IV. 145, (iii. 631)). Inasmuch as our prophet, therefore, advised that protection should not be given, he properly inserted his addition between the two strophes, as if the prophetic lamentation of the second strophe were the result of the refusal of protection which had then been made for a time. The mention of the important city Séla', xvi. 1, as belonging to the territory of Yuda, also points to the same period, since this city was again wrested from the Idumæans by King Amassya, 2 Kings xiv. 7. At all events, it is most natural to judge from the context that this Séla' belonged at that time to Yuda, since a still further indication points to such an early date. For it appears from xvi. 4 that the disturbances under Amassya had then been only just recently quelled in Yuda, and 'Uzzia had accordingly not been

long raised to the throne, although he had already fully approved himself as fitted to reign (comp. *History of Israel* IV.
142, (iii. 627 sq.)). We may, therefore, justly suppose that this
prophet laboured almost fifty years before Yesaya appeared
publicly in Jerusalem; and yet he certainly did not publish his
revised form of the older oracle quite in this detached shape.

3. This being the subject-matter of the older prophecy, it is
quite evident that Yesaya could easily apply it with a brief
supplement to his own time. The new and still more powerful
enemy and the final calamity which the older prophet had
anticipated as coming upon Môab, had not yet arrived, but
now, with the threatening position of the Assyrians, whose
further historical relations to Moab we unhappily cannot trace,
the fulfilment of the ancient prophecy seemed near and not to
be longer postponed. This is the one thought which Yesaya
adds in his own words, xvi. 13, 14.—This piece is subsequently
used in a free way by Yéremyá, ch. xlviii.

The High-Oracle concerning Môab.

1.

XV.

1　　　*Yea in the night when 'Ar-Môab was stormed, it is*
destroyed, | yea in the night Qîr-Môab was stormed,
it is destroyed. ‖ Habbáith and Dibon ascendeth
the Heights to weep, | upon Nebó and upon Mœdabá
Môab waileth, upon all its heads baldness, every
beard shorn; ‖ in its streets it hath girt on sack-
cloth, | upon its roofs and its markets waileth it
wholly, running down in weeping; ‖ and Heshbon
and El'ale lamenteth, unto Yáhass their voice is
heard; | therefore Môab's strong-ones shout alarm
—his soul shaketh in him!* ‖

---

* The Hebrew לו is rendered by the simple Germ. dative *ihm*. In English the
substitution of another prep. is necessary.—*Tr.*

5   *My heart lamenteth over Môab, whose fugitives*
unto Ssóar 'Eglath-Shelishiya, | because of Luc-
hith's ascent—with weeping it ascendeth it, because
they raise on the way to Horonáim a cry of death. ||
For Nimrim's waters* will become deserts, | for
grass drieth up, green vanisheth, herbage is at an
end. || Therefore the savings they have gotten | and
their stores—beyond the brook of the Steppes they
carry it. ||

    Yea the lamentation hath spread round Môab's
border, | unto Egláim is their wailing, unto Beér-
Elim their wailing! || Yea Dimôns waters† are full
of blood : | for I bring upon Dimón yet new things,
upon Môab's war-fugitives a lion, and upon the
survivors of the land. ||

2.

XVI.

1   " Send ye the lambs of the prince of the land Séla'
towards the desert | away to the mount of the daughter
Ssion !" || And as wandering birds, a nest driven out, |
are Môab's daughters, the fords of Arnon : || "bring ye
counsel, carry out arbitration, | make [O Ssion !] as the
night thy shadow at high noon-day, | shelter the
scattered, the fugitive betray not ! || let Môab's scat-
tered ones tarry with thee, be to them a shelter from
the spoiler ! | for the oppression hath ceased, the spoil-

---

    * As if one of our brooks was called *the Fair-waters.*

    † As if the brook were called *the Bloody,* or *the Blood.*

ing is at an end, the tormenters have vanished from the land, ‖ and with graciousness has the throne been established, and there sitteth thereupon by faithfulness in David's tent | a judge both seeking right and expert in justice." ‖—"We have heard the haughtiness of Môab the very haughty, | his pride and his haughtiness and his insolence, the insincerity of his pratings !" ‖

3.

Therefore let Môab wail for Môab, wholly let it wail, | for Qîr-Haréseth's grapes moan ye, solely smitten down !‖ for Heshbon's fields droop, Sibmah's vine—the Heathen-lords have beaten down its noble branches which reached unto Ya'zer, strayed through the desert, | its shoots which trailed, which went over the sea. ‖

Therefore let me with Ya'zer's weeping beweep Sibmah's vine, let me water thee with my tears, Heshbon and El'ale ! | for upon thy fruit- and thy corn-harvest fell the wild uproar, ‖ and joy and exultation is withdrawn from the fruit-fields, and in the vineyards there is no jubilation nor shouting, | wine in presses treadeth no treader, the wild uproar I still ! ‖

Therefore my feelings sound over Môab like the harp, | and my inward parts over Qîr-Háres. ‖ Yet when appeareth when awearieth himself—Môab upon the Height, | and cometh into his sanctuary to pray and is not able : ‖ [then he will wholly give up Kamôsh and learn humbly to apply to Yahvé. !]

This is the word which Yahvé spake to Môab
long ago ; ‖ but now Yahvé speaketh thus :
Within three years as a hireling's years | then will
Môab's glory be humbled with all the great tur-
moil, | and the remnant will be very small, not
great. ‖

1. Of the three smaller strophes, which are very distinctly
marked off by pauses, the *first*, vv. 1-4, considers the general
confusion and lamentation of the remainder of the land which
followed the terrible and sudden destruction of its two chief
cities. This strophe, therefore, deals with the immediate and
present condition of the time. The second and third strophes
then pass to further results, such as are already apparent,
namely, flight even beyond the border, and such as will in the
future come increasingly to light, namely, the fresh terrible
calamities which are threatening, the scorching up of the land,
as if it were smitten with the divine curse, vv. 5-7, and another
sanguinary destruction even of the few who had been saved, vv.
8, 9. These three short strophes, just as in an elegy, with a
successive diminution of the volume of the discourse, comp.
Dichter des A. B. I. *a*, p. 148 sq.—(1) Ar-Môab, ver. 1, is the
capital, strictly speaking, Qîr-Môab, properly Môab's *wall* or
fortress, appears to have been, as the strongest fortress, the
second capital, Χάρακα, 2 Macc. xii. 17. The hostile army
had, therefore, divided itself, according to a customary military
stratagem, into two armies, for the purpose of surprising both
capitals at the same time, in which they were successful. The
lamentations which followed appeared in every form, both by all
signs of mourning and weeping before the altars upon the mountains Nebô and Mædebá, and by loud wailing ; it appeared
everywhere, in all cities from Habbáith (probably the same
place which is further defined by *Bœth-Diblatháim*, Jer. xlviii.
22), and Dibon, from Heshbon and Elʻale, unto the north-

western border, near Yáhass [comp. *History of Israel*, II. 209 (II. p. 295)]; both upon the roofs of the houses and in the markets of all towns; it appears finally even amongst the warriors, the warriors of Môab, who are at all other times so stout, cry *murder* because in its inmost parts the soul of Môab *melteth*,* because the entire nation is convulsed with terror to its very bone and marrow, a play upon both the words and the thought (see vol. I. p. 69 *sq.*).—(2) Yea, the prophet himself is compelled to join in the lamentation when he sees how the fugitives hasten even unto Ssóar, unto Eglath Shelishiya (which is correctly used as the name of a place, Jer. xlviii. 34 also) on the south-western border, how in this direction *with weeping* they *ascend* the difficult *ascent* (elevation) of Luchith, on the opposite slope (Jer. xlviii. 5) of Horonáim lift up a cry of alarm and murder, ver. 5. Indeed, it seems as if nature herself were about from this time to assume an aspect of grief, the well-watered and verdant land of Môab becoming a barren desert! ver. 6, comp. xix. 5; xxxiii. 9; Hab. iii. 17; in the dread this causes both of the further wrath of their gods and of their enemies, the people of Môab seem now to be carrying off their entire moveable property over the Steppe-brook on the southern border, ver. 7, comp. Amos. vi. 14.—(3) Yea, as a fact, the loud lamentation has encircled the entire boundary of the land, unto Egláim and Beér Elim, *i.e.*, as far as into the southern boundary of Yuda, Ez. xlvii. 10 (however, these names rather than any other are chosen only for the sake of the paronomasia with the Hebrew word *wailing*), ver. 8 : for it is certain (and here for the first time the divine *I* appears), that the fortunes of this land are threatened with new and severe devastations, the river *Dimon* (as if it were named *the blood*) is full of blood, and will carry still more blood; Yahvé will bring a lion, a still more powerful and

---

* The author renders the paronomasia : " Mòabs Starke rufen *zeter*—seine seele *zittert* ihm." Cheyne (The Book of Isaiah Chronologically arranged by F. K. Cheyne, M.A., Fellow of Balliol College, Oxford. London, 1870) represents it by: " The valiant ones of Moab *shriek*, his soul *shrinketh* within him."—*Tr.*

overwhelming enemy, upon the warriors and others who have escaped the present peril! ver. 9, comp. 2 Kings iii. 22.

2. It is true, they will in the midst of such distress seek protection from their ancient protector and suzerain, the Davîdic king in Ssion. They are advised to send to Ssion the lambs (*i.e.*, the customary annual present, the tribute, 2 Kings iii. 4) of the prince of the land, which are his just due, from Séla', or with the Greek name, *Petra,* on the south of that border-river, xv. 7, in which large mercantile city they may be able to assemble and conveniently buy the tribute, ver. 1. And immediately, in trembling fright, like unprotected birds, the *daughters i.e.,* the individual communities of Môab, the fords, *i.e.,* the dwellers near the fords of the Arnon, the chief river of Môab, do actually hasten to Jerusalem with urgent petitions for counsel, for the putting into force of the inherent right of arbitrament (or intervention, by which a more powerful neighbour and former suzerain acts as umpire between two contending parties for the purpose of assisting the one that is without just cause oppressed), for protection in this hot day, and reception of the fugitives. vv. 2-4 *a.* But unhappily, the reason which they add for the hearing of their prayer, and the arrogant tone of their language, cannot but of itself betray the still-unreformed feeling and temper of the nation (so little is that which is invariably wrong able to conceal itself, even in the time of need) : they are of opinion that the former severe rule (which had led them to revolt, as their language insinuates) has now disappeared in Yuda, the throne, they say, is now established by grace and faithfulness, the two fundamental virtues of a good ruler, and a judge, as zealous as he is experienced in justice, sits upon Davîd's throne and in his house. But how does it become those who are seeking help to desire to palliate their former, in nowise excusable, faithlessness, by a pretext which is not even well founded ? Is *that* simple subjection to the former state of obedience ? Therefore, ver. 6, the answer is returned from the exalted

throne: we have heard their words, the haughty, insincere, ostentatious words, heard them, and that is enough! If Môab continues to show so little penitence, it cannot be assisted : and therefore, the prophet also, however greatly it grieves him, must

3. leave Môab to itself and its further chastisements, to see whether in the future it may perhaps recognize the helplessness of its gods and turn humbly to Yahvé. At present it cannot be assisted, and the prophet can only mourn over its destruction, which has commenced with such heavy blows; three times must the prophet lift up his lamentation afresh, although it has already become calmer, before it can be quite brought to end in peace. For it is a fruitful land, rich in vines and fruits of all kinds, a luxuriant nation, spreading itself far abroad ; it is as if a luxuriant vine, sending out its trailing branches in all directions, were smitten with all its fruit by a rough hand, and had now to wither away : and can one who is a prophet see that with pleasure? This is the principal picture of the first two strophes, comp. Hos. x. 1 ; Isa. v. 1-6 ; Ps. lxxx. 9 *sq.*—
(1) Therefore let Môab mourn over Môab, over itself! no one can render it any help ; over the grape-cakes (Cant. ii. 5 ; Hos. iii. 1), which can no longer be devoured, over the drooping fields (xv. 6), over the smitten vine, whose noble branches (Isa. v. 2) and luxuriant trailing shoots spread out far beyond the borders of the land towards the north or to Ya'zér (comp. *History of Israel*, II. 204, (II. 289)), and towards the desert and towards the east, or the Dead Sea, as if they would overgrow everything,—for these things let there be lamentation everywhere in the land, in Qîr-Haréseth, Heshbon, Sibma, places which have specially seen this luxuriance of the ground! vv. 7, 8. Yea,—(2) the prophet also must join in the lamentation of the places which have been deprived of their ornament : for a wild uproar, that of the enemy, fell with sudden destruction into the rich harvest and its wild uproar, and in the future the loud joy of the harvest will not again be heard in

10 *

these fruit-fields, because a Higher One (here the second and final *I* breaks in) will by that warlike uproar bring this peaceful one to silence (another paronomasia) vv. 9, 10.—(3) On that account, therefore, the prophet cannot remain quiet, his feelings are stirred, loudly sounding like a harp, ver. 11. Yet one hope remains—the eternal hope : when Môab, in the pressure of the further calamities of the future, again *appeareth* as now, (xv. 2,) in its idol-temple (the sacred term for going to the temple, i. 12) or rather *wearieth himself,* vainly wrings his hands (again a paronomasia) and in complete despair is unable even to pray—then he will be ashamed of his god Kamôsh and learn true humility in Yahvé ! But the last words, which are necessary to complete the sense, have been lost.

In vv. 13, 14, every syllable has Yesaya's majestic tone. *As the daylabourer's days, i.e.,* strictly measured, not longer, xxi. 16.

With regard to the geography of the land of Môab, which the oldest of the three prophets so graphically glances at, much fresh knowledge has been acquired during the last twenty or thirty years. We are especially indebted to the works of de Saulcy (*Voyage en terre sainte,* Paris, 1865) and H. B. Tristram (*The Land of Israel,* London, 1865) for this fuller knowledge. Comp. with regard to both of these works, *Gött. Gel. Anz.,* 1866, p. 429 *sq.*, 1565 *sq.* However, there is a good deal of the geography of these chapters about which we have but little definite knowledge, while, again, there are some points of it which have not been even examined. That *Qîr-Môab,* xv. 1, is the same as Qîr-Háres, or *Qir-Haréseth,* named at the commencement and also at the close of the third of the main strophes, xvi. 7, 11, and that the latter is only the primary name of the strong fortress, while the former is chosen merely for the sake of greater euphony, xvi. 11, was indicated in the *History of Israel,* IV. 89 (III. p. 557). We have thus an explanation of the fact that Jer. xlviii. the latter name only is found, vv. 31, 36. As to 'Ar-Môab, see Vol. I. p. 165. The locality of Nebó, xv. 2, according to the above most recent geographical books appears to have been at last certainly discovered. The name *Dibón*, xv. 2, alters its sound a little, ver. 9, to *Dimôn* to suit the paronomasia.

xv. 1. According to this understanding of the passage, it is merely the difference between being *subdued* (stormed) and *annihilated*, which is prominently brought forward: that the two chief cities appeared already destroyed by the terrible attack would be at that time the worst that could happen. It is true that the entire ver. 1 might be supposed to form only the protasis to vv. 2-4: in that case *laid waste . . . . . destroyed* would convey the feeling of great distress. But it seems difficult to conceive that all the events of vv. 2-4 are intended to have taken place in that one night. And yet it is probably correct, if the entire land had for some days been prepared beforehand for this night.

xv. 9. The word פליטה is certainly distinguished from שארית as denoting the warriors which have escaped from the battle, whilst the latter word denotes all the rest. What still more powerful enemy the oldest prophet intended by the *lion* it is hard to say: his successor might intend by it the King of Yuda, inasmuch as the lion was the emblem on the flags of Yuda (see *History of Israel*, III. 250 (III. 341)), and on that account be the more naturally induced to insert the following strophe in this place.

xvi. 4. The Massôra intend *a* and *b* to be understood thus: "let *my scattered ones* sojourn with thee, let *Môab—be a shelter to them !*" But it is much easier to read בְּדְחִי; comp. thereon *Gött. Gel. Anz.* 1832, p. 103.—Ver. 5, the elegant use of the conjunction וְ- וְ-, acc. § 359, should be observed: Yesaya himself does not affect it, but this instance shows how accurately he quoted the words of his predecessor.

xvi. 9. The ornate expression, " let me with Ya'zer's weeping beweep the vine of Sibma !" may be most naturally explained

by the transition from the previous strophe, ver. 8; but the
apparent frigidity of it disappears when it is remembered that
Ya'zer may signify the *helper*, as if the prophet desired to make
himself a helper by joining in the grief.—The similarity between the words ver. 10 and Joel i. 16 is not decisive enough
to warrant any inference therefrom. Both prophets belong to
nearly the same time.

With regard to the unusual words, xvi. 12, it is, on the one
hand, certain that they cannot be far from the end, because the
discourse while recurring to its commencement, xv. 2, at the
same time in point of meaning comes to a close: but, on the
other hand, the apodosis is plainly missing, since ולא יוכל
completely answers to נלאה in the first member. The true
concluding sentence, therefore, must have been lost by an
error in transcription, and perhaps Yéremyá had it before him
in his day, inasmuch as the words, וּבוֹשׁ מוֹאָב מִפְּמוֹשׁ xlviii.
13, comp. vv. 7, 35, would be quite suitable here.

The two following oracles, xxi. 11-17, were both of them
originally of the same extreme brevity, each of them consisting of but two verses; for whoever can recognise Yesaya's
own language will perceive that he is not speaking before
ver. 15, but then most certainly commences in his own most
characteristic language. We have here, therefore, oracles of a
very peculiar nature with regard to their form and style. We
find nowhere else oracles of such great brevity, and conveyed
in language of such an enigmatical complexion. It is as if
one still heard the most ancient voices, with their almost pro-
voking laconism and biting subtlety of utterance, which are
intended the more effectually to spur the hearer on to meditate
upon the meaning of what is thus put before him, and to search
out what the ultimate intention of the oracle is. In fact, these
oracles have in this respect a great deal of similarity with the
Heathen oracles, *e.g.*, those of the Greeks: and yet Yesaya

for good reasons deigned to appropriate and amplify them.
That they are very old follows from these characteristics. But
if we inquire more particularly as to their age and authorship,
we might be induced to suppose that they owe their origin to
the second of the prophets of Yuda mentioned above, to whom
we are indebted for the oracle xvi. 1-6, (1) because an oracle
concerning Edóm would appear to be more likely to come from
a prophet living in Jerusalem; but this reason is not free
from uncertainty, especially in the case of such a short piece;
(2) because the word נֹדֵד, *fugitive*, ver. 14, occurs in that
prophet as a very favourite expression, xvi. 2, 3; but Yesaya
also uses it here, ver. 15, and elsewhere, while in poetry generally it is by no means rare. In fact, we have every reason to
suppose in the case of these pieces, as in the case of the larger
of the previous ones, that an ancient prophet of the kingdom of
the Ten Tribes was their author, whether he was the same as
the author whom we found there, ch. xv.-xvi., or another in
any case very much like him. The forms אֵתָיוּ, בָּעָיָ, תִּבְעָיוּן,
ver. 12, הֵתָיוּ or more correctly הֵתִיוּ, ver. 14, comp. §§ 142*a*,
194*a*, are nowhere else so frequent as here;* the orthography
אֵתָא, ver. 12, is also peculiar. And the exceedingly brief and
pointed manner of the discourse seems to be very unlike the
soft and overflowing style of chapters xv. and xvi. We have,
here, therefore, perhaps the most ancient oracles that have
been preserved in the Old Testament of prophets after the
division of the Davídic kingdom.

If the heading, ver. 11, had been original, it might be supposed, first, that the Arabian tribe *Dûma*, which is mentioned
elsewhere only in Gen. xxv. 14, was visited in that early
period by some sudden but protracted calamity, probably the
same which the next oracle looks upon as affecting all other
Arabian tribes. But in order to understand the first words,
ver. 11, we should, secondly, have to suppose that the

---

* In Yesaya the form יְכָלָיוּן is found only in the pause (xvii. 12); xxxi. 3
(xxxiii. 7), and in that case not always, i. 28.

report of the calamity had reached the prophet by way of Seʿîr, *i.e.* Edóm. But in that case it does not appear why the prophet should merely commence with the mention of Seʿîr, and stop there; the words, ver. 11, indicate that Edóm had itself so severely suffered at that time that the prophet seemed to hear a loud voice, rising involuntarily from its midst, and calling to him for help and explanation, a voice which he feels compelled to answer. The LXX, two Hebrew MSS., and the *Arab. Polyg.* have actually preferred to read אֱדוֹם instead of דּוּמָה, as if we had here simply an oracle concerning *Edôm*. We do not know whether this was not purely a conjecture on their part, and we may rather suppose that the heading is intended to mean an *Oracle of Silence,* and owes its position here to the wit of a later reader, inasmuch as the import of the oracle at all events issues in the fact that the prophet who has been called upon to speak prefers to be as good as silent. In any case, we name the piece as the oracle,

3. Concerning Edom, ch. xxi. 11, 12.

This very smallest piece has the most beautiful prophetic import. Every genuine prophet, as we saw, Vol. I. p. 28, sq., must always stand upon his watch-tower, as it were, in the divine consideration of the fortunes of all men and nations, and must know what has shortly to come to pass. Accordingly it seems to our prophet precisely at this moment that a troubled voice is calling to him from the above district, enquiring whether the long terrible night (of calamity, Job xxxv. 10) is not yet past? what o'clock it is in the night?—But however glad he would be to return a pleasant answer, he finds it impossible. In accordance with the higher consideration that those nations which are so deeply sunk in heathenism must be much more seriously chastised before they will arrive at the truth, he is unable to give a favourable reply, and veils, with a certain degree of evasion, the mournful anticipation of a still longer duration of this night. The whole forms the shortest possible oracle, and is nevertheless pregnant with thought, clear, and finished.—As this prophet is, therefore, a very ancient one, we might even think that the attack upon Edóm proceeded at that time from Yuda (comp. *History of Israel*, IV. 54 (iii. 510 sq.)), and that our prophet as living in the Northern kingdom returned such a brief answer, for the very reason that this kingdom as hostile to Yuda might be easily considered by Edom as friendly to it. Yet the enemy might have been the same as that that appears in the next piece.

XXI.

High-Oracle of Silence.

11   *To me one calleth* from Se‘îr : " watchman, what of the night ? watchman, what of the night ? " ‖ The watchman saith : " The morning hath come—and also the night ! If ye will enquire, enquire ye ! return ye, come !" ‖*

The repetition of the question, ver. 11, pourtrays the distress of the enquirers. The answer, ver. 12, is already contained in the words: morning is come—and also night ! everything has its time, and if formerly there came a bright, cheerful morning, now the night is here and will not depart very soon : I cannot give you any better comfort. In order, however, to make it quite clear that this is all he has to say, he adds : *" if ye desire to ask, ask ye !* I have nothing to say against your enquiry of the prophet, but *return, come !* in the future when ye return put new enquiries ; for the present I have nothing further to say. Comp. *Jahrb. der Bibl. Wiss.* V. p. 246 sq.

Precisely this rare word בָּעָה is peculiar to our prophet, and

---

* Germ.: " Zu mir *ruft es.*" For the indefinite force of the part., see § 200.—*Tr.*

is found elsewhere only in the sense of to *search through*, Ob.
ver. 6.—לַיִל, ver. 11, has this form manifestly only on account
of the pause, § 146 *e*, yet that is also peculiar.

---

4.   Concerning the Arabians, ch. xxi. 13-17.

The caravans of the Arabian tribe Dedân, which had become
very rich and powerful by the trade of carrying, had been
evidently at the time of the older prophet attacked by superior
enemies and compelled to make an ignominious flight, so that
the proud tribe must be content in its complete helplessness to
receive the most necessary means of living from the favour of
others, *e.g.* of those dwelling in the land Tæmâ (Job vi. 19).
Inasmuch as these Arabs had already wandered far from the
true religion, it cannot be surprising that the older prophet
feels himself compelled to address to this tribe also no word of
consolation, but rather dismisses it with delicate irony.

But in Yesaya's days, the Assyrian power, endeavouring to
become a world-wide monarchy, threatened not in vain all these
Arab tribes also, as indeed Sancherhib is called also king of
the Arabs, Herod. ii. 141. Accordingly, Yesaya applies and
amplifies the old oracle in such a way that he expresses the anticipation, that upon the first defeat which the Arabs had then
already suffered from the Assyrians, a much greater humiliation
of all the predatory Arab tribes would soon follow : and he
comprehends all these tribes in an original manner under the
name of *Qedar*, which was at that time a prominent tribe.
When, therefore, that historical event of recent occurrence has
been brought forward in the first strophe, vv. 13-15, the real
prophetic anticipation is introduced in the second strophe, vv.
16, 17.

High-Oracle concerning the Steppe (Arabia).

1.

XXI.

13   *In the forest in steppes must ye pass the*

night, ye caravans of Dedán? ‖ *To meet*
the thirsty bring ye water, ye inhabitants of
the land Tæmá! with his bread anticipate
15   *the fugitive!* ‖ Because they fled before swords,
    | before the drawn sword and before the bent bow,
and before the stress of war! ‖

2.

For thus saith the Lord unto me : | Within a
year like a hireling's years—and all Qedar's glory
is at an end :‖ and the remnant of the bowmen's
force* of the brave sons of Qedar will be few! |
for Yahvé Israel's God hath spoken it. ‖

It cannot be too distinctly borne in mind that this Oracle,
when separated from its additions in the pure form in which
the old prophet uttered it, vv. 13, 14, is exactly like the
previous one in respect of its deterrent and sharp tone, notwithstanding its numerous dissimilarities. *In forests,* even *in
steppes,* (the last worse than the first) *must ye pass the night,*
without being able to find any caravansary or convenient places
for encamping ?   That is hard !   But I do not know anything
better for you ; and at best one can only call upon the neighbouring Tæmâ to meet the fugitive with water, with *his,* i.e.,
that which is necessary for him, bread of dependence : it is
hard to be compelled to accept such bread, but I know nothing
better ! Let no more be said ! The curtain descends, and it
is sufficiently indicated that they deserve nothing better.   The
manner of expression, therefore, is different from that of the
previous oracle, and yet it amounts to the same thing.   It is
remarkable with what tact Yesaya connects his further elucidation and application, ver. 15, with the last word ver. 14.

הֵיתָיוּ, ver. 14, is according to this pointing the *imper.*, §. 141 *a,*

* Germ.: *bogenzahl.—Tr.*

the *perf.*, would have to be הֵתִיו, acc. §. 142 *a*.   But later
punctuators must have misunderstood this and in consequence
have incorrectly written קִדְּמוּ instead of קַדְּמוּ; the accents also
of ver. 14 are incorrect.

It is evident on the very face of it that עֲרָב, ver. 13, in the
ancient oracle, cannot mean *Arabia,* but as equal to עֲרָבָה retains fully its primary meaning, *steppe.* That the Arabians came
gradually to be denominated from their *steppes,* is clearly a custom which did not arise before the 7th cent., and is first met with
in Jer. iii. 3 ; Ez. xxvii. 21, and later writers. Not before
this time, therefore, for this reason amongst others, can a new
editor of the book of Yesaya have added the heading *High-
Oracle on Arabia,* (the Arabs) ver. 13 : he took the word בַּעֲרָב
from the commencement of the piece, understood it in this more
modern sense, and could thus also connect the prep. בְּ־, in
accordance with an old usage (" Zech." ix. 1), with מַשָּׂא in a
new sense. In its original meaning the word must be understood acc. §. 176 *a*.

That the most northern Arabs (for in reality it is these only
who are intended in such cases) were distinguished bowmen,
ver. 17, is well known, Gen. xxi. 20.

IV.—YESAYA'S FOURTH BOOK.

But for the time Yesaya in vain summoned the nation, by
his moving representation, ch. i. and the entire previous book,
to repentance ; it still lacked the requisite earnestness and self-
denial, and soon had its attention attracted into another direction.   The Assyrians, without doubt because those small
nations referred to in ch. i. (see *ante* p. 119) were finally unable
to effect much against Jerusalem, sent an army against it, most
likely from the north-east, perhaps by the same road which our
prophet subsequently, x. 28-32, looked upon as the one to be
taken by an Assyrian army marching against Jerusalem.   An
army was sent from Jerusalem against the Assyrians, but at

the sight of these northern warriors, who were such as it had
never seen before, the army fled immediately, and in consequence the people of Jerusalem hastened to put an end to the
Assyrian devastation of the land by a treaty of peace. Indeed
it appeared in Jerusalem as if no calamity had occurred, and
there had been no great humiliation of the nation; it seemed
too, as if the people wished to defy the admonitions of the
prophet. As appears from xxii. 1 sq., the people on the conclusion of peace gave themselves up to the most uncontrolled
rejoicing, and the intoxication of material pleasures. It was
as if they wished to stifle by means of a whirl of wild extrava-
gance the irrepressible thought of the near destruction, and as
if they would drown the voice of the prophet with uproarious
amusements. But that was more than the prophet could bear.
He saw it, and was astonished. He collected himself, and proclaimed to the people, who were lost in wild joy, the mournful
thought which their conduct had given rise to within him.
Nothing is more disgraceful in itself, as nothing contains more
elements of future trouble, than for a nation to endeavour to
drown a disgrace, which it has brought upon itself, by means
of thoughtlessness and pleasure-hunting: and at that time
Yesaya must either give the lie to all his earlier efforts, or he
was compelled to labour still more zealously and unweariedly
for the same truths as he had hitherto defended. Accordingly
he laboured manifestly with the greater energy in all directions
during those days, sought to hold back the people from blindly
running into the yawning abyss which it had made for itself, and
endeavoured in a general way to labour for a genuine reform of
the whole kingdom, from its highest to its lowest members. We
still possess in the two pieces, ch. xxii. the most self-evident
records of his labours at that time, which were most unsuccessful, although they cost him the greatest effort. And inasmuch as these pieces are found precisely here just after the
end of the previous book, and then the piece, ch. xxiii. can
quite well follow, we may with reason conclude that Yesaya

very soon republished his former book with the addition of
these supplements, his assistants, mentioned above, p. 61,
without doubt again lending him their help.

---

1. *The Harangue against the People*, ch. xxii. 1-14.

This harangue comprises the essential things that Yesaya
had uttered face to face with the whole people on that day of
mad intoxication.   It is an oration born of human astonishment
and sorrow, which, however, as the depth of the matter comes
to be more closely considered, changes into an overwhelming
threat, such as does not elsewhere occur in our prophet, but
which the import of this moment fully justifies.   The prophet
cannot join in this noise, if for no other reasons, on account of
the shameful defeat which preceded it, and because he anticipates worse things from a no distant future, vv. 1-5 ; but when
he considers how little the nation was brought by the recent
great danger to fix its attention on better things, vv. 6-11 ;
when he considers how it now converts the serious call to repentance into an antithesis which mocks this call, and gives
itself over to wild rejoicing, thereby to escape from the divine
seriousness of the position,—he is compelled to declare that
there is here the greatest and most serious sin that men are
capable of, the sin against the Holy Spirit, vv. 12-14.—All
this in one outburst, yet in three short strophes, the last of
which closes in the greatest agitation, and with great rapidity
and brevity in consequence.   The later collector gave to the
piece, from ver. 5, the heading :—

High-oracle of the Oracle-valley.

1.

XXII.

1.   What hast thou then that thou art all-together
    gone up to the house-roofs? || O thou filled with
    clamours, thou noisy city jubilant place! | thy

slain are not the slain of the sword, not the fallen
in battle: ‖ all thy captains fled together from the
bow, were made prisoners, | all of thine who were
found were made prisoners all-together, sped far
away. ‖ Therefore say I: look away from me, let
me weep bitterly, | press not to comfort me on the
desolation of the daughter of my people! ‖ for a
day of alarm and assault and amazement hath the
Lord Yahvé of Hosts in the Oracle-valley! | to
carnage careereth Qîr, and Shôa is at the mount! ‖

2.

And 'Aelam carried the quiver in a line of
horsemen, | and Qîr made bare the shield; ‖ and
already were thy choicest valleys full of horse, | —
and the cavalry — yea they rushed against the
gates, ‖ and he uncovered Yuda's covering: | then
thou lookedst on that day at the armour of the
Forest-house, ‖ and the clefts of the Davîd city ye
saw how many they were, | and collected the water
of the lower pool, ‖ and the houses of Jerusalem
ye numbered, | and pulled down the houses to
fortify the wall, ‖ and a basin ye made between
the double-wall for the water of the old pool, | —
but ye looked not unto him that did it, and him
that formed it from afar ye saw not! ‖

3.

And the Lord Yahvé of Hosts called indeed on
that day | to weeping and to lamentation, and to
cutting off the hair and to putting on sackcloth: ‖
but behold joy and gladness, slaughtering oxen

and killing sheep, eating flesh and drinking wine, |
eating and drinking, for tomorrow we die! ‖ Thus
in mine ears revealed Yahvé of Hosts : | never
shall this sin be forgiven you, till ye die! saith
the Lord Yahvé of Hosts. ‖

1. The prophet as he appears in public unexpectedly beholds
the whole city upon the house-tops, for the purpose, as appears
from ver. 2, and further from ver. 13, of holding unusual feasts
of rejoicing, with unbounded merrriment, the inhabitants of
every house being accustomed on such occasions to assemble
upon their flat roofs, Judg. xvi. 27; Neh. viii. 16.   It is clear
that the holiday was the celebration of the dishonourable conclusion of peace with the Assyrians; for the first thing that
Yesaya speaks in opposition to the wild uproar (v. 14) of which
the city is too lavish, is that it has no ground for rejoicing,
inasmuch as its lost men did not fall in honourable battle, but
fled, together with their captains, disgracefully before the
Assyrian (ver. 6), or were taken prisoners in their flight, vv.
2, 3.   On that account he desires to be left to weep bitterly,
since he foresees at the same time that for his beloved native
city so much the greater suffering must soon follow the present
foolish joy, and that Yahvé had already in his mind a day when
every conceivable calamity would break over the sacred city,
when no help would be known against the wild hosts of those
who would fall suddenly upon the city and the enemy who
would attack the sacred hill in wild rage! vv. 4, 5.   And how
great was the prophet's grief that this must take place *in the
valley of vision,* i.e. acc. Vol. i. p. 33, *of the Oracle,* in the
lower part of the city of Jerusalem, where he himself and
many others before him had preached the divine word, alas,
generally in vain !

2. For when the nations farthest to the east ('Aelam) and to
the north (Qîr, Amos. i. 5) advanced in well-arranged and excel-

lently armed cavalry troops (comp. xxi. 9), when even the
fairest valleys around the city had been already occupied, the
horsemen made sallies even to the very gate of Jerusalem, yea,
when Yahvé *made bare the veil of Yuda, i.e.* showed wholly
without veil and openly the inmost secret condition, and accordingly the real weakness of the state to the enemy—then
the magnates of the kingdom did indeed look anxiously after
every form of external protection and defence, preparing themselves for a siege (which nevertheless did not come) : but to
the real originator of the calamity, to Yahvé who had long
since silently prepared and then announced it by his prophets,
to him they did not look, to discover and to do his will.

3. On the contrary, when they were at that time expressly
summoned by the prophet to serious repentance and penance,
instead of that they gave themselves up to the most unrestrained and senseless pleasure, as if by their thoughtlessness,
to defy the thought of the speedy fall as is graphically described, ver. 13 (1 Cor. xv. 32). But the prophet accordingly
hears sounding clearly in his ears the dreadful word of Yahvé
(v. 9), "this sin of intentional resistance of the Holy Spirit is
unpardonable, and must bring them step by step, without any
break, to ruin, so that nothing but death can put an end to the
process of destruction," ver. 14, comp. xxx. 13, 14.

---

xxii. 3. It is best, contrary to the accents, to connect מְקַשֵּׁת
with the foregoing words, comp. ver. 6.—The words, ver. 4,
even at the recollection of such a time of extreme distress, are
quite unusual, in order that what cannot in any way be described may be forcibly adumbrated : the English words *alarm
and assault and amazement,* are a weak imitation of the
Hebrew.* But this sound-painting extends to the last words

* The German language is better able to render the volume and force of Hebrew
words than the English. Ewald's words are : *bedrängung und bestürmung und
bestürzung.* Another English imitation would be : *distress and destruction and
dismay.*—*Tr.*

2   11

of the verse. In the first edition they were rendered: *by un-walling the wall and war-shout against the mountain !* But in the second vol. p. 301, the present rendering was already proposed. It is quite certain that *the mountain* as forming the antithesis to the above-named *ravine*, must be Ssion: but whether קִר is intended to correspond to this as one of its *sides*, or rather as its *wall*, is the more uncertain since Yesaya does not use it elsewhere. It is rather from the outset the more probable that it denotes in this passage a wild, warlike northern nation, which the Assyrians employed, answering to the Qîr mentioned, Vol. i. p. 159, inasmuch as it is immediately resumed, ver. 6, at the commencement of the next strophe; and that שׁוֹעַ was a nation of this kind will appear below at Ez. xxiii. 23. As indicating the signification of קִרְקֵר, Num. xxiv. 17 cannot be quoted, since it has in that place to give way to another reading; but the Arab. *rakâ to perforate, excavate, destroy*; and in any case, this very rare word is here used only for the sake of the paronomasia; from which fact it follows further that קִיר, as the principal word upon which the play is made, can only be taken as an important proper-name. The paronomasia is rendered freely in the translation.*

The word שִׁית ver. 7, as is shown by the context, cannot here mean, as Ps. iii. 7, to take up a firm position, or *to encamp*, but must signify *to attack* or *to storm*, like שִׂים, 1 Kings xx. 12; Ez. xxi. 21. With regard to the much misunderstood וַיְהִי at the commencement of ver. 7, see §. 345 *b*.— The figure *of uncovering the wrapper*, or the veil, *of a capital*, ver. 8, (and that Yuda was as appropriate in such a connexion as Jerusalem, follows from what was said vol. I. p. 189 *sq*.) was the more natural when in more elevated language it was the custom to speak of a capital as a *virgin*, comp. Arab. *kashafa*,

---

* Ewald's free rendering of מְקַרְקַר קִר is: *wie ein stier raset Qîr*, which owing to the slight difference of meaning between the English word *steer* and the Germ. *stier*, could not be reproduced in the translation of the Hebrew text. The rendering substituted is in any case not freer than the author's.—*Tr.*

Tab. I. p. 208. 3, *hataka sitra* or *tahattaka* Freytag's *Chrest.* p. 48. 7; Borhaneldin *enchir. stud.* p. 8, ver. 1, and the more rare Syriac words in the Carm. de Alex. p. 97. 7, 11, edit. Knös.

The preparations against the siege, vv. 8-11, are: (1) examination of the *forest-house*, *i.e.*, of the armoury built with cedars from the forest (Lebanon, Kings vii. 2-6; x. 17; Neh. iii. 19 (*History of Israel*, III., 249, (III. p. 341)); (2) examination of the condition of the walls of the citadel and the diversion of those pools which were in a too exposed position (*History of Israel*, III. 253 sq.; IV. 176 (III. 347 sq.; 672); (3) demolition of many of the houses which were built outside the walls and gates of the city, lest they should serve a besieging enemy as outworks against the city-walls; comp. *History of Israel*, IV. 272 (III. 805). (Comp. similar precautions, vii. 3 sq.)

The words, ver. 12, might seem to refer to the great oration, chap. i., and for that reason also we might be inclined to consider the enemies described in ch. i. as the same as those who are here meant, vv. 6-8. As was said above, the difference of date is in any case small; yet the words, ver. 12, rather point to an exhortation to repentance, and the way in which the enemies are described, ch. i., differs considerably from that found here. In any case, the orations of ch. xxii. are of later date than that of ch. i.; and the position of the three pieces of ch. xxii. and xxiii. is most easily explained by the supposition that we have in the book before us a new edition of that earlier book. Further, comp. *Jahrbb. der Bibl. wiss.* I. p. 40 sq.; VII. p. 129.

---

2. *The Harangue against Shebnâ.*

Probably about the same time Yesaya addressed the following harangue to a particular man in Jerusalem, one of the magnates, who had been in general terms often censured by the prophet,

and whose position was at that particular moment of the
greatest importance as regards the general affairs of the
realm. As appears from ver. 16 and the foreign sound of his
name, he was not a native Hebrew, but a foreigner, whom
probably the previous king Ahaz had raised to the great
dignity of a steward of the royal house and court, (comp.
History of Israel, III. p. 268 (III. p. 367), a dignity which he
retained for some time under the next king Hizqia. Yesaya's
words leave no doubt that the proud foreigner had in
many ways misused his dignity and power, *e g.*, by showing
favour to unworthy men (comp. vv. 23-25) ; and he was just
about to immortalize his name and family in Jerusalem by the
erection of a family tomb, the ancients setting much store by
the sanctity of such family tombs ; it seemed as if this man
would insolently defy the future, while his position in
Jerusalem had long been without any moral support. It was
then that Yesaya felt himself impelled by the spirit to deprive
him of this desire, by the prediction that instead of his doing
this a still more powerful hand would soon lay hold of him and
hurl him into exile, by the instrumentality of the Assyrian
whose new attack the previous piece, xxii. 5, had just anticipated, vv. 16-19, comp. Amos vii. 17. And because at the
same time another man in Jerusalem, of the name of Elyaqîm,
seemed to be more worthy of this position, the prophetic
anticipation goes on to represent him, vv. 20-24, as the man
chosen by Yahvé and found worthy to succeed to Shebnâ's
office, and closes, ver. 25, with the expectation that the
unworthy and injurious dependents of the latter will then also
fall, as an evident sign that the kingdom was then still more
seriously injured by the immoral favourites of the man than by
himself. The arrangement of the oration is, therefore, quite
the same as that of the preceding one ; as a whole it is a little
shorter.

It is obvious that the king Hizqia, although he might gladly
listen to the prophet, was not necessitated at once to quite dis-

miss the man on account of this merely prophetic harangue
and Divine threat ; the prophet speaks throughout in the form
of anticipation only, not as issuing commands.   At the same
time, we see from xxxvi. 3 ; xxxvii. 2, that a few years subsequently Elyaqîm was raised to this post, while Shebnâ was
removed to another ministerial position, whereby probably the
main complaint against him, that of having in the past
promoted unworthy favourites, was finally settled.   It is always
wrong to wish to precipitate a Minister if there is no better
substitute for him to be had.

1.

XXII.

15   Thus saith the Lord Yahvé of Hosts : Go
appear before this high officer, even before Shebnâ
the steward of the house : ‖ What hast thou here
and whom hast thou here, that thou hewest-out
for thee here a tomb, | hewing-out the height for
his tomb, hollowing in the rock a dwelling for himself? ‖ Behold Yahvé will hurl hurl thee thou great
man, | and grasp grasp thee, ‖ rolling-up as a ball
roll roll thee up | — into a wide-bordered land; |
there shalt thou die and there thy glorious chariots,
thou shame of the house of thy lord ! ‖ So I thrust
thee from thy post, | and from thy position will he
uproot thee. ‖

2.

20   But then on that day, | I summon my servant
Elyaqîm the son of Hilqia, ‖ and clothe him with
thy robe, and with thy girdle I gird him, | and thy
government I transfer to him, so that he will be a
father to Jerusalem's inhabitants and to Yuda's
house; ‖ and I lay the key of the house of Davîd

upon his shoulder, | so that he openeth while none shutteth, and shutteth while none openeth. ‖ And I drive him as a nail into a sure place, | so that he will be a seat of honour to his father's house, ‖ and upon him hangeth all the glory of his father's house, the shoots and the sprouts, all the dainty vessels, | alike the vessels of bowls and all the vessels of pitchers. ‖

3.

25   On that day, saith Yahvé of Hosts, will the nail which is driven into a sure place give way, | it will be cut off and falleth, and the burden which hangeth upon it will be destroyed: | for Yahvé said it. ‖

At the very commencement of the oration, ver. 15, its character is indicated, Shebnâ being called at once, quite contrary to Yesaya's customary manner, contemptuously *this* minister (comp. the Latin *iste*). And the first word addressed to him, ver. 16, forthwith inquires of the proud man, what rights and what ancestors he has, giving him a title to erect here a family tomb, as if he were a native, a man who will further establish his lasting residence (comp. xiv. 18 ; Ecc. xii. 5) upon the summit of a rock, as if he desired for all time to come to look proudly down upon the holy city, Job xxi. 32.   But precisely because thou, great man, (comp. on Ps. lii. 3*) art resolved to establish thyself here against the Divine will, he will seize thee with a mighty hand, and, rolling thee into a round mass (thou

---

* On this passage, *Dichter des A. B. I. b*, p. 174, the author maintains that גִּבּוֹר *hero*, as well as גֶּבֶר, Germ. *mann*, Eng. *strong man*, the word used by Yesaya, in later usage lost its ancient elevated and noble signification, through the fault of the deteriorated magnates, and gradually sank to the semi-bantering semi-malicious meaning which the ancient German name *held* (hero), sometimes now bears. Comp., perhaps our old English word, *worthy* = hero.—*Tr.*

mayest resist or not), hurl thee as a light ball far away out of
the holy land into a distant vast land, into a waste, together
with thy proud chariots (2 Sam. xv. 1), where thou, unworthy
man, whose position brings the royal house into disgrace,
mayest perish ! vv. 17-19, uttered at first vv. 17, 18*a*, with
uncommon force and annihilating severity, only towards the
end, ver. 19, becoming calmer, passing therefore also from the
first into the third person, as xiv. 30.—Afterwards Elyaqîm
may, from the divine point of view, be clothed with the official
insignia of this high dignity, the official vestment with the
broad and brilliant girdle, that he may be a provident father
to the whole country (ix. 5), and exercise in the royal house
the full privilege and the full authority to do and to leave un-
done, to open and to shut, as much as any other man who gets
laid upon his shoulder this no less important than difficult office
of the Keys (*i.e.*, house-stewardship), vv. 20-22. But he,
personally irreproachable and springing from a noble house,
will not be liable to such a fall as Shebnâ, but maintain his position like a nail driven into a secure place, so firmly that by his
throne and firm seat his entire paternal house also feels itself
honoured, and upon this nail the entire nobility of his family,
i.e., all the members of this magnificent family, will hang, and
be borne like a number of vessels upon a strong nail in a wall,
also the younger members of the house (Elyaqîm was
undoubtedly already advanced in life), or the shoots and the
sprouts like graceful vessels of all kinds, and the lowly as well
as the exalted ones of the wide-spread branches of the family,
as it were both the low, shallow bowls and the high pitchers.
Thus we have here figure upon figure ; the figure of the *nail*
is not very uncommon, Zech. x. 4; Ezra, ix. 8, 9: If the
dependants of the minister Shebnâ had not excited such
desires, the prophet would hardly have mentioned thus pro-
spectively the followers of his future successor : but he now
returns expressly, ver. 25, to the followers of Shebnâ, who
though at present he holds his place as a nail driven into a

sure place, (namely, in the Davîdic house) will soon violently
fall with the entire burden which he supports.

The Arab. phrase *thabatat lahu autâd*, Arab. Fâqih. p. 27
medio; 120, 9 *a fin.*, answers to the figure of a *nail.*—
It follows from ver. 21, that the official attire of the prime
minister was at that time kept in the royal palace and was
transmitted from one minister to another, just as the official
attire of the High Priest in the Persian and subsequent times
was always kept in the temple.

This piece is further remarkable inasmuch as it permits us to
see more closely into the relations of the principal parties in the
kingdom at that period.   In any kingdom in which the humour
and arbitrary will of a king and royal family are not suffered
to have the sway, but in which, on the contrary, especially law
and religion are designed to rule, and actually have ruled with
some degree of consistency, as was the case in the kingdom of
the people of Israel, and particularly in Jerusalem, the various
tendencies and efforts often take a distinct form and representative character in the hereditary principles of powerful houses
(or families), whose ancestors had fought and suffered, conquered and ruled in their cause.   In accordance with this fact,
it may also be observed that a new class of protectors and
dependants often arises, the relatives of the house and the
friends of the same principles attaching themselves gladly to
the head of a powerful family.   This is not the common and
legal relation of the *cliens* and *patronus* (see *Alterthümer* p.
287 (248) : it is an entirely free, unrestricted relation, which
must assume the form dictated by an understanding of the
higher principles of the kingdom and by the courage which men
have to identify themselves with them.   When such a relation
is established it may powerfully affect the history of a kingdom.   We shall subsequently find it recurring when we come
to the book of Yéremyá.

3.   *Concerning Tyre.*
Ch. xxiii.

Vv. 1-14 form a complete piece concerning Tyre ; it is a piece of three strophes complete in itself, and so far as its subject-matter is concerned may belong to the time of Yesaya. We know, in a somewhat more detailed form, from Josephus (*Antiq.* ix. 14), that Salmanassar conquered the whole of continental Phœnicia and laid siege to the island Tyre for a long period, although without ultimate success ; and the Assyrians, are expressly named, ver. 13, as the dangerous enemy.   Just at the commencement, when Assyria advanced with a great force against Phœnicia, a prophet may have thus spoken : and that the island Tyre was in the end not conquered, detracts nothing from the true prophetic import and value of the utterance.   For that which really calls forth the righteous threats of the prophet against Tyre, is its greed of gain, its arrogance, and its oppression of foreign lands, the three fundamental vices of this mercantile state, which was then at the climax of its prosperity ; and the prophetic utterance falls into three strophes of medium length having reference to these three sins, vv. 1-5 ; 6-9 ; 10-14. The prophet might indeed lament over the downfall of so much power and glory ; and, as a fact, the whole piece bears more especially the character of a prophetic elegy upon the certain fall of the Phœnician rule, each strophe beginning, or, as is more suitable for the last two, closing with a summons to lamentation.   To this extent the piece is a cry of lamentation over Tyre, in relation (1) to the destruction of trade, (2) to the destruction of the world-wide dominions of these luxurious people, (3) to the destruction of her oppression of even foreign countries.   But precisely as a prophet, he could not fail to see clearly the eternal necessity of the downfall of a power which reposed upon such foundations, and must overcome his first human astonishment at this fall the moment he reflected upon the divine causes which were

here at work.   They are ever valid and know no change, and
in conformity with these Tyre was necessitated sooner or later
to lose its power; or if it did not wholly lose it so soon as the
prophet then anticipated, and if it recovered from the first
blow for a few centuries, there was nevertheless (as subsequent
history has shown) no firm condition of things which could
defy all attacks.

The poetical art of the piece is in a very high degree
finished. Since the whole takes the form of a cry of woe, the
first strophe, and the second also almost immediately, begins
with it; but as the first note of this woe, beginning with
the proud Tarshîsh ships, forms the key-note of the whole,
it occurs again at the end of the first, second, and the third
strophes.   It is true, it is now not found after ver. 9, but for
the additional reason that each of the three strophes ought
clearly to have five verses, it must have dropped out. Further,
Tarshîsh occurs at the head of each strophe appropriately.

Whether, however, this prophet of the Assyrian period
was Yesaya, is very doubtful.   It is true, there are many
Yesayanic words and thoughts scattered through the piece,
e.g., ver. 4 רוֹמֵם and גֵּדֵל, as i. 2; עֲלִיזָה vv. 7, 12, as v.
14; xxii. 2; xxxii. 13; הָקֵל ver. 9, as viii. 23; ידו נטה ver.
11, as v. 25; ver. 13 especially has a strongly Yesayanic ring,
comp. xxxii. 14; xvii. 1.   On the other hand, other expressions we should not expect, as אִי *coast*, vv. 2, 6, here denotes
the island of Tyre as opposed to the whole of Sidonia, *i.e.*,
Phœnicia, vv. 2, 4, while in Yesaya's usage, xx. 5, it
signifies simply the whole Phœnician coast. Besides, the
elevation, magnificence, and energetic brevity of Yesaya are
wholly wanting.   It looks, therefore, as if a younger contemporary and disciple of Yesaya were the author, just as in ch.
xxxiii. a similar supposition has to be made; and inasmuch as
these disciples, acc. viii. 16, took a considerable part in commit-
ting to writing and preserving in a literary form the orations
of Yesaya, it is not difficult to understand how some oracles of

the disciples should find their way into the same book.—It might also be conjectured that the piece was first written on Nabukodrossor's* siege; yet no sufficient reason can be produced to justify such a conjecture, not even this, that the word *Kanaanites,* ver. 8, in the meaning of *merchants,* appears to be according to a somewhat later usage, Prov. xxxi. 24; Job xl. 30; and against the conjecture is, that in the entire book of Yesaya as we have it there is no piece from the Chaldæan period.

On the other hand, the last verses, vv. 15-18, can belong neither to the time of Salmanassar nor of Nabukodrossor, the latter of whom besieged the island Tyre a second time and for a longer period. These verses prophesy that Tyre will be forgotten for 70 years, remain, therefore, almost completely powerless and ruined, but after that time will rise again to some degree of power; yet its wealth, gained by universal trade, will in the end be devoted to the requirements of the true religion. This thought has no real connexion with the previous prophecy of the destruction of the island fortress; for then the idea of such a resuscitation of the ruined Tyre is not in the most distant manner on the horizon of the prophet's vision, and while its three strophes form a complete and distinct whole, this postscript has not been in any way prepared for or rendered possible, neither by the subject-matter, nor by the figures and images of the foregoing prophecy. On the contrary, it cannot have been an earlier prophet than one living at the commencement of the Persian period who could write thus. At the close of the Chaldæan rule, which lasted in round numbers 70 years, all the countries which had up to that time been oppressed revived, and Tyre attained a tolerable degree of prosperity once more. The number 70 was at that time in prevailing use in such connexions, Zech. i. 12, and at that period when the new Jerusalem was very poor and in necessi-

---

* On the orthography of the name, see *Hist. of Israel,* iv. 256 (III. 782 note).—*Tr.*

tous circumstances, and the Messianic hopes were nevertheless
excited in a high degree, this anticipation and this wish are
quite intelligible, that the sanctuary at Jerusalem would finally
reap the benefit of Tyre's actual wealth, when Tyre, together
with all other heathen nations, should turn to the true God.
Indeed, it appeared at length the necessary supplement to the
ancient oracle, that Tyre should again rise from its ruins and
resort to its former mercantile arts, from which it appeared
that it could not desist, but only for the divine end, that in
this way also the final prosperity of the divine kingdom might
be promoted. The language also points to this period. We
have here, therefore, a postscript or appendix, of a similar kind
and of the same age as ch. xii. (see *infra* p. 239) ; and both
additions are attached to the older pieces, as well as it could be
managed; nor is there any doubt but that they are both from
the same hand, see vol. I. p. 95.

High-oracle concerning Tyre.

1.

XXIII.

1   *Wail ye Tarshish-ships !* | for "it is laid waste
so that there is no house, no entry!" is from the
land of the Kittim announced to them. ‖ — Be
dumb ye inhabitants of the coast, | which Sidonia's
merchant the sea-farer replenished, ‖ and whose
gain was the Nile's seed, the river's harvest upon
many waters, | so that she became a mart of the
nations. ‖ — Be ashamed Sidonia, for the Sea, the
Sea's stronghold spake thus : " I have not travailed
nor brought forth, not reared youths nor brought-
5   up virgins!" ‖ — When the report cometh to
Egypt, they will tremble there, | when the report of
Tyrus. ‖

2.

Migrate to Tarshîsh, | wail inhabitants of the coast! || — " Is this your exultant [city], whose origin is from the days of the past, | whose feet carry her far away to sojourn? || Who hath counselled this concerning Tyre the bestower of crowns, | whose merchants [are] princes, whose traders the honoured of the earth?" || Yahvé of Hosts hath counselled it, to profane the pride of all splendour, to humble all the honoured of the earth! || [*Wail ye Tarshish-ships, that your fortress is destroyed!*]

3.

10   Spread over thy land like the Nile, | thou daughter Tarshîsh! there is no more a bridle. || His hand he stretched over the Sea, made kingdoms quake, | Yahvé commanded concerning Kanáan to destroy its strongholds; || and said: " thou shalt not go on longer to exult, thou violated virgin daughter Ssidon! | to the Kittim arise migrate! neither there will it be peaceful for thee." || — " Behold the land of the Kanáanites—this people is no more, Asshur hath made it a desert; | they raised their watch-towers, built their palaces: he hath laid it in ruins!" || — *Wail ye Tarshîsh-ships,* | *that your stronghold is destroyed!* ||

15   But on that day—then will Tyre be forgotten seventy years like the years of one king; | after seventy years it will fare with Tyre as in the song concerning the harlot: ||
take the harp, go round the city,—thou forgotten harlot!
play well, sing much—that thou mayest be remembered.
For after seventy years Yahvé will visit Tyre, so that she cometh again to

her harlot-hire; | and she playeth the harlot then with all kingdoms on the face of the earth. || — Yet her gains and harlot-hire will be consecrated to Yahvé, not laid-up nor hoarded: | but to those who dwell before Yahvé her gains will come, to eat to fulness and for stately attire. ||

1. Wail, become dumb with terror, blush and tremble, must all who are immediately or distantly connected with the prosperity of this over-rich Tyre. The prophet takes a wide glance that he may include everything: (1) the great Tartessus-ships must wail (ii. 16), to which on their homeward voyage from Spain, when they have only reached the Kittim-land, *i.e.*, Kypros, the powerful Phœnician colony, the evil tidings are announced, that everything is destroyed to the very foundation, without leaving a house, an entrance where they might find protection, ver. 1.—(2) The inhabitants of the strong Tyrian island must be filled with alarm, which being filled with seafaring merchants, and especially busied with the rich trade in Egyptian corn (comp. ver. 5), was a market for all nations, vv. 2, 3. — (3) All Sidonia (*i.e.*, the entire Sidonian-Phœnician federated state) must blush, inasmuch as its strongest protection, the island Tyre, is laid waste, inasmuch as the sea itself, therefore, or rather the sea's fortress (ver. 14), as it were, cries out in lamentation, that she has in vain brought up children, is now desolate, ruined, ver. 4. That the name *Ssidôn* is here used in the general sense, follows also from ver 12.—(4) Egypt especially will tremble when it hears the tidings about Tyre, ver. 5; with which sentence, uttered in a more relaxed manner, the first strophe fittingly closes. That the Tyrians very early traded beyond the Egyptian coast is *per se* very probable, and may be gathered from Herod. ii. 112, and Gen. x. 6-20.

2. In the first strophe the human lamentation was so predominant that scarcely a hint as to the causes of it could force its way: it is only the greed of gain which is in a distant way touched upon. But now as the prophet already sees in his spirit the flight of the Tyrians to the distant colonies, luxury and arrogancy are more distinctly brought forward as a second

sin. The very ancient and proud city, which distributed the crowns of distant cities and countries, and whose traders are equal to princes and kings (Jer. xxv. 22), she must now shamefully flee; the prophet himself must counsel her to do so, ver. 6 ; and if any one in astonishment enquires after the cause of this dishonour and the author of this punishment, vv. 7, 8, the prophet is aware that ultimately it is no other than Yahvé who brings it upon her, and not without cause; her unbounded pride, like all earthly pride, must be humbled ! ver. 9.

3. And, further, her oppression of foreign countries, and colonies, *e.g.*, Tartessus, is next censured. Tartessus, freely and without hindrance overflow thy land, as the Nile overflows Egypt without hindrance, Amos viii. 8 ; ix. 5 ; there is no more a bridle in the hand of Tyre to restrain thee, ver. 10 ! Stretching his hand even over the sea, Yahvé hath shaken wide kingdoms by the command to destroy the Phœnician strongholds ! the virgin of Phœnicia, Tyre, up to the present unconquered, but now violated, conquered, shall not continue to exult as formerly (ver. 6), but, as was said ver. 5 sq., shall flee, at first to Kypros, but only to find no rest there ! vv. 11, 12. This brief image of the violated virgin, ver. 12, is without doubt the precursor of Nah. iii. 5-7, "Isa." xlvii. 1-5. The reason of the sudden daring of the Kittim and the flight of the Tarshîsh ships before them, is given, ver. 13, in the language of the Kittim themselves (just as our prophet, ver. 1, and vv. 7, 8, has introduced other persons of this kind as speaking) : land and people of the Phœnicians, they pronounce, is already as good as annihilated by the Assyrians, with all the fair watchtowers (garden-towers, xxxii. 14) and palaces (xxxii. 14) which they erected. Therefore, wail, as was said, ver. 1, ye ships, ver. 14. In this way the discourse treating the entire matter, and hastening to a close at ver. 13, is fully explained.

When, ver. 15, the seventy years are explained by the days of *one* king, *i.e.*, about as long as one king may live and rule, it may be that the author had the instance of Nabukodrossor,

as that nearest at hand, before his eyes, this king having as a
fact had a very long life and reign, while he became early the
standing representative of the Chaldean rule.—The conception
which pervades this appendix, namely, that of a great heathen
mercantile city as a harlot, is as foreign to the previous
prophecy as to the entire age of Yesaya, it being found first, Nah.
iii. 4. But it supplies here an excellent application of the chief
thought. As an old harlot cannot well cease from her trade, and
though chastised for a time still returns again to her profitable
traffic as soon as she regains her freedom : so Tyre, after she
has been long forgotten, as soon as Yahvé visits her with his
liberating grace, will endeavour to return to her beloved and
seductive trade and traffic with all nations, as is said in that
well-known satirical song concerning the old harlot, vv. 15-17.
Yet the wealth which is thus won will not be hoarded up again
for such a long time and in such quantities as was the case in
the ancient Tyre, but will very soon find its way, by the conversion of Tyre, to the poor of the holy city, who are now
scarcely able to eat till they have had enough, or to clothe
themselves decently (comp. "Isa." xlix. 22, 23; lx. 9-12;
Haggai and Zech. vi. 10, 11.)

On vv. 2, 3. Although the direct address to the *coast*, ver.
2, passes with greater calmness into the third person in the
continuation of it, ver. 3, the whole from סֹחֵר to the end is a
relative sentence to אִי.

On ver. 10. מֵזַח from the Arab, *zaḥama* and *ḥazama* to
make close, firm, whether it be a girdle or a bridle as here,
comp. Arab. *ḥaṭama* and *khaṭamaʿ*; *ḥizâm* used of a *bridle* in
Lebîd's Moʿall, ver. 58.

On ver. 13. When it is considered how accurately the two
threes of the members of this verse correspond, how the third
answers to the sixth (צִיִּים = צִיָּה waste, acc. § 179 *b*), the

fourth to the fifth (הקים=עֲרֵר), and how accordingly the first and second members must correspond, there can be no doubt that כשדים is an early copyist's error for פְּנָעֲנִים, as was more at length remarked, *Gött. Gel. Anz.* 1837, p. 1799. לֹא היה as xv. 6; Job iii. 16; Ez. xxi. 32.

On מְבַסֶּה ver. 18, comp. § 160 *e.* In general such forms are revived in later writers, and this word belongs manifestly less to the age of Yesaya than to that of the prophet who will come under our notice at " Isa." xiv. 11.

V.—YESAYA'S FIFTH BOOK.

Ch. xxviii.-xxxii.

This long oration is complete in itself and finished; a no less important than extensive piece, in which the prophetic views and judgments with regard to an important question of that age are exhaustively handled from every possible point of view.   The time in which this oration falls is at once indicated by the commencement, xxviii. 1-6.   Samaria had not yet been taken, but was evidently very imminently threatened, and was clearly approaching its destruction.   Nor is there anything in the other part of the long piece which contradicts this date. The Assyrians made themselves felt very oppressively at Jerusalem, xxx. 27-33; xxxi. 8, 9, inasmuch as tribute had to be paid to them: but at that time Yuda was not at war with them, and they are not in this piece named plunderers and robbers in such violent language as is used in later orations; neither is it intimated that they had already greatly exceeded their divine commission to chastise Yuda, as is the case, x. 5 sq.; xvii. 14; xxxiii. 1-24: on the contrary, the threat is made, that they will overflow the land and closely besiege Jerusalem, xxix. 1-8; xxx. 16, 17; comp. Mic. iv. 10 sq., Mikha's book in general belonging to almost the same time. ·

It was at this time that many magnates of the land, alarmed by the constantly growing power of the Assyrians, and probably also with a view to getting rid of their obligations to pay them tribute, very seriously meditated an alliance with Egypt against Assyria, Egypt for its part also being anxious for such alliances.   That Yesaya with his powerful voice was against this and all similar alliances was known to these magnates; they therefore altogether avoided asking him and the other true prophets for their advice on the matter, xxix. 15; xxx. 1; xxxi. 1, as, in fact, they endeavoured on other occasions to put on one side every true prophet who publicly proclaimed the truth,

xxix. 21 ; xxx. 9-11 ; on the other hand, they found less conscientious prophets and priests of Yahvé who on all matters
spoke and acted as they desired, and with whose help they
hoped to have spread a sacred halo around their project and to
have escaped all danger for the future, xxviii. 14, 15 ; xxix.
13, 14, and, in fact, the affair seems to have already made good
progress ; at all events, representatives were already on their
way to Egypt, xxx. 6 ; and imagining that they were safe, they
with their accomplices, the false teachers, gave themselves up
the more fully to their revels and other follies, xxviii. 7 sq.

But while Yesaya could not justify the degenerate government of the Assyrians, the truth was equally clear to his mind,
that an Egyptian alliance was both useless and pernicious,
because it was really only from the want of pure spiritual
strength and genuine confidence that such external aids were
sought after at a moment of disgraceful embarrassment. In
this time of growing confusion too, his faith, that in Yahvé
alone is prosperity and deliverance, remained immovable as a
rock. And as he found eternal stability and secure help
neither in Assyria nor in Egypt, nor anywhere else but in
Yahvé ; and as, further, he saw in the sanctuary at Ssion the
image of this imperishable religion, and had himself already
experienced in his earlier life how securely this sanctuary could
withstand threatening dangers, ch. vii.—ix. 6 : so now in the
darknesses of this time the new light was kindled before his
prophetic eye, namely, that Ssion would it is true be severely
besieged by the Assyrians, as, for instance, Samaria then was,
and as a punishment for so many sins and perverse aims, *e.g.,*
this very confidence in Egypt; but that when it was humbled to
the uttermost it would evince an imperishable strength, and
be gloriously redeemed by Yahvé as the commencement of the
new reformed age. In the light of this thought all the darknesses of the time disappeared : neither will Egypt deliver nor
Assyria destroy Ssion ; on the contrary, there is coming a
severe time of trial and of destruction of thoughtlessness, but

12 *

the blessed age will come too, a commencement of reformation may appear shortly. Thus the prophet was able to contend against the false hope, seriously to threaten the false teachers and their followers, and also, which was at that time very necessary in order to sustain the confidence of the wavering, to promise the best comfort. The earlier anticipations as to the form the future may assume give way somewhat to this firmer and still more glorious conception, and it is not until the end of the discourse, xxxii. 9 sq., that they are repeated in a less altered form.

With these wholly heterodox and hitherto unheard-of forebodings and views, Yesaya, whom the people desired to ignore, boldly appeared in the midst of the luxuriating magnates and false teachers, annihilated with the marvellous power of his oratory both the ridicule with which they received him and their entire view of life and of the future, and placed before them his own view, while, on the one hand, he censured, and on the other, comforted and exhorted them. We may also safely suppose that it was greatly due to his exertions that the alliance was not actually formed, although the desire for it continued to be felt by many in Jerusalem, ch. xx., and it appears subsequently to have been revived to that extent that it became known also to the Assyrians, xxxvi. 6.

When we examine the structure and artistic form of the book which Yesaya published upon the basis of that appearance in the assembly, it is clear, and confirmed by the prophet's own words (xxx. 8 sq.), that he cannot have written it until some time after that event. But it is equally certain that it followed the appearance as soon as possible. The book is without narrative in any form : for it bears the marks of having been written while everything was quite fresh in the memory of all, and for the purpose of supplying what the prophet had been unable to bring forward in that severe public collision with his opponents. But although it originated in the midst of a new crisis in the history of the kingdom and of the influential labours of the prophet, in order that if possible that object, which he probably could not have fully accomplished by a publicly spoken word, might be attained more effectively by a written book, it still presents the position of affairs with no less stormy emphasis than calm and instructive copiousness, and enables us most clearly to see how the literary and the oral labours of the prophet are related to each other. There is no other book of the prophet which handles a particular question with such completeness and from all points of view at the very moment when it was agitating the minds of the people as is the case with this book; in this respect it is a model that cannot be surpassed, and shows us the prophet at work in the fulness of his strength. How on that day he took by surprise the intoxicated spirits, annihilated their aims and hopes, and reestablished truths which accord with the Divine will,—of this he gives the most vivid picture in two sections, of the same structure and extent, and each consisting of four strophes, ch. xxviii. and ch. xxix. 1—xxx. 7, in order that in a third section of five strophes, xxx. 8—xxxii. 8, he may add whatever else is needful to be said at this time; and a final single strophe, xxxii. 9-20, proceeding from the true Divine oracle concerning the luxurious women, supplies the last word.

The most noteworthy feature of this great oration, with the high tension of its tone and execution, is the wise distinction everywhere made between the various classes of the opponents against whom the oration is directed. The preference for Egypt and the hope that was based on this country was in the air in the kingdom of Yuda, and this preference was the more generally fascinating and deceptive inasmuch as the disadvantages of Ahaz's Assyrian proclivities were then being painfully felt. The mass of the people also, and even the excellent king Hizqia, had been plainly enough brought over to this side, partly of their own accord and partly by that powerful faction which was openly opposed to our prophet: and Yesaya with a few more intimate friends stood probably quite alone on the other side.   His public opposition was, therefore, all the more difficult.   But in this most difficult situation he chose the right word in a masterly manner. . He knew well that the body of the people erred in this as in most instances rather from weakness and fear of the world than intentionally, and that only individual, defiantly rash magnates had so miserably gone astray in their aims and calculations.   Accordingly, he varies with great prudence and firm discrimination the tone and manner of his discourse, according as he wishes to speak simply against and concerning the leaders of the affairs of the nation, or to the people themselves and concerning themselves.   As in the first case the words of God cannot come from his mouth with a sufficiently crushing force, in the second, they are as full of gentle but serious admonition and overflowing with hope and consolation ; whilst he never forgets the idea of the whole nation, which is elevated beyond all the individual members of the community of the true God.   Not until the true Oracle of God has thus cast its light upon all sides, does it find repose.   It is impossible to understand this long oration, which is the highest model of its kind, with regard to its agitation or even its long sections, unless all these points are carefully considered.

This book was manifestly circulated immediately in a separate form during that time of depression, and, as far as we can see, was always preserved in a separate form, without even a heading.   Nor was a heading needed in the case of a book the origin of which from Yesaya any reader in those days could discern plainly enough in every word.—Whether the short piece ch. xx., was written at the same time in conjunction with our book, will be considered below.

1. The drunkenness and perversity of the leaders of the nation.   Ch. xxviii.

That he may combat the drunken, irrational prophets and

their followers, Yesaya does not at once commence with them and their folly: he begins with a matter of apparently more distant interest, although it was of importance at that time and would be gladly listened to. With captivating and eloquent words he touches upon the mad frivolity of the magnates of Samaria, who were throwing themselves into all kinds of giddy pleasures although their country was just advancing headlong to manifest destruction, vv. 1-6. The people of Jerusalem are certain to listen willingly to a charge against Samaria: but they have hardly begun to attend to Yesaya's discourse, when he suddenly turns the severe censure against themselves, especially against the false prophets and priests and against other leaders of the people who are equally irrational, and who further (which is the worst crime of all!) ridicule the voice of truth — who, however, as the just punishment for this sin against the Holy Spirit, will soon themselves be terribly mocked and put to confusion by Him whom they now deride, by Yahvé, vv. 7-13. Having thus suddenly reached the heart of the matter, with a rapid climax surprising and overwhelming with the fire of prophetic zeal in a moment all enemies, he then prepares calmly to combat his opponents, although his opposition soon resumes its former fire: he confronts their false pretences and undertakings with the truth with regard to their future, vv. 14-21. The discourse, which has been of this stormy character through the second and even the third strophes, descends finally to gentler language, for the purpose of teaching the already vanquished opponents who are the friends of that immoderation which will not receive instruction from the prophet, that there must be moderation in all things, the form of the language being that of the calm, sententious proverb, vv. 22-29. Therefore four strophes of nearly equal length, the introductory one only being somewhat shorter and seeming at the end to be abruptly broken off.

XXVIII.   1.

1   O proud crown of the drunkards of Ephráim,
and faded flowers of his glorious adornment, | which
is upon the head of the fat valley, of those stunned
with wine ! ‖ behold the Lord hath a mighty and
powerful one, | as a tempest of hail and destroying
storm, as a tempest of mightily overflowing waters :
he casteth them to the earth by force ! ‖ With the
feet it will be trodden down | the proud crown of
the drunkards of Ephráim, ‖ and the fading flower
of his glorious adornment which is upon the head
of the fat hill | becometh as an early fig before the
summer, which one seeth, scarcely is it in his hand,
5   swalloweth. ‖ —On that day will Yahvé of Hosts
be for an adorning crown and for a glorious wreath |
to the remnant of his people, ‖ both for a spirit of
judgment to those who sit on the judgment-seat,
and for might to those who drive back war to the
gate.‖

2.

But these also—in wine they reel and in mead
they stagger, | the priest and the prophet reeled
in mead are overcome of wine, staggered from
mead reeled in the oracle tottered in the decision ! ‖
yea all tables are full of filthy vomit | so that
there is no more room . . . . ! ‖—" Whom
teacheth he wisdom, and to whom declareth he
revelation ? them that are weaned from the milk,
10   taken from the breast ? ‖ that rule on rule rule
on rule, rod on rod rod on rod, | now here now

there!" ‖ . . . . Yea with stammering words
and with another tongue | will he speak to this
people : ‖ he who said unto them "this is the
place of rest: give rest to the weary ! and this is
the refreshment!" | but they would not hear: ‖
therefore Yahvé's word will be to them rule on
rule rule on rule, rod on rod rod on rod, now
here now there, | in order that they may go and
stumble backwards and break their limbs, and
ensnare and take themselves! ‖

3.

Therefore hear Yahvé's word, ye men of
scorning, | rulers of this people which is in Jeru-
15 salem : ‖ because ye think: "we formed a covenant
with death, and with hell we made an oracle; | the
overflowing scourge when it cometh up will not
reach us, because we made a lie our refuge and in
deceit hide ourselves:" ‖ therefore saith the Lord
Yahvé thus: behold I have founded in Ssion a
stone, | a tried precious corner-stone of firmest
foundation: whoever believeth will not flee ! ‖ and
I make judgment as a rule and righteousness as a
balance, | so that the hail teareth away the refuge
of a lie, the covert of deceit the waters overflow, ‖
and your covenant with death will be blotted out,
and your oracle with hell standeth not : | the
overflowing scourge when it cometh up, then ye
will serve it for crushing;‖ as often as it cometh up
it will seize you, | for every morning it will come up,
by day and by night, | so that it is pure terror to

20   receive revelation. ‖ — For " too short is the bed
to stretch oneself, | and the covering too narrow
when one will compose oneself !" ‖ because as on
the mount Perassim Yahvé will arise, as in the
valley at Gibeon tremble, | to execute his work—
his strange work, and to perform his occupation—
his unheard-of occupation ! ‖

4.

So therefore make no scorners, lest your bands
become fast ! | for an end and decision have I
heard from the Lord Yahvé of Hosts concerning
the whole earth. ‖ Observe and hear my voice, |
attend and hear my words : ‖

Is then the ploughman always ploughing that he
may sow, | looseneth and harroweth his ground? ‖
25   when he hath levelled his surface, doth he not then
scatter dill or sow cummin, | and setteth wheat
upon the best land and barley upon the rough and
spelt upon its borders ? ‖ Thus instructeth him to
judgment, his God teacheth him. ‖

Surely with a sledge dill is not threshed, neither
is a cartwheel drawn over cummin, | but with the
staff dill is beaten and cummin with the stick. ‖
Corn is threshed : | yet not for ever doth one
thresh it and drive on his cart's axle and his
horses, he doth not thresh it away. ‖ — This also
is uttered by Yahvé of Hosts; | wonderful counsel
hath he, great wisdom.

1. Samaria, the glorious ornament, or the proud royal residence, the honour and crown of Ephráim, is situated upon a

mountain, which in the physical sense also rises like a pretty wreath over a fat, fruitful valley, Amos iv. 1; Mic. i. 6; 1 Kings xvi. 24; yet inasmuch as drunken people sit at table with wreaths on their heads, and the magnates of Ephraim are always as it were drunk (comp. ix. 8), there is from the commencement mixed with this figure the related and still more expressive one of the proud crown upon the head of the Ephráimite as he is stunned* with wine, and both figures are carried on together from the commencement to the close, vv. 3, 4, accurately and beautifully, only in such a way that the figure of drunkenness, which is here the more important, takes the precedence. The wreath upon the head of the drunkard swings to and fro with its wearer, and may easily be cast into the dust; the flowers of the splendid wreath upon the head of the fat valley are already faded, ready to fall off: in both forms of it the wreath may, therefore, be easily torn off, and Yahvé has actually in readiness a mighty one (the Assyrian), who, approaching like a destructive hailstorm, or like a tempest of overwhelming rain-deluge hurled upon the earth by Yahvé, with a mighty hand tears off and tears down both wreaths at the same time by the conquest of Samaria, and who especially swallows down the attractive royal city like an early-fig which one has been fortunate enough to meet with (Hos. ix. 10; Mic. vii. 1 sq.; Mark xi. 13, 14). But the day when that will take place is (as is added, vv. 5, 6, in order to at once say all that is necessary here) nevertheless not a day of pure calamity: it is intended to be, according to the divine mind and aim, at the same time the commencement of that better age when Yahvé alone will be to the regenerated of his nation for a genuine ornament and for a royal adornment, to him who sits upon the seat of judgment for a spirit (not of wrong, as is at present the case in Samaria, but) of right, and to the noble warriors, who repulse the attacks of the enemy even into his

---

* Compare οἰνοπλήξ and *mero saucius.*—*Tr.*

own city and his own gate, for a true strength, when all, therefore, however various their callings and occupations, will be
impelled towards the same good end by the same Yahvé.

2. But the magnates here in Jerusalem also are as drunken
and giddy as any of those in Samaria, especially is this the case
with those who ought to be the most sober and temperate,
priests and prophets tope and tumble in the midst of their
prophesying, their judicial decisions; one has only to enter
their assemblies, and, behold, what revelries and abomina-
tions beyond all limits ! ver. 8, comp. v. 8.—But with the last
words, ver. 8, one hears (with such graphic life does Yesaya
here reproduce what then actually occurred), the verse and the
entire oration suddenly interrupted : entirely different voices
with equal abruptness are heard, vv. 9, 10.   Scarcely a genuine
prophet can approach them to explain the truth but they scoff
at him and the divine word in the most shameful manner,
asking him whether they are then such children (and wholly
uninstructed people) that he should propose to teach them
oracles, when they are grown and unusually wise men and
highly enlightened prophets, ridiculing by mimicry his strong
and surprising oration with its numerous repetitions of certain
offensive words, ver. 7, while as drunken people they are only
able to speak as stammerers in half-words, and thus giving him
to understand what a miserable, insignificant schoolmaster, who
stammers owing to his undue zeal, he is, that he is perpetually
and everywhere finding nothing but occasions for censure and
correction, is always endeavouring to smother them and deafen
them with his *scale of justice* and his *measuring line* (*i.e.* with
everlasting admonitions), never leaving them in peace, having
somewhat to censure sometimes here sometimes there !   (We
must conceive the abrupt, intentionally short, reiterated, and
almost childish words, ver. 10, as spoken in mimicry, with a
mocking motion of the head, and in a childish, stammering,
taunting tone, comp. lvii. 4).   With such taunting mimicry
they desire to confound and trouble the true prophet, and to

reject the word of truth and therewith their correcting God ; but the very opposite of this their godless intention must take place ! Did they really think that they were able to ridicule the prophet not simply as a man but the God who speaks from within him, inasmuch as they looked upon the former as an unduly zealous, stammering, dogmatic person ? But because with such derision they only wish to escape from him from whom they can never escape, least of all now when they are so thoughtlessly rejecting his plain truth, they will soon be compelled to hear in an entirely different manner the language which they wish not to hear : with stammering, confounding words, and in a new language which they have never heard before, Yahvé, whose mild clear words, which never demand too much, and whose admonitions to spare the poor they would not obey, will himself address them, returning them their mimic derision, that is, in the language of the thunder and of the terrible punishment which can no longer be put off, he will visit them, so that they who wished to confound him will themselves be cast down in their own confusion, and meet their destruction ! comp. viii. 15, and as a further elucidation the words that immediately follow, vv. 18-22.

3. With such presence of mind and such overwhelming energy is Yesaya able with the most telling precision to turn against themselves the thoughts and words with which they intended to deride him (or rather, when we consider the real fact, the God within him). But after he has thus uttered at the right moment the strongest thing that he could say, he is equally able to speak with calmness : and it is marvellous to observe with what a degree of self-possession he now directs his words to them in the next strophe : therefore hear ye further, and more calmly what Yahvé now saith, ye mockers and magnates of the land who are easily overcome by him whom ye desire to deride ! I will lay bare before your eyes your inmost thoughts which ye desire to conceal, and I will declare what Yahvé saith with regard to them. Ye imagine

that ye have secured yourselves by lying and deceit (*e. g.*, by
an alliance with Egypt (xxix. 15 sq.) which is kept hidden from
Yahvé and the light, concluded in secret, and still kept from
the public) against any future national calamity, against the
advancing scourge of the divine chastisements which will over-
whelm the land (viii. 7, 8; Job ix. 23); nay, more, ye imagine
that, in view of the approaching times of mortal danger, which
are feared even by you, ye have concluded a covenant with
death and hell that they are not to lay hold upon you, confiding
in certain black arts and oracular formulas from which ye look
for this magic power to conjure danger and death in your
favour, ver. 15 (comp. viii. 19 although the prophets here
intended, who imagined that they could conjure death by their
oracles and sacrifices, might be false prophets of Yahvé himself): but Yahvé has long ago established another defence,
another sure stone of refuge, namely, the Sanctuary in Ssion,
the long tested, precious foundation-stone of surest foundation,
and faith in the true God who is worshipped therein; so that
it may also be briefly said, *whoever* holdeth fast (to this
Eternal, *believeth*, has faith), he *will not flee* when threatened
by calamity, but in the midst of danger find a firm position and
an indestructible fortress, ver. 16, comp. xxix. 1-8; viii. 14;
xiv. 32; with regard, however, to the precise form the future
will assume, what the false prophets and their followers
imagine they have gained will be of no avail, but God will
take justice and righteousness alone as the rule and scale of all
human actions, and the irresistible punishment mentioned
before in connexion with Samaria, ver. 2, will carry away your
refuge, wipe out your prophetically hallowed covenant with
death, so that ye will rather serve for trampling upon to the
scourge ye fear (the Assyrian, *e. g.*), vv. 17, 18. Indeed, as
often as the divine chastisement in the time of the great
decision cometh up (and it will come up in incessant blows), it
will seize and smite you (Ps. xlix. 16), so that then it will no
more occur to you to deride the oracle which will come with

every blow (for the divine truth will then be the more perceptible and urgent with every successive blow, Rev. xiv. 6) ;
for, as is said in the proverb of the bed and the coverlet, people
will then feel themselves too confined and too cold, finding
rest nowhere (ver. 12), because, in one word, the rising of
Yahvé will be as terrible as at any time in the ancient days
when he arose to punish the Kanáanites—for the purpose of
completing a work such as men have never before seen or
experienced ! xxix. 14.—The great ancient days at Perassim
and Gibeon are not probably those of 2 Sam. v. 20, 25, but
rather such as are mentioned Josh. x. 20 sq., because the prophets of this period did not yet borrow such examples from
the history of Davîd. The description, ver. 19, is further, on
too great a scale to allow the supposition that the Assyrians
are alone intended.

4. And yet once more, and this time if possible with greater
calmness, Yesaya with all earnestness admonishes them not to
continue their derision, lest the bands of evil in which they
were already snared become still faster and quite indissoluble ;
indeed, he has clearly heard from Yahvé, that nothing less
than destruction and decision, therefore the destruction of all
sinners in pursuance of a judicial and unalterable divine
decision, awaits the whole earth from Yahvé (comp. x. 22, 23) ;
there can then be no jesting and mockery ! May they who
formerly despised his teaching listen now to it ! ver. 23 ; he is
about quite calmly to place before them by way of conclusion
a few proverbs taken from simple country life, leaving it to the
superior wisdom of the wise magnates of the capital to discover
their application to themselves. If one attends only to the
common labours of the husbandman in their two main aspects,
sowing and reaping, (hence the two short strophes, vv. 24-26 ;
27-29), one soon observes that he does nothing without regard
to its proper manner and measure : he does not keep on
ploughing and harrowing incessantly that he may sow on some
indefinite future day, he sows also at the proper time, and sows

everything in the right place, on the land that is in each case
suitable, *e.g.*, wheat on the best land, barley on the poorer and
rougher land, spelt somewhere near this, on a piece between
the barley and the wheat land; he proceeds with his harvest
with equal consideration, not threshing, *e.g.*, the small and
finer seeds, dill, cummin, in the same rough manner as he does
the larger, the proper corn, but the former he beats out more
carefully with a staff (xxvii. 12), while he draws over the latter
only in the rougher manner the threshing sledge with wheels
and horses; however, he does not drag this over them for
ever, because he would then only grind to pieces and lose
everything. All this is done by the simple husbandman,
instructed by God to observe order and propriety! But ye
magnates and philosophers, who imagine yourselves to be far
more than a husbandman, will ye observe no moderation and
propriety? will ye go on in your wild, irrational life?
Assuredly it is the one thing needful and the only proper
course in all hidden and difficult matters to attend to God and
to his action, which is manifested in history, and to follow in
all things his guidance. But Yesaya leaves them to make this
application to themselves, that he may not again fall into the
language of severity; and, ver. 29, closes quite calmly with the
observation, that this instruction also comes from him who has
infinite wisdom and imparts it to the man who looks to him.

How the construction of the construct cases, ver. 1 *b* and
ver. 4, which is in many ways involved, is to be explained,
appears from § 287 *b* and § 289 *a*. The difference between
צִיץ ver. 1, and צִיצַת ver. 4, is with respect to the general
sense of the passage not great, but it should not, acc. § 176 *a*,
be overlooked, and may be indicated in the translation.* In
any case, it is not necessary to alter the reading; but if in
ver. 2 the alteration וְהִנִיח is made the gain in respect of
meaning and connexion is immense, comp. § 346 *b*.

* In the German, *Geblüme* and *Blume.—Tr.*

The words, vv. 6, 7, have the greatest similarity, with respect to the opening of the strophe, their tone, and their entire meaning, to iv. 2 : but the particular allusion to the good *judge*, or rather king, who was then ruling, ver. 6 *a*, and to the army of brave defenders of their country, ver. 6 *b*, as it was then to be wished that they might prove, flows from the new circumstances of the time, and recurs quite similarly below, towards the end of the long oration, xxxii. 1 sq., with Messianic elevation. With reference to the phrase *to drive back the war*, *i.e.*, the enemy, *to the gate*, comp. Ps. cxxvii. 5 ; Nah. iii. 13.

רָאָה ver. 7, and חֹזֶה ver. 15, to which חָזוּת corresponds ver. 18, receive further explanation §. 156 *e*.—In ver. 8 it must not be overlooked that the line and prophet's words themselves are intentionally cut short.

The meaning of the two words, צָו and קַו, which are here placed together manifestly on account of the similarity of their sound, vv. 10, 13, would be determined with more difficulty had not Yesaya himself in the course of his oration, and especially ver. 17, alluded to them and come back to them almost verbally. The meaning of קַו as a *line* appears clearly from ver. 17: and צָו, like Arab. *sûwatun* (or *sûwah*), *suwan* (or *suwâ*) Hamâsa, p. 156, ver. 6, may denote something that is *placed upright*, or what stands up, as we have already met with it in the meaning of a *post*, or pale, Hosea v. 11, comp. iv. 12 (see Vol. I. p. 261) ; for צָוָה *to command* is also properly *to set up, to erect*, and the Arab. *swb* (as radical) is related to it. It could therefore as a *straight piece of wood*, a *rule*, also signify the beam of a scale, like κάνων, but was without doubt an antiquated word which was very little used in Jerusalem, and is therefore itself explained, ver. 17, by the usual word for *scale*. Taken in this sense, the word קַו as a *string* or *measuring line* bore very much the same meaning, both ideas really interchanging, ver. 17 and 2 Kings xxi. 13 ; and in the above translation they are represented by the words *rule* and *rod* [Germ. *richte* and *ruthe*] only that the assonance may appear. If both words thus express

2 13

the idea that the prophet seems to these people to be only like
a schoolmaster who is incessantly dinning them with his rule
and his rod, it is clearly intended that by this rattling
combination of sounds they wish to mimic the language of
Yesaya himself, who had just before, ver. 7, six times repeated
words of a similar sound פְּקַי שָׁעֵי תָּעֵי, becoming, however, in
the mouth of these drunken people only half-intelligible,
stammered sounds, to which allusion is made immediately,
vv. 11 sq., and at the end of the great oration, xxxii. 4, and
again intentionally in the latter place, in order to refer the
hearer at the end once more to the beginning. These facts
determine clearly enough the signification of the two words and
of the whole passage; and if the words of God, vv. 11, 13, are
meant to convey only a reciprocated taunt, there is therein no
allusion whatever to a foreign human language, *e.g.*, that of the
Assyrians, or to the approach of these people, and the passage
referring to them, xxxiii. 19, can with the less reason be produced here to show this, inasmuch as the piece, ch. xxxiii.
does not belong to our book or originate from Yesaya. The
לְעֵגֵי שָׂפָה are also naturally in conformity with ordinary
usage simply *stammering sounds,* not people of a stammering (barbarian) speech, as if it came from a לָעֵג; such an
one is elsewhere called לוֹעֵז; see on xxxiii. 19; and the translation, 1 Cor. xiv. 21, is taken quite loosely from the LXX.*

---

* The author adds the following note on this passage in the second edition of his
work, *Die drei ersten Evangelien und die Apostelgeschichte* (Göttingen, 1872), Vol.
II. p. 66 :—"What I have said in my Commentary on the Prophets on this passage
(Isa. xxviii. 11 sq.) is on the whole correct: yet it is possible that Yesaya referred
ultimately when he spoke of the stammering words and the strange language with
which God was about to speak to the people, to the Assyrians and their incessant,
terrible commands and demands in a strange tongue, and that the piece in which
he explained this more fully has not come down to us. The reason for supposing
that the Assyrians are also intended here as an instrument in Yahvé's hand (as
Yesaya says elsewhere), is that Yesaya must have had something definite in his
mind when he spoke of the means by which Yahvé would as it were himself deride
and punish those who were deriding him in his prophet: this could not be anything
else than the Assyrians. He refers, therefore, here ch. xxviii. 11 sq., in a distant
way to them; but, in accordance with his custom, he then without doubt explained

The *st. constr.*, ver. 16 *b*, extends even further than that in vv. 1, 4, through as many as five words; on מוּסָד מוּסָד see §. 313 *c*. It is probable that ver. 17 שֶׁקֶר acc. ver. 15, has fallen out after סֵתֶר, the meaning requiring its suppletion.— The language of the portion vv. 16-18 is on another account (see Vol. I. p. 21) remarkable, inasmuch as it shows very vividly how inseparably in the minds of the ancients the *Oracle* (and sacrifice) was connected with every important national undertaking, *e.g.*, the conclusion of an alliance, so much so that both ideas here interchange. This, however, was the case in all religions, and is mentioned here in this way only as the feeling of those thoughtless people.

There is no doubt but that the words ver. 20 embody an ancient proverb : but vv. 24-29 Yesaya shows how well he knows how to make use of proverbial and didactic poetry where he deems it in place ; in this respect he prepares for the transition to Christ and the Gospels.

The word שׂוֹרָה, ver. 25, appears to be an agricultural term, derived from שׂר, the first man, prince, (Germ. *fürst.*), נִסְמָן is probably the rougher, coarser, less productive, land, being *part. Nif.* from סמן, acc. §. 51 *c*=סמר prickly, bristly, rough ; at least there is at present no better explanation. It is necessary ver. 28 to read יוּדַשׁ instead of יוּדַק.

---

2. *The Truth with regard to the Future presented as an Enigma and as actual Fact.*

Ch. xxix. 1—xxx. 7.

How totally unlike its commencement the end of the previous piece became ! It seems as if those hearers who at first rose in drunken defiance and derision against the word of the prophet, had now become by the irresistible power and truth of

---

his reference in a special piece, which has now been lost. But that we have then to understand the words לַעֲגֵי שָׂפָה as meaning *stammering speakers* from לָעֵג, is not correct, as ver. 13 shows.

his word growingly calmer and more serious, and as if they
were already listening in silence and sober attention to that
word of God upon which at first they could not heap sufficient
scorn. But scarcely have they been brought thus far, when
the prophet after a brief pause commences again from an
entirely different point of view, although he is at the same
time only completing all that he had said before : he comes
now to present his own prophetic anticipation and therein the
pure divine truth with regard to the future. But at once the
whole of his conceptions with regard to the true future and
its necessary unfolding are gathered up and concentrated in a
single compressed figure and a short description, while the
truth, upon which these conceptions are based, is expressed in
a single new name, which contains everything as it were in a
wonderful germ, and from which therefore everything now
proceeds. This is the name *Ariel*, i.e., *Lion of God*, the lion
that is strong and valorous by God's help. If Ssion (for the
prophet really intends Ssion by this new name) is this Lion, as
Yesaya supposes it to be in his prophetic anticipation, there
lies in the mysterious depths of this higher, divine name the
truth of the city's entire future. It may, on the one hand, be
attacked and greatly distressed by powerful and destructive
enemies (the Assyrians), and as a fact will very soon, within one
or two years (xxix. 1, 17; xxxii. 10) be closely besieged ; but,
on the other hand, the more threatening the danger the more
will it approve itself the invincible Lion of God, the more
triumphantly and quickly will it be rescued by Yahvé (as, for
instance, all Israel was once rescued by Yahvé's succouring
presence in Egypt). Yesaya wishes at the opening of his long
oration to excite in the highest degree the attention of his
hearers with regard to the new view of the true solution of the
problem of the future, and also by the way once more to place
in a clear light the folly of the false prophets, beyond whose
reach this truth lies. He accordingly prefaces his oration with
his prophetic view of the future, clothing it in an enigmatical

form, as a strange narrative of a divine miracle, proposing to the false prophets as it were an enigma, to see if they understood the strange utterance with regard to this marvellous history of Ariel and his divine power and deliverance — of which they have no conception, neither, considering their past habits, can have, and at which they must be overwhelmed with helpless amazement! And not until in the first strophe, xxix. 1-8, the enigmatical oracle has been uttered, and in the second, xxix. 9-14, the stupid amazement of the false prophets which it causes has been properly chastised, does the prophet begin to explain more fully this enigma, as if it were now time to supply the simple interpretation of it with the greater calmness and completeness. But this interpretation consists precisely in the censure of the obstinacy and the false confidence of those who are now without faith in Ssion and Yahvé and are turning secretly to Egypt for help, while they ought to find wisdom, faithfulness and confidence in Yahvé, who alone has the will and the power to promote the weal of Ssion, and who certainly will do it in quite another way than these men imagine. But scarcely has the prophet begun in this way to speak concerning the true authors of the evil proposal, when his heart compels him in the third strophe, vv. 15-24, to turn especially to the mass of the nation, who are quite innocent of the proposal, with words of consolation, so that the severest utterance of censure does not fall upon those whom it primarily concerns before the fourth strophe, xxx. 1-7. Thus the arrangement of this piece, notwithstanding the great dissimilarity of its matter, is like that of the previous one, both with regard to the number of the strophes and its entire development. Like the former, it begins in the first strophe with something which appears quite foreign, but only in order that in the second strophe it may with the more overwhelming force strike those against whom it is aimed, and then in the last two fully exhaust the thought.

1.

XXIX.

1   O God's-lioness God's-lioness, city where David
encamped ! | add year to year, let the feasts re-
volve, || then will I make it strait for God's-lioness,
so that she becometh sighs and sighing : | —but
then will she be to me as God's-lioness. || —For I
encamp as a ring around thee, | and enclose around
thee a rampart and set up against thee bulwarks : ||
then thou wilt speak humbly from the ground, and
from the dust thy words whisper, | as of a ghost
from the ground will thy voice be, and from the
5   dust thy words chirp. || Yet like fine dust shall be
the throng of thine enemies, and like flying chaff
the throng of the mighty-ones ; | and it will come
to pass on a sudden suddenly || —From Yahvé of
Hosts shall she be visited with crashing and thun-·
der and great noise, | storm and tempest and flame of
devouring fire; || and as a dream a night-vision will
be the throng of all the Heathen who contend against
God's-lioness. || And all they who fight against her
and her fortress and who distress her— | well, as
when he who is hungry dreameth that he eateth,
and awaketh and empty is his stomach, | and as
when he who is thirsty dreameth that he drinketh,
and awaketh and seeth himself languishing and his
soul longing, | thus will be the throng of all the
Heathen who contend against Mount Ssion. ||

2.

Be astounded and astonished ! be blinded and

blind ! | they are drunken but without wine,
10   stunned but without mead! || for Yahvé hath
poured a spirit of intoxication upon you, and
closed your eyes* and covered your seeing heads, ||
so that the prophecy concerning everything became like the words of the sealed book, which men
give to the book-scholar saying " pray read this"! |
but he saith "I cannot, because it is sealed;" ||
or as when a book is given to one who doth not
understand written characters, saying " pray read
this" | and he saith "I know nothing of books"! ||
—So then the Lord hath said: Because this nation
approached with its mouth and with its lips
honouring me, but its heart strayeth far from me, |
so that their fear towards me became a command-
ment of men got by heart : || therefore will I
further deal marvellously with this people, mar-
vellously and a marvel, | so that the wisdom of its
wise men perisheth, and the intelligence of its
intelligent men concealeth itself.

3.

15   O they who desire to hide deep from Yahvé coun-
sel, that their deeds may be in darkness, | and say
" who seeth us and who knoweth us?" || How
perverse are ye ! or as the clay is the framer to be
esteemed, | that a work should say to its master
" he hath not made me," and a thing framed say of
its framer " he understandeth it not"! || —Yea a
very little while longer—and Lebanon is turned

* *The Prophets.*

into a fruit-field | and the fruit-field will be deemed the forest, ‖ and there will hear on that day the deaf the words of a book, | and out of obscurity and darkness the eyes of the blind will see, ‖ and sufferers have greater joy in Yahvé, | and helpless

20 people exult in the Holy One of Israel. ‖ For the violent one vanisheth and the scorner ceaseth, | and all that wake for evil are cut off, ‖ who condemn men for a word, for him that reproveth in the market-place lay snares | and by inanity overthrow the just. ‖ —Therefore thus saith Yahvé unto the House of Yaqob, he that redeemed Abraham: | thenceforth Yaqob will not any more blush, and thenceforth his countenance no more wax pale: ‖ but when he seeth his children as the work of my hands in his midst, people will hallow my name, | hallow the Holy One of Yaqob and profoundly fear Israel's God ; ‖ and the erring in spirit know understanding, | and the hardened learn education. ‖

4.

XXX.

1   O rebellious sons, saith Yahvé, to execute a counsel and not from me, and to weave a web without my spirit, | in order to heap sin upon sin! ‖ they who go down to Egypt, without having enquired of my mouth, | to fortify themselves in Pharaoh's fortress, and to flee into Egypt's shadow! ‖ So Pharaoh's fortress will become your shame, | and the flight into Egypt's shadow your confusion. ‖ Though his princes are in Tanis, | and

though his messengers reach unto Hanés: ‖ every-
one blusheth at people who help him not, | who
are not there for help nor for profit, but for shame
and also for reproach. ‖ —*Through a land of
distress and straitness, whence lioness and lion,
adder and flying dragon, | they carry upon the
shoulders of young asses their wealth and upon the
humps of camels their treasures | —to people who
do not profit! ‖ But Egypt helpeth idly and
vainly: ‖ therefore I call this *Boastful* [Rahab]
that is *Slothful!* ‖

1. vv. 1-8. The strange and wonderful name must from the
first supply some indication of its meaning, and accordingly
Ariel is at once, ver. 1, designated as the place, in fact, more
definitely, as *the* city, where Davîd once encamped during his
wars; but it is not until the end, ver. 8, that the artistic
structure of this strophe suffers the real name to appear, when
it is a surprise to the hearer, though it has been gradually
prepared for. And the enigma of the entire historical marvel
is similarly presented at first in the most pointed form, vv. 1, 2,
to be gradually hinted at and described with increasing particularity, vv. 3-5, vv. 6-8. At the commencement, therefore,
with great brevity: let another year pass, the feasts again
revolve, then will I so straiten the *Lioness of God* that she
will become nothing but grief without preserving any of the
characteristics of a Lioness of God; but it is then precisely
that she will become to me the true Lioness of God, approve
herself as one who is invincible through me. For, it is further
said, vv. 3-5, that in the Assyrians, who will enclose and
straiten her after the best method of besieging, it is in reality
Yahvé himself who comes to inflict punishment, as if he

* *Oracle of the Beasts of the South;* comp. Vol. I. p. 89.

besieged her, which she must then discover in the fact that she
will be brought to extremities, and is scarcely able with
ghostly, hollow voice (viii. 18) to whimper, sunk in the profoundest grief; yet suddenly (when it is to be hoped that she
will then at least have been converted) all her enemies will be
scattered like dust.   For Yahvé himself, vv. 6-8, will visit her
in a storm, as he once visited Israel in Egypt, for instance, and
so dash to pieces the barbarians who desire to destroy the true
sanctuary, were they never so many, that they vanish like the
forms of a dream (which alarm but do not injure), Ps. lxxiii.
20, while their greed to destroy Ssion, very unlike the case of
xxviii. 4, will be deceived like that of a man who has appeased
his appetite merely in a dream.   Comp. the way in which this
is explained below, xxx. 27-33; xxxi. 4-9.

.2. Vv. 9-14.   The prophet sees his former opponents
astonished, amazed and confounded at his strange oration.
But with great presence of mind and remarkable force he
immediately turns their astonishment against themselves and
sees in it a new proof of their folly, which he had before been
compelled to charge them with, ch. xxviii.   Yes, be amazed
and blind as much as you like !   Here men are intoxicated and
stupefied by quite another than the ordinary process, that of
wine! ver. 9, with reference to xxviii. 7.   Yahvé himself has
blinded you with your eyes open, and, instead of the true
prophetic spirit, poured upon you a spirit of intoxication, so
that ye cannot now understand a genuine oracle concerning
any matter whatsoever (as that is which I have just delivered
to you), as if prophecy concerning any matter had become to
you already like the contents of a sealed book, which although
a man understands writing he cannot read (Rev. v. 1 sq.), or
as if ye were even like those who are unable to read any book
(even an open one), vv. 10-12, comp. xix. 14.   But just
because the entire nation of the present time, misled by such
prophets, even when it appears, as now, before Yahvé, and
comes to his sanctuary with sacrifices (i. 12), and professes to

honour him, really in its inmost heart wanders far from him,
and their fear cf him, of which they make a display, is not an
impulse of the heart and a voluntary and joyous resolve, but
merely an acquired commandment of men, a following of the
laws and customs which have once for all been prescribed by
priests and prophets ;—precisely on this account, will Yahvé
deal once more with this people in a very marvellous manner,
as he did in ancient times, that is, in some such manner as is
described, vv. 1-8, so that the wisdom of the nation's wise men,
which is unable to understand true spiritual marvels of this
kind, must shamefully perish.

3. If the naked fact, however, instead of the enigma must be
declared, it is especially, as follows at once from what has just
been said, the folly of the originators of the Egyptian proposal
which deserves to be severely blamed, their folly in the present
instance consisting in the belief that they are able to plan and
execute a matter (*e.g.*, the alliance with Egypt) in secret
without Yahvé's knowledge : which is so perverse, inasmuch
as the creature cannot excel the Creator in point of power and
knowledge, vv. 15, 16.—But since such folly really flows from
pusillanimity and a certain suspicion regarding Yahvé's power,
a failing in which unhappily the misled masses of the people
share, the discourse turns off to them, and declares, as if
animated by profound compassion, that Yahvé, on the contrary,
will even within a short time change the entire condition of the
world (ver. 17, comp. xxxii. 15, 16, in a tropical sense, *forest*,
desert = Lebanon, Ps. cxxxii. 6 ; Hag. i. 8), and by a great
action, which will make even the deaf hear and the blind see
(and put an end to the present folly, ver. 9), deliver the helpless
sufferers, since it is surely impossible that the violent one, *i.e.*,
the tyrant, the Assyrian, ver. 5, or the insolent mocker in
Israel itself, xxviii. 14, and all the keen transgressors should
continue, who, *e.g.*, condemn the true prophets and faithful
monitors on account of a mere word, and prepare for them all
kinds of fatal traps on frivolous grounds when they appear in

public, vv. 17-21; with ver. 21, comp. xxx. 10, 11; ver. 20 as
xxxii. 10 *b,* 14.—Let, therefore, Israel in its present liability to
despair comfort itself with the sure promise of the redeemer of
Abraham, that its youngest tribal father, Yaqob himself, who
though he now looks down upon it from his elevation in glory
can feel only grief and shame, will then at the sight of his trans-
figured nation (*the work of my hands,* comp. xix. 25) no more
blush; the experience of the great miraculous succour, xxviii.
21, and their own redemption, will forcibly impel all really to
consider the Holy One holy and to fear him (viii. 12, 13), will
therefore promote the spiritual regeneration, and people of an
erring, hardened spirit also, as those described, vv. 9-12, 18,
and especially xxviii. 7, will then receive sound doctrine, to
which they are now insensible, vv. 22-24.

4. But, finally, it is time to speak quite openly of those
who boasted to the common people that they were the true
statesmen, xxx. 1-7. That the counsel which they execute, the
web which they *weave,* will not succeed, that Egypt will not
help them, follows (1) precisely from the fact that the plan is
conceived against Yahvé; therefore the alliance with Egypt
will bring them nothing but disgrace, ver. 3; if Egypt is
really as great and powerful as is said, although it embraces
the north (where the royal residence was in Tanis) and the
centre of the territory of the Nile, so that its messengers (the
ambassadors of the kingdom with the royal commands, Nah.
ii. 14) reach to Hanés ("Ανυσις, Herod. ii. 137, now Ehnés):
yet it brings to a man only shame to hope for help from such a
land! vv. 4, 5.—But (2) it also lies in the nature of the vain
Egyptians not to keep their promises, not to render assistance,
so that one might call the kingdom, which gives itself the high
name Ráhab, *i.e.* as translated into Hebrew, *Defiance, Violence,*
(comp. the note on Ps. lxxxvii. 4, *Dichter des A. B.* I. *b,* p. 389)
or, for the sake of the paronomasia, *Boastful,* rather by the
name of *Shébeth, i.e. Sitting,* or staying still, *Stillness,* according to the common experience that the most haughty and

boastful people, when action and assistance are required, are
the most cowardly and dilatory. What folly, therefore, to
carry the most costly presents through the terrors of the wil-
derness to such people, vv. 6, 7! The paronomasia might also
be rendered *Precipitancy*, that is, *Sitting-still*, or *Crocodile that
is Stay-a-while*. It is clearly Yesaya's purpose to conduct the
thread of the discourse in such a way that it shall conclude
with a witty paronomasia, which may allow the severe seriousness of the entire transaction to be relieved at last by a ray of
humour, and also serve to compress into a brief witty utterance,
that can be easily remembered, the real gist of the whole
matter as regards its immediate application to the present.
It is also very suitable that the same piece whose first word is
the enigmatical Ariel and its interpretation, should end with
the directly opposite enigmatical Ráhab and its explanation.

That *Ariel*, xxix. 1, denotes the *fire-hearth* (altar) *of God*,
cannot at most be made more than probable from the words
with which Yesaya, xxxi. 9, closes a strophe; Ez. xliii. 15, 16,
cannot be quoted for this interpretation, as will appear *in loco*:
but a root אָרָה and יָרָה = *to burn*, is possible (see *History
of Israel*, II. 206 (II. 291). But here, vv. 1-8, it is manifestly
the invincible, *i.e.* lion-like, character of this city to which
prominence is given; and how natural the image of a lion was
as applied to the Jerusalem of that time is explained, *History
of Israel*, III. 250 (III. 341). But Yesaya unquestionably recurs
to this image, xxxi. 4-9.

The word מֻצָּב, xxix. 3, is certainly taken most correctly by the
LXX., Vulg., Sym., Pesch., as denoting something like a rampart and mound, which is *closed*, *i.e.* carried round, the city;
properly something thrown up, as *agger*, comp. Zech. viii. 8,
elsewhere with a slight difference סֹלְלָה Isa. xxxvii. 31; Jer.
xxxiii. 4; different from these are the מְצֻרוֹת, *i.e.*, proper bul-
warks, towers constructed for a siege.

xxix. 7. The discourse would become unnecessarily languid

if *b* were closely connected with *a*. It is much better to
begin a long new sentence with it, which is continued in ver.
8: this has also the recommendation that in that case the entire
third and last main section of the oration vv. 6-8 will consist of
only two similar long sentences, the first of which closes like
ver. 2 with Ariel, the second with the corresponding word
Ssion. It is true, this involves an alteration in the division of
the verses.

xxix. 10. The LXX. already read the words את הנביאים,
only misinterpreted them as they did so many others. But if
they are to be considered genuine, they would have to be more
closely connected, acc. §. 290 *d*, and translated your *prophet-
eyes*, or rather, in consideration of the repeated את, *your eyes the
prophetic ones*. But even then the sense would not be so simple
as it clearly must be according to the second member, compared
with vi. 9, 10; xxxii. 3; and the chief point is that it is not
the prophets alone who can here be referred to, according to
the general meaning of the entire discourse; for they are
included, acc. xxviii. 7 sq., but are by no means alone intended,
as also immediately appears v. 11 sq. The words must therefore be looked upon as a later addition, (see vol. I. p. 89),
although, like the addition with a similar meaning and object
ix. 14, it may have been found in the manuscript as early as
Yéremyá's time.

On the other hand, care must be taken not to misunderstand
the sublime words, xxix. 23, or to find in them anything
superfluous; in the *History of Israel* I. 296 (I. 424) it was
shown how truly they accord in thought and language with the
primitive ideas of the Patriarchs, and particularly of the last
of them Yaqob.

The sense of the difficult words xxx. 4, is not evident until
it is observed that this כי forms, acc. §. 362 *b.*, a mere protasis
and antithesis to ver. 5.

The three concluding words xxx. 7, רהב הם שבת will remain
obscure as long as it is not perceived that they are intended to

supply a short proverbial utterance, to be retained in the memory, or even to be written in great letters upon a public writing slab as a monument, as is here forthwith pre-supposed at the commencement of the next section, ver. 8. Accordingly חז must signify merely the *Germ. das ist, that is,* or *which is ;* the הז therefore has here, as ver. 6 and elsewhere, the force of *it,* acc. §. 172 *b,* and the plural may be used here and ver. 6 because in the case of any country the people of it may be understood, but this does not affect the real force of the word here.

---

3. *The Prophet's further Anticipations and Admonitions.* ch. xxx. 8—xxxii. 8.

At this point the prophet becomes silent : his opponents are also quite silent, although their silence may be due rather to the irresistible force of his words for the moment than to genuine conviction. Nor does Yesaya deceive himself in this respect. But as the Spirit of God had impelled him thus to appear in public and to speak as he had done, so now he was led by the same Spirit to feel that it was not well just then to speak further publicly, that he must withdraw into privacy leaving his words to gradually produce their full effect, not with a view of giving up the cause which he had defended, but to labour in it further at home by the means which were there at his command and accordant with the divine will. Thus the production of this entire book, together with similar efforts, was simply the natural continuation of his public labours in the arduous cause of the time, and by a very easy transition he subjoins in this *third* section all that he had further to say from his retirement, whether it was admonition or prophetic anticipation, threat or consolation, severe reproof or mild instruction, with the design of explaining and giving the highest meaning to the two-edged sharpness of his public oration. On this account the discourse which now opens, as a third great section at the close of the entire book and as a supplement of the two preceding sections, is of greater length, becoming a highly important closing oration of five strophes. It commences slowly and softly, but early in the first strophe the real opponents are from general points of view severely enough censured; it soon turns in the second and third strophes to the mass of the nation, comforting them and holding forth with growing force and precision the consummation of the Messianic hope; but this is done only in order that from this elevation the real opponents may in the fourth strophe be once more pointed out and profound errors of their policy displayed, and the entire piece be closed in the fifth with the calmest and sweetest Messianic hope and doctrine.

It is in this section, which originated as a literary composition, that Yesaya for the first time speaks quite openly against Assyria xxx. 31-33; subsequently he does this the more frequently the greater their haughtiness becomes. Another indication that this third section, as from the first a written production, is later than the public orations of the previous sections may be seen in the words xxxi. 2, as will be shown below.

1.

XXX.

8   Now go home write it upon a slab before them, and note it in a book, | that it may be to a later day for a witness for ever! || —For it is a stubborn nation, apostate sons, | sons who will not hear

10   Yahvé's doctrine, || who said to the seers "ye shall not see!" and to the presagers " ye shall not presage unto us straightforwardness ! | speak unto us flatteries, presage delusions; || get ye out of the way, turn aside from the path, | make the Holy One of Israel to rest before us!" || —Wherefore

thus saith the Holy One of Israel : Because ye
disdained this word, | but trusted in violence and
crooked ways and stayed yourselves thereon: ‖
therefore this transgression will be to you as a
falling rent swelling out in a highbuilt wall | whose
breach cometh on a sudden suddenly, ‖ and
breaking it as when an earthen pitcher is broken
shattered without pity. | and there is not found in
its shivers a sherd to take fire from the hearth, or
to draw water from the fountain. ‖ For thus saith

15   the Lord Yahvé the Holy One of Israel " in quiet
and rest shall ye be saved, in peace and in confi-
dence will be your strength !" | but ye would not ‖
and said : " no, but upon *fleet-steeds* will we *fly !*"
therefore shall ye *flee ;* | " and upon *chargers* will
we ride !" therefore shall your pursuers *charge !* ‖
a thousand at the threat of one, at the threat of
five will ye flee, | till ye remain over as the pole
upon the top of the mountain, and as the standard
upon the hill. ‖

2.

And therefore Yahvé delayeth to be gracious
unto you, and therefore he stirreth not to have
pity upon you : | for a God of justice is Yahvé ;
blessed are all who wait for him ! ‖ —For O people
which dwellest in Ssion, in Jerusalem ! | weep
weep shalt thou not, pity pity will he have upon
thee as soon as thou callest, as soon as he heareth

20   it he hath already answered thee ; ‖ but if the
Lord giveth you bread of distress and water of

affliction, | then will thy teacher no more hide
himself, but thine eyes will continually see thy
teacher, ‖ and thine ears will hear words behind
thee saying | " there is the way, walk ye in it !"
when ye turn to the right and when ye turn to the
left; ‖ then thou defilest the covering of thy
silver graven-images and the fine-work of thy
golden molten-image, | thou wilt spurn them as a
loathsome thing, saying to it " hence"! ‖ Then
giveth he rain for thy seed with which thou sowest
the ground, and the bread of the produce of the
ground—it is nourishing and fat; | thy herd will
feed on that day in a wide pasture, ‖ and the oxen
and young asses which work the ground eat salted
mixed-fodder | which has been winnowed with the
25 fan and shovel; ‖ and upon every high mountain and upon every lofty hill are streams flowing
with water, | —on the day of the great battle,
when towers fall. ‖ Then will the pale moonlight
be as the glow light, and the glow-light is seven-
fold as the light of seven days | —on the day when
Yahvé bindeth up the wound of his people, and
healeth the hurt of its blow. ‖

3.

Behold Yahvé's name cometh from afar, burning
with anger and with violent uprising, | his lips full
of wrath, and his tongue like devouring fire, ‖
while his breath is like an overflowing torrent
which reacheth unto the neck to toss heathen with
the fan of delusion, | and a misleading bridle is

upon the cheeks of the nations. ‖ —The song will
be to you as in the night of the solemnisation of the
feast, | and joy of heart as when one journeyeth to
the pipe towards Yahvé's mount unto the rock of
30 Israel ; ‖ and Yahvé causeth his grand thunder to
peal, and showeth the lighting-down of his arm |
in the heat of his anger and flame of devouring
fire, a crashing and tempest and hailstones. ‖
Yea at the thunder of Yahvé Assur will crash
down, | from the staff wherewith he smiteth
it; ‖ and whenever there passeth over the rod of
doom which Yahve letteth down upon him | with
tabrets and guitars and with battles of swing-
sacrifices will they fight against it. ‖ —Long ago
indeed was the pile got ready, even for the king
also is it prepared deep and broad; | it can contain
much fire and wood: | Yahvé's breath like a
torrent of brimstone kindleth it. ‖

4.

XXXI.

1   O they who go down to Egypt for help, upon
horses staying themselves, | and trust in horsemen
that there are many of them, and in riders that they
are very numerous, ‖ without ever looking to the
Holy One of Israel, and without ever seeking
Yahvé! ‖ Yet he also is wise and announced evil
and hath never changed his words, | but ariseth
against the house of the evil, and against the help
of the workers of iniquity. ‖ But Egyptians are
men and not God, and their horses flesh not spirit, |

14 *

and Yahvé will stretch out his hand so that the
helper stumbleth and the helped falleth, and
together they all perish. ‖ — For thus saith Yahvé
unto me : Just as the lion and the young-lion
growleth over his prey, against whom a multitude
of shepherds is called—at their voice he trembleth
not, and at their noise he croucheth not — : | so
will Yahvé of Hosts come down with his host

5   upon mount Ssion and upon its hill, ‖ as fluttering
birds, so will Yahvé of Hosts shield Jerusalem, |
shield and so deliver, pass over and so redeem. ‖ —
O return ye unto him whom they deeply injured, sons of Israel! ‖ for on. that day they shall.
each one reject his silver idols and his golden
idols, | which your hands made you for a sin, ‖ and
Assur falleth by no man's sword and no man's
sword will devour him: | he fleeth before the
sword, and his brave ones are for servitude, ‖ and
his rock he misseth from terror, and his princes
run trembling from the standard, | saith Yahvé who
hath a fire in Ssion, and a hearth in Jerusalem. ‖

5.

XXXII.

1.   Behold according to justice will the ruler rule, |
and the governors—according to equity govern, ‖ so
that each one is as a hiding-place from the storm
and a covert from the tempest, | as water-brooks
in a drought, as a mighty rock's shadow in a languishing land. ‖ And the eyes of those who see
are then not closed, | the ears of those who hear

are attentive, ‖ and the heart of the rash hath wise
understanding, | and the tongue of stammerers
5   speaketh clearly with readiness. ‖ No more is the
worthless man called nobleman, | nor is the in-
triguer greeted as Worthy; ‖ for a worthless man
speaketh worthless things, and his heart prepareth
evil, | to work unholiness and to speak against
Yahvé folly, to let the soul of the hungry famish
and to take away the drink of the thirsty; ‖ and
an *intriguer*—his *intricacies* are evil, | he adviseth
to misdeeds, to destroy the suffering with lying
words, and thereby that he prosecuteth the help-
less: ‖ the noble adviseth to noble things; | and he
will stand to noble things. ‖

1. xxx. 8-17.   Unexpectedly one of the most important
portions of the entire oration had just been brought forward, the oracle of the certainty that Egypt will not render
assistance.   It is true, at present people will not believe that;
but Yesaya has received the assurance of it from Yahvé,
and now hears further, after that the great word has gone
forth, in perfect calmness the higher command to write down
this oracle at home, that is, to set up the brief enigmatical word
with which the previous oration closed upon a tablet before
the eyes of those who now refuse to believe it, and to write all
the rest in a book, in order that both tablet and book may subsequently serve when the fulfilment comes as an eternal testimony to the prophetic truth, ver. 8, comp. viii. 1, 16.   They
are indeed at present (and here echoes of the former powerful
oration occur, i. 2 sq.) rebellious sons, denying their God and
benefactor, sons who cannot even endure the genuine prophetic
word, because it places before their eyes the Holy One, while
they wish that the genuine prophets would not speak at all, or
in any case falsely and insincerely, forsaking the eternal path,

vv. 9-11.   But they must still hear the divine word, in order
that precisely this contempt of the prophetic word and their
dishonest violence in the government may finally issue in a
complete overthrow, with as much certainty as a rent, perhaps
hitherto quite hidden, in a high wall goes deeper and deeper,
and swells out until suddenly it precipitates the whole of the
lofty wall in ruins, just as when a poor man's earthenware is
dashed to pieces, so that he has not even a sherd left for the
simplest necessities of life, vv. 12-14.   For long ago Yahvé
pronounced peace, possession of mind, and trust in him the
only available means of your deliverance, comp. ch. vii. : but
ye preferred commotion and haughtiness, to pursue upon
Egyptian chargers and racers (Hos. xiv. 4) ; well, then, ye
shall run from your enemies (the Assyrians) in the most disgraceful manner and fall, until ye remain as solitary in the land
as a lonely memorial sign upon the mountains, vv. 15-17,
comp. xvii. 6 ; v. 26.—But this precisely the source whence

2. the present mournful condition of indecision comes, of
the impossibility that Yahvé should be able, however much he
may desire to do it, at once to save you : for as the Just One
he cannot endure for ever the great injustice which now prevails upon the earth through the Assyrians ; he is already preparing himself to restore justice and help the pious sufferers,
sooner or later the deliverer comes, blessed, therefore, are all
who patiently wait for him !   Thus ver. 18 forms the transition
to the new strophe, in which the prophet passes entirely to the
consolation of the faithful.   For in any case (thus the discourse
rises again with new life, ver. 19, the very address quivering
with the fire of the blessed hope, which here for the first time
breaks forth without restraint), thou nation in Ssion shalt not
perish calling in repentance and humility upon thy God, comp.
xxix. 4, but precisely in the deepest trouble, when the Lord
presents to you as bread and water nothing but distress (*i.e.*
in the siege, 1 Kings xxii. 27), then will he, who now hides
himself from you, and whom you do not see, be quite near

and perceptible to you as the true teacher and leader, that ye may always see and hear Him, and then, therefore, knowingly cast away with a true and profound abomination your splendid idols as something loathsome, since ye have then found the true eternal God, vv. 19-22.   And how glorious will be that time of harmony between Yahvé and men! even the ground will be more fruitful, the toiling cattle less poorly kept, and barren mountains flooded with water, vv. 22-25, comp. iv. 2 ; Joel iv. 18; and if humbler things become more glorious, how much more higher things, the light from above, so that the moon then will be as the glow-light, *i.e.* sunlight, and the sun as if the glow of seven days as they now are shone at the same time, ver. 26, comp. iv. 5 sq.; Rev. xxi. 11, 23.   But at the end of the last two verses the fact is referred to with great significance and beauty, that the happiness cannot come before the great day of decision and conflict, when on the one hand towers fall (in this connexion, therefore, somewhat different from ii. 15, so that everything high, including what is high amongst men, may be understood, comp. ver. 33), on the other, the wounds of the genuine kingdom will be removed, i. 5; which forms the transition to the next strophe,

3. vv. 27-33, which is a description in more exalted language of the great moment of the decision itself, as the prophetic imagination conceives it according to the model of the great deliverance of ancient times, Ex. ch. xiv. and xv.   The *name* of Yahvé, Yahvé as far as he can become visibly manifest, will come from the distant heaven, appearing as in clouds of fire, terrible and alarming (Ps. l. 3) : with these figures a description is commenced, ver. 27, which notwithstanding the models that had preceded it, is as unique as the unfolding of the great Assyrian drama itself, which was then commencing.   That the Assyrians would dash themselves against the Temple in blind rage, was foreseen by Yesaya (comp. xxix. 1-7 ; x. 28-34) ; but his firm faith in the indestructibility of the true Sanctuary and an upward glance to the true God, brought most clearly before

his clarified eye the knowledge that this day will become a
high festival, such as had not been experienced before, when
Yahvé himself, amidst the rejoicing of his people, will choose
out the Assyrian for himself as an offering, when his breath,
like a mountain-torrent suddenly rising to men's necks (viii.
8), will seize the Heathen, in order that, laying hold upon them
with a *swing*, or fan, of *delusion*, and with a subduing but misleading cheek-bridle, with which wild beasts are tamed (xxxvii.
29), it may hurl them to the Sanctuary, ver. 28, that they may
not find what they desire to destroy, Ps. lix. 12; whilst the
Redeemed sing and rejoice, as on the joyous feast when great
multitudes journey up to the Temple, to the rock of Israel,
i.e. to Yahvé, amid endless exultation, Yahvé will appear in
conflict from above in the majestic tempest, with which he
terrifies and destroys the ungodly, vv. 29, 30.   Yea, to declare
it most plainly, the Assyrian shall so tremble at Yahvé's thunder
and his rod that every stroke which falls upon him from above
is greeted from below with unmixed delight, and not with weak
but mightily swinging battles of sacrifices the war is carried
on against him, vv. 31, 32.—For as the rod or chastisement of
Yahvé, was already, ver. 32, said to be firmly established, un-
avoidably decreed, the punishment has been long necessary, so
the pile is prepared, even for the Assyrian king himself if it is
needful, a deep and broad pile, whose circumference or enclosure
is much fire and wood: then it needs only the fiery breath of
Yahvé, ver. 27, to kindle it ! ver. 33, with which this strophe
returning to the figure at the commencement, vv. 27, 28, most
fittingly closes.

4. Chap. xxxi. By the three foregoing strophes, which have
gradually attained the greatest elevation, the preparation has
been made for a descent from this height upon the matter which
is of first concern, and once more with still greater force than
in the last strophe of the previous section, xxx. 1-7, to rebuke
the false confidence which they who are here chiefly opposed
place in external, material things, in this case the Egyptians

and their numerous chariots and horses. How mistaken and unnecessary this is, this strophe proves in the most complete manner. How mistaken it is, appears not only from the thing itself, but still more from the consideration that Yahvé, whom they have thereby not considered although he alone deserves their confidence, is after all, however wise they imagine themselves to be in the air of mystery they put on toward him, xxix. 15, much wiser, and sees through their perversity. Hence Yahvé has already *brought, i.e.,* announced evil by Yesaya, acc. xxx. 3-7, and, since he never alters his words, will certainly execute this threatened punishment on both parties, the evildoers who seek such help and the Egyptians, vv. 1-3. That it is unnecessary appears from Yahvé's solemn promise, xxix. 1-7, that he intends himself to help; and if ever so many Heathen gathered in a threatening manner around the sanctuary upon the hill of Ssion, he descends with power upon it, (to repeat the image from xxix. 1-7) like a fearless lion with a terrible roar upon the prey which he has in his eye, or rather as birds which flutter around their nests, protecting and defending them, Deut. xxxii. 11, and his simple protection, his gracious passing-by, as formerly at the Pascha (to which there is here even a verbal allusion, Exod. xii. 13), is deliverance and redemption itself, vv. 4, 5. O return, therefore, with penitence to him who has been deeply injured (properly, with regard to whom they have deeply revolted, i. 5), while there is yet time! for then it is too late, then every one casts his idols, which he has made to his own guilt, away, ii. 18-22, and the Assyrian with his army falls then by the sword of a Higher One, before the approaching judge Yahvé, as is described xxx. 27-33, with such terror that in blind and hurried flight he misses his own fortress and his princes in like fright abandon their standard that they may by some means escape (comp. *e.g.,* Job xv. 23, 24). For, as is significantly added at the end, not in vain has Yahvé his hearth in Ssion.

5. xxxii. 1-8. The closing strophe the more naturally falls

again, with a change of tone, into the description of the
blessed time, inasmuch as this had not received its due treatment in the previous long section.   One aspect of this description which, after the brief allusion xxviii. 6, had not been
definitely brought forward, is here very appropriately supplied, namely, that then the government and executive itself,
the axis of the kingdom, will be improved from its very basis :
which is not elaborated here in such exalted imagery as xi. 1-9,
but is on that very account the more applicable to the thoughtless magnates who opposed the prophet ; it is in a style which
stoops to the hearers' necessities, becoming simply didactic at
times, and the description is continued until the verses required
to make a strophe have been supplied.   King and princes
will then be what their vocation requires them to be, giving
protection and refreshment by righteous decisions in every
matter, vv. 1, 2 ; obduracy towards the truth and inability to
fill their offices, as is at present the case with the blind and
deaf, drunken and stammering magnates, xxviii. 7-10 ; xxix.
9-12, will not then be found, vv. 3, 4, comp. a similar state-
ment xxix. 18, 24 ; and the confusion of ideas and positions,
according to which at present the most worthless man, or
" windbag," is decorated with the most honourable names, will
be then unknown, ver. 5 : but that this mischievous confusion
is now really made, admits of no doubt, one has only to
examine the ideas closely ! a worthless man, one inwardly
corrupt (in Hebrew properly a *fool*), and nothing more, is he
who speaks and meditates evil, to sin both against Yahvé and
his helpless neighbour, and an intriguer is he who counsels to
empty and evil methods with a view to carrying out the injustice which seems to be useful, although such a worthless man
or such an intriguer may wear a high name in the state ; a
truly noble man does not merely purpose to do noble things
but will stand to his purpose, and in the end conquer, has in
any case the divine promise on his side (with which a concise
and powerful conclusion is made), vv. 6-8.

xxx. 8, instead of לָעַד *for ever*, which before the following *unto eternity* would in this case be somewhat superfluous and cumbrous, it is better to read with the Vulgate לְעֵד, comp. viii. 2; xix. 20.

xxx. 16, the various paronomasiæ are represented in the translation.—Ver. 18, it is necessary to read יָדוּם or יְדוּם instead of יָרוּם, *he is high*, which would not make sense here.

In the beautiful description, xxx. 20-22, מוֹרֶיךָ *sing*. as well as מִקְנֶיךָ ver. 23, must be taken acc. § 256 *b*; דוּחַ acc. to Job vi. 7, זרח is Aram. *zᵉrô* and Arab. *zará* (not Arab. *dhará*), Numb. xi. 20.

If זֹרֶה xxx. 24, § 169 *d*, is held to be the part. Pual, it is on the supposition that according to Prov. xx. 8, 26, זָרָה rather than זָרָה denotes *to sift* as an art; but it is true that after the relative אֲשֶׁר the perf. זֹרָה would then be more natural here.

xxx. 27, בֹּעֵר אַפּוֹ is a subordinate condition-sentence, [see Ewald's *Introductory Hebrew Grammar*, §§ 306, 341, and Driver, *On the Use of the Tenses in Hebrew*, (Oxford, 1874), App. I.] as 2 Sam. xv. 32, § 288 *c*, and כֹּבֶד מַשָּׂאָה *with violence of uprising*, is subordinated still more concisely in the simple accusative, acc. § 279 *d*; but the word מַשָּׂאָה has certainly the meaning found in Judg. xx. 38 of the *Germ. Schwall*, the swell of rising waves and storms, a column growing higher and higher.

The unusual figures, xxx. 28, comp. ver. 32, can be understood only as it is remembered, (1) that הֵנִיף both here and ver. 32 is an expression explained by the considerations given in the *Alterthümer*, p. 98 sq. (85 sq.); (2) that שָׁוְא both here and v. 18 retains its primary meaning of *vanity, delusion*, corresponding to the following מַתְעֶה *misleading*, and that the *swing* or *fan, of delusion* and this *misleading bridle* form a popular mythical image resembling our fabulous coat of darkness; (3) that, in as far as ultimately the experience of unusual violent transportations and legends arising therefrom have had great influence here, the entire illustration is taken from *the breath* of a whirlwind, or a similar storm.—Ver. 31 *b*, the present reading *Assur who smiteth* like a slave-driver *with the staff*, would have to be understood after the analogy of such phrases as x. 5, 24: but such phrases are suitable in their own connexion, while they are not here appropriate; besides in this place the phrase would be extremely abrupt and unfinished, even if יֻכֶּה were restored according to x. 24. Besides, from the structure of the strophes and because the idea of שבט is plainly carried on, ver. 32, by מטה, it is necessary to read here מִשְׁבֶט and יֻכֶּהָ, the fem. suff. in the latter word, as in בָּהּ, ver. 32, being explained by the fact that Assur, like all names of countries, may be construed as either masculine or feminine: still it might be easier to read יֻכֵּם in ver. 31 with the LXX. and בָּם ver. 32, with numerous authorities, just as the sing. and plur. interchange in the similar case, x. 5, 28, 29. With regard to ver. 32, where the accents must be altered, comp. further §§ 319 *b*, 345 *b*, and on ver. 33, §§ 173 *g*, 319 *b*. Since the originally fem. תפתה becomes also a masculine, the genders here alternate beautifully with the verse-members, in the same way as the plur. and sing. of the address, where both are permissible, vv. 19-21, most naturally interchange with the verse-members.

xxxi. 1, the וְ before עֵל סוּסִים יִשָּׁעֵנוּ must be removed, as is done in good MSS., giving greater symmetry to the verse-structure.—In xxxi. 2, *to bring* may denote in prophetic language *to announce*, as also in poetic language, see on Ps.lxxi. 16.— לִצְבֹּא ver. 4, which is added more for the sake of the paronomasia merely, has not erroneously been connected by the Massorites with עַל, although the sense is here different from that it bears in xxix. 8.

xxxii. 3, if תשעינה had been correctly pointed, לא would have to be read as לוֹ, *and to Him* (God) *will they who* see look, and they who hear give heed; but this reference to God does not lie in the context. We must therefore read תִּשְׁעֶינָה, acc. xxix. 9, 18; vi. 10.

The word פִּילַי, which becomes כְּלַי in ver. 7, merely for the sake of the paronomasia, derived from פִּיל = כַּיְד Arab. *kaid*, is exactly what is in German called a *Ränkemacher*, intriguer, plotter of mischief; and from the description it is evident that the crime of the פִּילַי is supposed to lie in the counsel which he gives, while that of the נָבָל consists in the ideas and feelings according to which he acts. With regard to דְּבֶּ רמְשָׁפֵּט, see § 283 *d*; 2 Kings xxv. 6 may probably be taken in the same sense, only אֹרוֹ is to be read. Comp. the *Jahrbb. der Bibl. Wiss.* I., p. 100.

---

4. EPISODICAL ORATION ADDRESSED TO THE WOMEN.
CONCLUSION. Ch. xxxii. 9-20.

Yesaya adds here, as in a side-corner, a similarly earnest word against the careless, luxurious women of the capital, without doubt reproducing a discourse which he had upon some recent occasion publicly delivered. This has similarity with the discourse of the earliest book, iii. 16 sq. : but although he deems a similar admonition necessary, vv. 9-13, he recurs in this case earlier than he did then to the main subject of the entire book, his agitated voice rising and falling here also between the threatening and the consolation of the prophecy, until it finds its goal in a suitable exhortation, ver. 14; 15-18; 19-20.

Careless women, rise hear ye my voice, | ye secure
10 daughters, mark my speech ! || After a year and a day shall ye secure ones tremble ! | for the vintage hath perished, the fruit-harvest cometh not in. || Be alarmed ye careless ones, tremble ye secure ones, | strip yourselves naked, and put the girdle upon your loins ! || upon the *fair* breast will they soon smite | on account of the pleasant *fare*, on account of the fruitful vine : || upon the ground of my people will

thorn and thistle come up, | yea upon all houses of
pleasure, of the joyous city. ‖ —For the palace will
be forsaken, the throng of the city be made desert, |
Hillside and Pleasure-tower serveth instead of
caves for ever, as a joy of wild asses as a pasture

15 of flocks ‖ —until there be poured upon us a spirit
from on high, | and the desert becometh a fruit-
field and the fruit-field is counted as forest, ‖ and
in the desert dwelleth justice, | and righteousness
in the fruit-field maketh abode, ‖ the fruit of
righteousness is peace, | and the profit of righteous-
ness quiet and security for ever, ‖ and my people
maketh abode in the pasture of peace, | in secure
dwellings and in careless resting-places. ‖ — But
hail will come down when the forest *cometh down* |
and to the ground will the city be abased. ‖

20 Blessed are ye who sow by all waters, | who put
in motion the foot of the ox and the ass ! ‖

The women, they who still live carelessly and luxuriously notwithstanding the growing seriousness of the time, shall soon be
touched most acutely by that which primarily concerns them
with their household cares—by unfruitfulness and laying waste
of the cultivated soil, so that great scarcity is felt in the houses
vv. 9, 10, comp. v. 10, 17; vii. 23-25. Yea, cries the
prophet to them in still more threatening tones, ver. 11,
tremble, and instead of your own ornaments, which have been
carried off by the barbarous enemy, place sackcloth upon the
bare body, comp. iii. 24; very soon there will be beating upon
the breast (in the well-known manner, *plangere*, Nah. ii. 8), at
the loss of the beautiful fruitful fields, upon which, as well as
even upon the ruins of the city which is now so full of joy and
luxury (xxii. 2), nothing but weeds will grow, vv. 12, 13.—For

it is indeed true, as Yesaya but briefly urges again from his earlier oracles, that on that spot where now the wild, uproarious joy of Jerusalem reigns, desert, waste loneliness will arise, and where now on a *slope* of the temple-hill ('*Ophel* Neh. iii. 27; Mic. iv. 8) the most ornamental pleasure-turrets rise, there there will be caverns for wild beasts, ver. 14—for an indefinite period, until at length there comes from above the spiritual transformation and amendment, which permeates lower things, filling the entire land, desert and fruit-field, with righteousness and its fair fruits—quiet and peace, vv. 15-18, comp. xxix. 17; Joel iii. 1.—But, it must be once more finally added, severe punishments and tempests must first come; *but it will hail* (briefly repeated from xxviii. 2; xxix. 6; xxx. 30), when forest and city, *i.e.*, everything that is high and proud in the land, falls and is deeply bowed down, therefore when the punishment cometh, ver. 19 (a paronomasia adds further force to the concise, incisive language, city=citadel, Mic. v. 13): blessed are they therefore who cultivate their fields in the most fitting spots (anywhere where there is water), and industriously (driving to their work the ox and the ass, which are used in husbandry, xxx. 24), in order that they may some day reap a good harvest! Since the judgment is the matter spoken of, it follows as a matter of course that the illustration is to be understood morally of the pursuit of duty; it is only he who sows near abundance of water who does not sow upon unproductive ground, it is only he who spares no pains and labour who can expect to reap; and the figure was the more natural, since just before, vv. 13, 14, the barren field had been spoken of as the punishment of sin.

All the imperatives רְגָזָה‎, חֲרָדָה‎, etc. ver. 11, must acc. § 226 *a*, have suffered in this case contraction from רְגַזְנָה‎, חֲרְדְנָה‎, etc., a formation which does not occur elsewhere, but is possible in the language of the people and is sufficiently clear in this instance, Yesaya probably making the change from the common form of ver. 9 for the sake of imitating the affected language of such women.

The rendering of the words *upon the breasts will they soon smite on account of the pleasant fields,* ver. 12, is free, in order that the forcible paronomasia of the Hebrew may not be left unrepresented.*

" Hail will *come down"* is instead of the simple *it will hail,* ver. 19, to bring out the paronomasia. Another German rendering would be "aber *stürmen (wird's)* wann *stürzt* der Wald und in den grund versinkt die Stadt."

Finally, the prophecy of the complete destruction of Jerusalem, vv. 13, 14, 19, might seem to contradict that of the deliverance of Ssion, xxix. 1-9, did not one bear in mind that Yesaya after all only brings forward again what he had already said chap. vii., and that the idea of Ssion as far as it is something indestructible leads up of itself into higher regions. Comp. further on this subject the commentary on Micah, chaps. iv. and v. below.

---

* The author's rendering in the text is : " Auf *leib und brust* wird man bald schlagen | ob der verlornen *leibgerichte."—Tr.*

VI.—YESAYA'S SIXTH BOOK.

Ch. x. 5—xii. 6; xiv. 24-27; xvii. 12—xviii. 7; xx.

Meanwhile Samaria actually fell in the year 719 : and the whole power of the Assyrians was thrown with the more oppressive weight upon the remaining kingdom with its head at Jerusalem. There came now the troubled times of the chastising hand of God upon this kingdom, of which Yesaya had prophesied in all his earlier books : they did not come at once in the special form of a severe siege of Jerusalem as he had most recently prophesied, xxix. 1-8, and yet times of the same oppresive and continued calamity had only too truly arrived. The Assyrians had manifestly long sought a pretext for taking the strong fortress of Jerusalem into their hands, and for destroying the kingdom of Yuda, as they had done that of Samaria, its religion being as unintelligible to them as that of the Northern Kingdom. The hopes which many magnates in Jerusalem still continued to place upon Egypt and the Æthiopic kingdom which had at that time become powerful, might supply them with the desired pretext. And the new reign of Sancherib aimed more violently and unsparingly than any former one at finally putting into execution the Assyrian plans of conquest against all the Southern Nations (Herod. ii. 141). It was under the pressure of this threatened evil that the whole land of Yuda had been suffering now for years ; the well-meaning, gentle king Hizqia was exposed to increasing demands and dishonour ; the whole house of Davîd, and with it what was in those times the firmest stay of all Messianic hope, seemed with growing clearness to be advancing to its destruction. But amid those wholly altered circumstances Yesaya preserved the true glance and the imperturbable strength of a genuine prophet; and in what way he then laboured is most clearly shown to us by this his sixth book. It must have been published about

2.   15

the year 713 B.C., and appears to have been preserved in a
fairly complete form, so far as its main portions are concerned.
We have but to correctly separate and arrange its constituent
pieces. Its main piece was without doubt the following oracle.

1.—The Oracle concerning the Kingdom of the Assyrian and the Kingdom of the Messiah.

Ch. x. 5—xii. 6.

It introduces us at once to an entirely different period. For
this great oration presupposes all the earlier ones of our prophet, especially the last long one ; and the brief expressions,
x. 12, 23, refer plainly to the more detailed explanations which
had been given in earlier passages, xxix. 1-8, 23 ; xxviii. 21, 22 ;
the destruction of Samaria is also referred to as past, x. 11.
But whilst Yesaya had continued, even in the last of the previous pieces, to anticipate further chastisements of Israel by
means of the Assyrian, foreseeing at the same time with equal
clearness his overthrow, in the present piece the prophet's mind
beholds him so far advanced in the immoderation of cruelty and
in the pure love of destruction which is the result of unrestrained unrighteousness, that he can no longer look upon him
as an instrument of divine punishment, but must think of him
as himself the great example of divine chastisement. This is
the new element of the present discourse : and therewith is connected the fact, that Yesaya no longer anticipates, as he had
done, ch. xxviii-xxxii., a close environment and long siege of
Jerusalem by the Assyrian, but on the contrary his rapid
overthrow, as soon as ever, with hasty step, eager to destroy,
and with insolent threats, he arrives before the sanctuary, x.
28-34, comp. xvii. 14. In fact, this is the first oration aimed
directly and solely against the Assyrian, and it must have been
occasioned by some new evidence of Assyrian inhumanity ; the
oration scarcely glances incidentally at the perversities which
were still to be found in Yuda, x. 20-23. On the contrary, the

oration, notwithstanding its violent commencement against the Assyrian, is occupied throughout its course in comforting and encouraging the oppressed and distressed people, and beyond any of its predecessors issues in lovely and cheering pictures of the blessed age. After the first of the five strophes, x. 5-15, has sufficiently chastised the haughtiness of the Assyrian, the second handles the impending divine judgment, both as a general and as a special judgment, x. 16-23, so that the last three are occupied entirely with imparting consolation, first, with the consideration of the certainty of the overthrow of the Assyrian at the very moment when he thinks that he has with his insolent hand destroyed the last Sanctuary and asylum of the earth, x. 24-34, then still more with the consideration of the blessed age which is then possible, both with respect to its internal nature, xi. 1-9, and its relation to the world without, xi. 10-16. The relation to the world without leading to reference to the Assyrians again, the discourse is brought round at its close to its starting point. The six verses that follow are an addition by a much later prophet.

But if in the course of this oration Yesaya sketches a picture of the Messianic age and especially of the Messiah himself, which, in respect of charming and graphic clearness, as well as of blessed repose and enchanting beauty, surpasses all that he had ever thought well to describe in any of his earlier writings, a sufficient explanation is found in the vast and direct contrast in which he was compelled to place the reign of the Messiah, which had never before been so longed for as now, with that of the Assyrians, which had at this time been fully experienced. The more painful the experience of this had been, so much the more clearly and intensely could people long for its most direct opposite, and the more was the prophet compelled to raise up those who had been so long bowed down by the certain hope in the consummation of the theocracy and by the brightest pictures of this consummation. And if he knew well that this consummation in its perfection could be but gradually attained

15 *

to and at that time was still in a backward state, yet this
would only compel him the more definitely to present the
form it must some time certainly assume, and its essential
characteristics.

1.

X.

5   O Assur thou staff of my anger, | and who exe-
cuteth as a rod my wrath! || against an unholy
nation I send him, and against people of my indig-
nation I appoint him, | to prey upon the prey and
to plunder the plunder, and to trample it small like
the mire of the streets: || yet he thinketh not so,
and his heart reckoneth not so, | but to destroy is
in his mind, and to cut off not a few nations; ||
since he saith: | "are not my princes as a body
kings! || is not Kalno as Karkemîsh? | or Hamâth
10   not as Arpad? or Samaria not as Damascus? || as
my hand reached to the idol-countries, | whose
images are more than those of Jerusalem and
Samaria, || — yea as I did unto Samaria and its
idols, | so will I do to Jerusalem and its gods!" ||
But when Yahvé shall finish his whole work upon
Mount Ssion and in Jerusalem, | — I will visit the
fruit of the haughtiness of the Assyrian king and
the vainglory of his proud eyes, || in that he saith
"by the strength of mine hand I did it, and by
my wisdom because I am intelligent, | remove the
boundaries of the nations, and plunder their stores |
and cast down as a God the enthroned: || yea my
hand found as a nest the wealth of the nations,
and as one gathereth forsaken eggs I gathered the

whole earth, | while there was not one with a flut-
tering wing, and opening its mouth and chirp-
15　ing!" || — O then doth the axe boast itself against
him that heweth therewith, or doth the saw brag
against him that swingeth it ? | as if the staff
should swing him that raiseth it, as if the rod
should raise that which is not wood !—

2.

Therefore will the Lord Yahvé of Hosts send
into his fat limbs consumption, | and under his
glory will a flame flame forth as fire flameth, ||
Israel's light will be a fire and his Holy One a
flame : | which kindleth and devoureth his thorns
and thistles in a day, || and the majesty of his
forest and fruitfield will he consume from the soul
to the body, | so that it is as when a sick man sick-
eneth away ; || but the remnant of his forest-trees
will be soon counted, | and a boy would write them
20　down. || — Then on that day the remnant of Israel
and the residue of the House of Yaqob will no
longer stay itself upon him that smiteth it, | but
stay itself upon Yahvé the Holy One of Israel with
faithfulness. || *The remnant will return, the rem-
nant of Yaqob* | to the Hero-God ! || for if thy
people O Israel were even as the sand of the sea : |
a remnant will return of it, | destruction is decided,
overflowing with righteousnes; ; || for an end and
decision will the Lord Yahvé of Hosts perform in
the midst of the whole earth. ||

3.

Therefore thus saith the Lord Yahvé of Hosts:
Fear not my people dwelling in Ssion on account
of Assur, | who smiteth thee with the staff and
raiseth his rod over thee in the Egyptian manner: ||
25   for yet a little a little while,—and the wrath is
passed: and my anger is for their wasting; || and
Yahvé of Hosts moveth over him a scourge as he
smote Midyan at the rock of the ravens, | and his
rod over the sea—he raiseth it in the Egyptian
manner. || Then on that day will his burden de-
part from off thy shoulder, and his yoke from thy
neck: | for destroyed is a youth by fat. || — He
cometh by 'Aiyâth, marcheth through Migron, | at
Mikmash he layeth up his baggage; || they pass
through the Pass, Géba' they make the night-camp, |
Harâma trembleth, Gibeah of Saul fleeth, || —
30   shriek aloud, daughter Gallim, | hearken Láischa,
answer her Anathoth! — || in motion is Madmena, |
the inhabitants of Gæbim flit; || yet to-day he
must rest in Nob, | he swingeth on high his hand
against the mountain of the daughter Ssion, the
hill of Jerusalem: || — behold the Lord Yahvé of
Hosts cleaveth the crown with sudden fright, | and
those high of stature have been hewn down, the
lofty are humbled; || smitten down are the thickets
of the forest with iron, | and the Lebanon felled
by a Majestical One.

4.

XI.
1   Then will a shoot from Ishaï's worn stem sprout

forth, | and a green branch burst forth from his roots : || and there resteth upon him Yahvé's spirit, | the spirit of wisdom and reason, the spirit of counsel and valour, the spirit of knowledge and fear of Yahvé; || and his breathing is in Yahvé's fear, | and not after the sight of his eyes judgeth he, nor after the hearing of his ears giveth he decision, || but judgeth after justice the oppressed, and giveth decision after equity to the sufferers of the earth; | he smiteth then the earth with the staff of his mouth, and slayeth by the breath of his lips the

5   wicked, || so that justice is the girdle of his waist, | and faithfulness the girdle of his loins. || Then the wolf lodgeth with the lamb, and the leopard reposeth with the kid, | and calf and young lion and fatling are together, led by the youngest child; || cow and she-bear will pasture, their young repose together, | and the lion like the ox eateth straw; || and a suckling stroketh the adder's feeler, | and over the cerast's flashing eye hath a weaned child stretched his hand. || They will not do evil nor commit wickedness upon all my holy mountain : | because the earth is full of the knowledge of Yahvé as the waters cover the sea. ||

5.

10   And on that day the rootshoot of Ishaï, which standeth as a banner of the nations, will be sought by the Heathen, | and his resting-place will be honour. || And on that day will Yahvé again a second time cause his hand to redeem the remnant

of his people, | which is left from Assur and from
Egypt and from Pathros and from Kûsh, and from
'Aelâm and from Shin'ar, and from Hamâth and
from the islands of the sea : || he raiseth a banner
to the Heathen, and gathereth the dispersed of
Israel, | and the scattered of Yuda assembleth he
men and women from the four corners of the earth. ||
Then the jealousy of Ephráim departeth and the
restless ones of Yuda will be cut off, | Ephráim
will not envy Yuda, and Yuda will not disturb
Ephráim: || and they fly upon the shoulders of the
Philistines towards the sea, together they plunder
the sons of the Easterns, | Edóm and Môab are
the seizure of their hand, the children of Ammon
15   their obedience. || — And Yahvé curseth the
tongue of the Egyptian sea, and swingeth his hand
over the Euphrates with the burning of his breath, |
smiteth it into seven streams, and causeth it to be
trodden with shoes, || so that a road hath the rem-
nant of his people which is left from Assur, | just
as Israel had it when it marched up out of Egypt.

XII.

1   And thou singest on that day :—

> I will praise thee Yahvé! for thou wast angry with me,
>> thine anger is allayed and thou comfortest me ;
> behold the God of my salvation,
>> I trust and tremble not,
> for my boast and my song is Yah Yahvé,
>> and he became my salvation.

Thus ye draw water with delight | from the wells of salvation || and sing on
that day :—

Give thanks unto Yahvé, call upon his name,
  proclaim among the nations his deeds,
  boast that his name is exalted !
play unto Yahvé, that he did great things ;
  let this be known in all the earth !
Rejoice aloud thou citizen Ssion,
  that great amongst you is Israel's Holy One !

1. The very first words issue from the fundamental thought
of the entire oration. The Assyrian is in Yahvé's sight simply
the instrument to execute his terrible anger ; he has received
all his present power from Yahvé (not from himself), as something lent to him for a definite commission and purpose,
namely, to spoil and to subdue, within the limits defined in
ver. 6, the nations who deserve punishment.   That is a divine
appointment or the will of Yahvé concerning him ; hence the
pres. ver. 6.   But then he desires to be something on his own
account, to determine his own destination ; he intends to
execute destruction, and the destruction of as many nations as
possible, ver. 7, in haughty pride over-estimating his power,
boasting that he is the king of kings, whose princes (courtiers)
are all equal to kings, and vaunting that all foreign lands (with
regard to the names, ver. 9, comp. *History of Israel*, IV. 150
(III. 638), without distinction met the same doom from him
and his omnipotence, so that if all the Heathen kingdoms
beginning from the extreme north had been subdued by him,
although in his view their gods had been much more numerous
and more powerful than those of the Israelite kingdoms, yea,
if even Samaria's gods had not been able to stand against him,
surely little Yuda, with its very few, really hardly visible, idol-
images, will form no exception ! vv. 8-11, comp. xxxvi. 6, 7, 19 ;
xxxvii. 13.   As a Heathen he speaks as if he knew in all kingdoms nothing but idols, powerful or weak ones, many or few,
according to the material greatness of the countries ; although
the Hebrew distinction of the Heathen or idol kingdoms
appears, vv. 10, 11.—Yet Yahvé (the prophetic language inter-

rupting the exposition of the Assyrian's thought) will at the right time, when he will finish the entire work which he has promised (ver. 12 as xxviii. 21) punish this insolent pride, that he imagines that he has done everything by his own power and wisdom, and boasts that he has in his hands as a God the fate of nations and kings, or that like a mischievous boy he can destroy nests while nothing dares to stir against him ! vv. 12-14 : but has one ever heard that the instrument boasts itself against its owner and master ? that would be in reality as if it should put in motion that which moves it, as if the wooden rod should raise that which is verily quite different from wood, the arm that raises it ! Thus the discourse returns, ver. 15, with a severe, taunting proof to its fundamental thought and even to its first words, ver. 5.

2. The deserved punishment must therefore overtake him, vv. 16-19, which is now more particularly described, while it had been hardly indicated, ver. 12, and there was no further space for its fuller description in the first strophe. It is true that the Assyrian armies are at present there as in close, fat columns (repeated Ps. lxxviii. 31) : but as a consumption soon consumes even the fattest body, so Yahvé sends into the fat limbs of the Assyrian an insidious disease, so that he soon declines, xvii. 4 ; or rather a sudden fire, namely, the wrath of Yahvé heated to a fire, is enkindled under his majesty and splendour (the commander at the head of the army), quickly seizing everything, both what is low, the rapidly consumed thorns and thistles, and what is high, the lofty forest and fruit trees, comp. ix. 13, 17 ; xxxii. 15, 16. These two figures appear, ver. 16, side by side, but subsequently, vv. 17-19, they are more closely interwoven, in accordance with a frequent custom of Yesaya's, yet in such a way that the more forcible one of fire takes the lead. Then the reformed and purified remnant of the nation will possess without interruption the true confidence in the true helper, and no more in such helpers as the Assyrians who were once called in by Ahaz, who are

really its destroyers, ver. 20; yea (the discourse breaks out
with joyous emotion), the thought upon which all hope is based
remains, that the remnant of the ancient community will yet
be converted to the Hero-God, the true helper (ix. 5), ver. 21
—it is true, not more than a remnant, a very small number;
destruction is once for all unalterably decided, bringing in
righteousness in full streams (for all sinners without distinction, including the many in Jerusalem), ver. 22, for precisely
in the centre of the earth, at Ssion, will Yahvé hold this judgment, ver. 23, how few will then be able to stand! comp.
xxxiii. 13-16, and ch. xviii. This would be the place to speak
more fully about the internal shortcomings of the nation which
still remain unamended; but Yesaya is satisfied to make only
these few backward references, spoken however with great
emotion, to earlier prophecies, xxviii. and xxii., since the
discourse hastens rather to console the nation in its state of
overwhelming distress.

3. Therefore, because the punishment of the Assyrian is so
certain, have no fear of him who now, as the Egyptian formerly, brandishes over you the slave-driver's stick! ver. 24:
for in a little time (acc. xxix. 17) the trying, hot hour of the
divine wrath passes over from Israel, vv. 5, 6, and directs itself
on the contrary against the Assyrians, to destroy them; and as
Yahvé formerly chastised Midyan, ix. 3, or rather as he chastised the Egyptian and the Red Sea in the time of Moses, so
will he now swing his scourge over the Assyrian; and if the
Assyrian's tyranny is now Egyptian, so will he also feel the
Egyptian rod which was once brandished over the Red Sea, vv.
25, 26. If it is therefore an old proverb, "ruined is a *youth*
by fat," and if children who suffer from a too rapid accumulation
of fat more easily perish, so will that Assyrian body, which acc.
ver. 16, has long ago grown too fat, quickly waste away, so
that Israel will get free of his *yoke* just as formerly it was freed
from that of Egypt. This is expressed in ver. 27 in a paronomasia between *yoke* [Germ. *joch*] and *youth* [Germ. *junge*],

which is much more perceptible in Hebrew than in our language.—It is probable enough that he may advance with a well
armed host, and in rapid marches, against the Sanctuary,
spreading terror everywhere by his approach, yea, he may in
the presence of it raise his insolent hand threateningly against
it, vv. 28-32 : but at that moment there descends suddenly
upon him what seems to be an overwhelming tempest from on
high, discrowning even the loftiest trees, and soon hewing
down as with an axe all that proud forest which was mentioned
ver. 18, were it not really a *Most Exalted One*, or a Most
Mighty One, namely Yahvé himself, the Hero-God, ver. 21,
who hurls them down and for ever humbles their pride, vv. 33,
34, comp. vv. 17, 18 ; ix. 18 ; ii. 9 ; "Zech." xi. 1, 3. The
vivid description of the enemy falls of itself in conformity with
the phenomena of the march into three parts : (1) he comes
rapidly from the north-east over the Yordan, enters at 'Aiyath
Yuda's territory, and soon sends his baggage by another way,
that he may surprise Jerusalem more quickly, ver. 28 ; (2)
while he is coming on the first day as far as Géba', all the
neighbouring places tremble, one place has to proclaim the
terrible news to another as it were in responsive chorus (for
what they have to do is to flee as quickly as they can), already
all are in the greatest confusion, and carry off whatever they
can get away, vv. 29-31 ; (3) yet he hastens on the second day
as rapidly as he can still further, must before this day is gone
rest at Nob, near Jerusalem, in order that on the third day
he may attack it early, yea, already he sees the Sanctuary, and
swings his hand threateningly against it, ver. 32. To fully
understand the description, it would be necessary to know
accurately the position of the various places mentioned therein ;
a contribution towards the fuller knowledge has now been
made by E. Robinson, *Zeitschrift für die Kunde des Morgenlandes*, Vol. ii. p. 354 sq., and in his two well-known works,
Biblical Researches. It is clear from the context that Yesaya
is here describing a future march as his imagination depicts it ;

the perfect tense prevails merely to produce greater vividness of description. But the fact that he could describe this future march with such particularity and accuracy, is fully explained only when we suppose that he had experienced similar marches in the past; the imagination is only able to expand and intensify what has already been presented to the mind, but cannot weave pictures that have never come within the range of experience and perception. However, we saw, xxii. 1-14, that the Assyrians had on a former occasion made incursions as far as the gates of Jerusalem.

4. xi. 1-9. After this great decision, when, as is said x. 20-23, the longed-for return and reformation of those in the community who are spared from the judgment has taken place, the blessed time will be possible in all its glory, and with it the coming of the Messiah. From the ancient stem of Davîd, which is now fallen very low, a new green branch as from the hidden ineradicable roots of a trunk will vigorously shoot forth (acc. vii.-ix. 6), upon whom Yahvé's spirit constantly rests, that spirit which looked at with reference to its nature is the spirit of wisdom and reason, looked at with reference to its activity is the spirit which adopts secure counsel in every case and then executes it, looked at with reference to its motives and ends is the spirit of knowledge and the fear of Yahvé, and in the triple alliance of true theory, practice and religion includes everything and is able to attain all divine ends, vv. 1, 2. If then this spirit rests upon him, he lives and moves every moment in the fear of Yahvé alone, as in the common and necessary air he breathes, not therefore in following the lusts of his own flesh and his own personal desires and passions: which in his capacity of judge forthwith manifests itself therein, that he dispenses justice and gives to the oppressed their right not according to what pleases his eyes or his ears, but only according to what is just and equitable before Yahvé; whilst he himself by all this possesses such inward divine strength, that but a bare word from him affects

the resisting, unholy earth like the strongest blow of a ruler's
sceptre, and a mere breath from his mouth slays like a pestilence
the wicked, he therefore has no need at all of those weapons
with which unjust and inefficient rulers have to protect their
government, inasmuch as his best preparations for battle are
justice and faithfulness themselves, vv. 3-5. But the further
consequence of this must be a marvellous growth of peace and
prosperity : all the savage and wild things of the earth cast off
their destructiveness (which may already be seen everywhere
as true culture advances), even the wild animals become as
tame as grazing cattle and a child that is hardly weaned
stretches out its hand in play to seize the flashing eyes and
beautiful feelers of poisonous snakes without receiving injury,
vv. 6-8. Sinners (in one word) will finally not be found in
Ssion, because the knowledge of Yahvé is then no longer dim
and weak as is now the case, but as inexhaustible as the profoundest ocean-deeps themselves, Hab. ii. 14.

5. But once more to the starting-point! As the discourse
started from the foreign relations of the nation, it must return
to them. Outside the sacred land itself, this *root*, or new
root-sprout (liii. 2), of the ancient trunk is celebrated and
honoured far and wide on account of such virtues, standing as
an exalted banner to which the eyes of all Heathen are
directed, to which they flock, seeking from it oracles and decisions, ver. 10, following ii. 2-4. But the prosperity which thus
becomes possible must according to the circumstances of the
time assume successively the following forms : (1) with regard
to the numerous prisoners which had been led away captive
into all quarters of the earth, Yahvé will cause his mighty
hand again to redeem all who shall have survived the time of
punishment, as formerly in Egypt, by showing to the Heathen
an exalted banner which they must acknowledge and fear,
namely, the Messiah as had been said, ver. 10, on account of
whom the Heathen release all his fellow countrymen so that
they are able to collect together again from the dispersions in

the holy land, vv. 11, 12.   The two principal tribes may therefore continue to exist side by side, without the conquest of the
one by the other : but, and that is—(2) further necessary as the
next stage, the mutual jealousy and enmity between them,
which has been the cause of so many of the evils that have
hitherto arisen (and especially the recent destruction of Samaria) must cease, ver. 13, so that then further—(3) as in
Davîd's time, with united forces all the nations which since
Davîd's time belong rightfully to the kingdom submit themselves again on the west and the east, ver. 14.   (The
shoulders of the Philistines is primarily the strip of coast
belonging to this people which rises from the sea, but in this
connexion the phrase is also taken figuratively from the eagle
as it flies with its prey upon its shoulder, and thus shows its
power over it, comp. Abulfeda's *Historia anteislamica*, pp. 84-5 ;
a seizure of their hand i.e., subject to them, so that they can use
them as owners use whatever belongs to them, which they
have merely to seize).—And to come back finally more directly
to Assyria and Egypt of which so much was said above, and
which as they are at present constituted seem to present the
greatest obstacles to the realisation of such a picture, all that
remains to be said is, that neither are they able to hinder
Yahvé's work : a wrathful word from him suffices to curse the
Red Sea, a threat of his hand with a burning, withering breath
of his anger is all that is required so to chastise the Euphrates
that it separates into seven small fordable streams, and thus
for the greater portion of the captives, namely, those led into
the Assyrian territory beyond the Euphrates, as easy a return
will be made as formerly for their forefathers from Egypt,
vv. 15, 16, "Zech." x. 11.

The passage xii. 1-6, with its two snatches of hymns, cannot
be by Yesaya : words, figures, turns of thought, as well as the
entire matter and spirit, are not Yesaya's, which is so evident
that further proof would be superfluous.   Besides, the foregoing discourse is of itself quite complete and finished ; it only

loses some of its beauty and force by this addition. The tone
and style of the passage point clearly to the period immediately
succeeding the work, "Isa." xl-lxvi. and it is possible that at
that time a copyist or reader, who beheld with joy a fulfilment
of the words xi. 15, 16, in the deliverance from the Babylonian
exile, supplemented the oracle of Yesaya with these jubilant
words ; see further on the passage, Vol. I. p. 95 sq. The connexion was easily enough established, although the very first
words, which were at that time quite common, *and thou singest
on that day*, are not in the style of Yesaya. Ver. 2 is from
Ex. xv. 2.

---

x. 5. The second verse-member is literally, acc. § 351 *a*,
and thou rod which is in their hand, *i.e.* who brandish it, *as my
wrath*, or my punishment. According to the well-known Hebrew
idiom the last words might also be construed *as the* (rod) *of
my wrath*. It is true that then there is a slight change of the
thought as it was most simply expressed in the first member,
and recurs again in the last words of this strophe, ver. 15 *b* :
but such a variation accords well with the structure of the
verse-members, and the same turn of the thought occurs again,
24 sq.; nor is there any reason for considering the words
הוא בידם to be a later addition. It should be remembered,
moreover, that the words which have been inserted in Yesaya's
books by subsequent hands are of an entirely different character, see Vol. I. p. 88 sq.

On the tenses of וְאָסִיר and וְאוֹרִיד, ver. 13, with which רְ שׁוֹשֵׁתִי
alternates according to rule, see § 343 *b*. The reading כַּבִּיר in
this verse would signify *the most powerful of the Rulers* : but
in this connexion, where the numerous individual kingdoms
and rulers are spoken of, that would yield a poor sense ; and
as poetry the *K'thîb* כְּאַבִּיר, *i.e. as a celestial being*, as a God,
comp. i. 24 ; Ps. lxxviii. 25, harmonises much better with the
whole context.

As when a sick man sickeneth away, is a somewhat free

rendering, to permit the reproduction of the assonance, ver. 18. [Cheyne has: "Like the sinking of strength in sickness."]

If the word עֹל, ver. 27, is considered to signify a *yoke*, we must suppose that there is in the words *for* (acc. § 353 a) *ruined is the yoke by fat* an allusion to the fact, that even in the case of the common yoke-ox, the fatter and more powerful he becomes, so much the more easily is his yoke broken by the expanding force that fills it, so that it may therefore be the same in the case of the nation which is at present enslaved as it grows more powerful. However, according to the common view of the prophets, a yoke of this kind is rather *broken* or *removed* by God himself in a moment. Since, then, Yesaya employs many paronomasiæ in this part of his discourse, it seems more probable that he alludes in the word *fat* to ver. 16, and in עֹל to עֹלֹו, and that עֹל is only a slight variation of the vocalisation עוּל, comp. *Jahrbb. der Bibl. Wiss.*, VI. p. 108. The use of the word חֶבֶל would accord better with this supposition, xxxii. 7; Mic. ii. 10; Job xvii. 1. Only it must especially be remembered that the phrase becomes plain only on the supposition that it is the application in this place of a well-known proverb.

In the translation scarcely any attempt has been made to render the numerous paronomasiæ which are used, vv. 28—32, to give life to the list of dry geographical names; comp. Vol. I. p. 70. Probably a paronomasia is intended also, ver. 30, between קוֹל and גַּלִּים or *Gālim*. Instead of עֲנִיָּה "*unhappy is Anathôth*," it is better to read with the LXX. עֲנִיָה, preserving the symmetry of the small sentences of the context.

It is easy to perceive that the true God is called, ver. 21, the *Hero-God*, and ver. 34, the *Majestic One*, that he may be placed in direct opposition to the Assyrian monarch with his ambition to rule the world. And since the first name in ver. 21 is used in the closest connexion with the Messianic force of the name Sheâr-Yashûb, *ante*, p. 75, Yesaya intends it to refer back to the

words concerning the Messiah, ix. 5 ; but it does not follow
from this that he is not thinking, in ver. 21, of Yahvé himself,
since it is to him that all that is said, ver. 20, and has further
to be said, vv. 33, 34, refers, and the Messiah is not brought
forward before the following strophe, ch. xi. For that the
Messiah could not come at once was felt at that time more
deeply by Yesaya than formerly, and he indicates this clearly,
xi. 1, when he describes him as appearing at first but as a very
young shoot from the Davîdic trunk in its weather-beaten
condition : the Davîdic kingdom as it then was must therefore
first fall into ruin. *The Root of Ishaï* is then, xi. 10, the briefest
expression of this expectation, since the young shoot of an
old weather-beaten tree is itself at first but a kind of root,
comp. Arab. *aṣl* Lebîd M. ver. 21 (?).

On לַיִּם, ver. 9, see § 292 *e*.   The חֹר, ver. 8, is a place
through which the light penetrates, *window*, Cant. v. 4 ; hence,
in the case of men, the hole of the eye, Zech. xiv. 12 ; and can
thus in the case of snakes very well signify their windows, *i. e.*
eyes, or also their feelers, just as מְאוּרָה instrument of light
= eye.

xi. 11. יוֹסִיף יָדוֹ is briefly said for *Yahvé* יָתֵן עוֹד.—Of foreign
countries 7-8 are named here again (comp. Vol. I. p. 319), at
the head of them Assyria and Egypt, as that age demanded, and
from them the series returns by the south and east to the north
and west, completing the circuit.   On כָּתֵף, ver. 14, see § 290 *e*.

The citizeness Ssion, xii. 6, is but one of the numerous new
names which gradually grew up from the poetical one of
daughter Ssion, Vol. I. p. 184 : according to all appearances,
Mikha, i. 11-15, was the first to introduce it ; it was not com-
monly repeated, as in the present instance, before the time of
Yéremyá, xlvi. 19 ; xlviii. 18, 19.   The introduction of lyrics
and pieces of lyrics, as well as the rapid transition from prophetic words to them, is a characteristic of the later prophets.

2. The Oracle concerning Ethiopia.

Ch. xvii. 12—xviii. 7 ; xiv. 24—27.

These two pieces, which are now separated, were probably originally connected in such a way that the second piece formed the conclusion; at all events in point of meaning their connexion yields all that can be desired, and we obtain then an oracle complete in itself. It is true that xviii. 1-7 would form a long strophe of a kind frequently met with in Yesaya's writings, so that we might suppose that we have here simply fragments of one or more longer orations : but the very excellent sense which arises from the connexion as we have above taken it, speaks against that possibility. The words, xvii. 12-14, which plainly belong to this later period, cannot be supposed to form a distinct piece, and fit excellently into ch. xviii. The other half strophe, xiv. 24-27, may have got displaced into its present position, because the later prophet, to whom we owe the Oracle concerning Babylon, xiii. 2—xiv. 23, desired to make it really the basis of his own piece; it is at all events more improbable that it formed the original conclusion to ch. xi., since the piece, ch. x. 5—xi., is a whole complete in itself, and, in fact, a somewhat different tone and style of discourse prevails in the passage before us : to which must be added, that no piece of Yesaya's has in direct succession above five strophes (iii. 16 is a marked subsection, in the same way as xxxii. 9).

The piece falls clearly only a short time later than the preceding piece. The main thoughts of the foregoing long oracle concerning the Assyrians recur here on a new occasion in almost exactly the same way, merely being put with greater brevity and precision. It appears from xviii. 1 that ambassadors had arrived at Jerusalem from the distant Ethiopia, for the purpose of observing on the spot the state of Assyrian and Hebrew affairs, certainly also to offer to the Hebrews help and an alliance against the Assyrians (comp. above on xiv. 32, p. 135). It follows also from xxxvii. 9, comp. Strab. 1. xv.

16*

ad in., that this took place a short time before the fall of
Sancherib.   The prophet could not think or speak disdainfully
with regard to this offer : for the Ethiopians, a people of good
repute generally amongst the nations of antiquity, could not be
by any means regarded by the Hebrews with the same suspicion as the Egyytians were.   Still he could not approve from
the Divine point of view : for here also he felt the force of the
principle, that true help could not come in this external way,
and that the Sanctuary of Yahvé would be preserved by Yahvé
himself.   According to ch. xxix it had already become an
established conviction in his mind, that the Assyrian would
soon fall by the Divine righteousness, that he would fall precisely at the temple of Yahvé, or, as is here more generally
said, in the holy land.   Well, then, the Ethiopians and other
Heathen, that is the conclusion and the new prophetic thought,
may rather look for the speedy fall of the Assyrian in the holy
land without their assistance, and in that way become acquainted with the true power and greatness of Yahvé and learn
to do him homage, which all lies in the Divine plan ! and the
ambassadors may proclaim everywhere the speedy overthrow
of the Assyrian !   When the eternal hope, notwithstanding all
the storms which at the present shake the world, has, therefore,
been powerfully presented at the opening, xvii. 11-14, Yesaya
utters, as the central fact of the entire piece and the original
element of it, his oracle concerning the Ethiopians, with-
holding from them no honour or commendation, and yet sacri-
ficing nothing of the higher dignity of Yahvé, xviii. 1-3, 4-6, 7,
and concludes with the strongest reiteration of the truth concerning the Assyrian, xiv. 24-27, as the plainest declaration of
his opinion.   Comp. *Gött. Gel. Anz.,* 1834, p. 914 sq.

The plan of the piece is therefore similar to that of another
prophet, which was explained Vol. I., pp. 325 sq.

XVII.

12   O murmur of many peoples, which murmur

like the murmuring of seas | and roar of nations
which roar like the roar of mighty waters ! ||
Nations roar as many waters roar : | but if He
rebuketh him, he fleeth afar off, | and becometh as
chaff of the mountains before the wind, and as a
dust-whirl chased before a storm. || Towards
evening—behold mortal-terror : before the dawn
—he is gone ; that is the portion of them who
plunder us, and the lot of them that rob us. ||

XVIII.

1   O land of winged boats, which art along
the rivers of Kûsh ; || which sendest ambas-
sadors by the sea, and in reed-ships over the
waters' face! | — go ye swift messengers to
the nation tall and nimble, to the people
dreaded since it arose until now, | the nation
of great power and conquest, whose land
rivers divide : || "all ye inhabitants of the
world and dwellers on the earth ! | if one
raiseth an ensign of the mountains behold ye,
and if one bloweth the trumpet hear ye ! " ||
— For thus said Yahvé to me : I will rest
and look on in my station, | as sultry heat
above sunshine, as dew-clouds in harvest-
5   heat ! || For before the harvest when the
blossom is over, and the flower becometh a
ripening grape, | he cutteth the branches with
pruning-knives, and the shoots he heweth.
away ; || they will be left together to the
eagles of the mountains and to the wild-
beasts of the land, | and the eagles summer

upon it, and all wild beasts of the earth
winter upon it. ‖ — In that time homage will
be brought unto Yahvé of Hosts by the
people tall and nimble, and by the people
dreaded since it arose until now, | the nation
of great power and conquest, whose land
rivers divide, | to the place of the name of
Yahvé of Hosts, the mount Ssion. ‖

XIV.

24   Yahvé of Hosts sweareth thus : | Verily as I
have thought it so it cometh to pass, and as I have
counselled it that will stand : ‖ that I break Assur
in my land, and subdue him upon my mountain, |
in order that his yoke may depart from them, and
his burden depart from their shoulders ! ‖ This is
the counsel which is counselled over all the earth, |
and this the hand which is stretched out over all
Heathen ! ‖ for Yahvé of Hosts hath counselled
it, and who will break it ? | and his hand is that
which is stretched out, and who will hinder it ? ‖

1. Everywhere is now heard the uproarious noise of the nations,
like the dashing of the sea, ver. 12, comp. Ps. xlvi. 3, 7 ; lxv.
8 : but let them roar—a stern word from Him is sufficient to
chase the Assyrian far away, ver. 13, a single night is enough
for utterly annihilating him, in the evening a fatal alarm sent
from Yahvé—and he has vanished before the morning has
dawned ! ver. 14, comp. Ps. xlvi. 6. The sing. masc., into
which there is a rapid change when the enemy is spoken of,
vv. 13, 14, points of itself to the Assyrian as the great object
so much spoken of in those days ; this is, however, a peculiarity
of the oracle before us, comp. xviii. 6 *b*.

2. xviii. 1-3. This truth that the Assyrian will very shortly

fall in the holy land by the hand of Yahvé, and that a
tremendous event is impending, let the Ethiopians give heed
to, let the messengers, which this nation with its marvellously
rapid movements has now sent to Jerusalem, proclaim when they
return thence, wherever they go calling to all to attend carefully to the next signal of alarm which will be given in the
distance (ver. 3, comp. xiii. 2; v. 26; xi. 12): it is the signal
that the great event which the prophet here foretells has taken
place in the holy land, the event which the following words immediately elucidate, vv. 4-6.   Thus the extraordinary and distant
nation, which sends its messengers with such rapidity in Papyrus-
boats over the Nile, may even serve to spread more quickly
the fame of Yahvé; nothing seems therefore at this moment
more important to the prophet than precisely its rapidity of
movement, he calls it accordingly at the commencement a nation
of boats with wings, possessing winged ships, comp. xi. 14, a
nation which although it dwells along the rivers of Ethiopia,
i.e., very far off, can yet send very rapid messengers and other
things by means of its light Nile-boats of Papyrus (Job ix. 26;
scholia to Lucian's *De dea Syra, cap.* vii., Heeren's *Historische
Werke* part xiv. p. 374; Layard's *Discoveries* p. 552; Heuglin in
Ausland for 1857, p. 1185).   For though at the present
moment it seems as if Yahvé will calmly look on from his
station in heaven, and wait for the proper time, yet it is really
as when, in the hottest summer days at the approaching harvest,
sultry heat with bright dew-clouds for a long time hangs over
the sunshine: the sultry heat will not subside, rain will not
come, but unexpectedly a tempest arises and then causes the
greater destruction.   For this tempest, as is said to limit the
time, ver. 5, must burst before the harvest; the Assyrians have
already such a position that little remains for them to attempt,
their grapes are just about to ripen: nevertheless before they
ripen Yahvé will destroy the entire vineyard, so completely
cut off the proud and luxuriant branches and vines that they
lose the harvest; thus, ver. 5, there is a rapid change to the

new figure of cutting off with the sickle (acc. Joel iv. 13,
comp. xvii. 10, 11) ; and the next verse, ver. 6, immediately
explains that this divine sickle casts to the ground a mighty
army of men, which is so immensely great that the birds and
beasts of prey feast upon its carcases a whole year or more,
comp. Ps. lxxvi. 13. But then the honoured nation of the
Ethiopians may and will at last bring its homage to the place
where the *name* of Yahvé, who has done these things, is called
upon and resides, ver. 7.

3. Yea, the Assyrian (here plainly mentioned for the first
time), shall fall in the holy land, the discourse continues, returning to its commencement; with the most sacred oath this
is here declared, and who will be able to hinder it ? xiv. 24-28,
comp. xviii. 3, and ix. 3 ; x. 27 ; v. 25 ; vii. 7 ; viii. 10. These
verses have completely the appearance of being the conclusion
of a larger whole : they cannot form an independent oracle,
because neither the Assyrian nor Israel is addressed. In view
of this peculiarity also it has the appearance of being the conclusion to the foregoing piece, in which the language and the
thoughts bear upon a third party—the Ethiopians.

---

xviii. 1-7. מֵעֵבֶר is in this place *along*, properly *opposite*,
as all such land in general lies opposite the rivers, just as Josh.
xii. 7, יָמָּה — בְּעֵבֶר over against the Yordan *towards the
West*, *i.e.*, westward of the Yordan ; whilst when the land
which lies beyond a river is alone intended, it is more distinctly
described as situated *on the other side, beyond ;* but our word
can never signify that which lies on *this side,* or the opposite of
what is on *that side,* (comp. *Jahrbb. der Bibl. Wiss.* VII. p. 211
sq ; Origen on Matt. xxiv. 10 (tom. iii. p. 858, ed. Delarue), it
is true, explains the Ethiopians *beyond the river* to mean only
that they were the most distant people of this name). Who
are in the prophet's mind he himself explains at the end :
"whose land streams divide." The translation "land of *fluttering*

of wings," *i.e.*, of fluttering wings, rapidly arriving at a place,
would supply a partial interpretation of the word צלצל; but
since the LXX, although they did not understand the whole
passage, nevertheless translated the word by πλοῖα, as if
they had a clear knowledge of its force, since further the Arab.
az-zolzol, Qam. p. 1495, is explained by *as-sufun* and the root
salla in Ethiopic is actually used of *swimming* wood, the signification of *ships*, which suits the context best, is without doubt
the true one: they must have been, however, a special kind of
small ships or boats.   In respect of its radicals (§. 49 *b*) the
Arab. *kalkal*, (hence the more modern *kelek*) in Edrîsi 3, 5
under Qolzum, is related.—It appears from the opening that
the ambassadors which are to go to the distant nation had been
sent by the nation itself.   The nation is described in terms of
deserved respect : (1) *tall* (lit. *extended*), which was true of the
Ethiopians, xlv. 14 ; Herod. iii. 20, 114, and yet *nimble*, not
sluggish, but as is proved by their ships very quick and agile,
comp. Arab. *amrat*, smooth, light, nimble, *Notices et Extr.* tom.
xii. p. 644 ; (2) *dreaded* by other nations *since it is*, since its
origin, *and further*, until now, §. 297 *c ;* (3) a nation of *great
power and trampling* that can subdue whatever it desires, which
again is in agreement with the descriptions which the Ancients
give of the Ethiopians, Herod. iii. 17-25 ; and (4) whose land
is divided by *streams*, which is also a great advantage in
southern countries, while with this particular the description
comes back to its commencement, ver. 1.

On ver. xviii. 7*a*.   On account of the similarity of the
details of the description we must conclude that מִן has fallen
out before עַם, as elsewhere מֵעַם and מִן alternate with the verse-
members.

3. The typical warning for Egyptians and Ethiopians.
ch. xx.

It may be easily imagined that Yesaya often spoke with
reference to the trust in Egypt as we have heard him, xxx. 1-7 ;

xxxi. 1-3. He would do this at all times and on every occasion
both openly and by signs. For the hankering after such an
alliance which the people in Jerusalem could not let go,
received fresh encouragement from Ethiopia, inasmuch as this
kingdom, which was at that time very powerful and comprehended the south of Egypt (comp. above on xxx. 4), was no
less than Egypt alarmed at the progress of Assyria, and still
more energetically than Egypt prepared for war against it,
comp. ch. xviii.—When, therefore, the Assyrian king Sargon,
who is mentioned here, ver. 1, only, and probably succeeded
Salmanassar soon after the fall of Samaria, sent his general
Tartan (2 Kings xviii. 17) against the Philistine city Ashdôd, a
very strong fortress and the key to Egypt, Yesaya not only
anticipated its fall, but also that the Assyrians soon after the
capture of the border fortress would carry devastation into
Africa itself. This was what no one in Jerusalem would
seriously believe. But it seemed to Yesaya that they would in
the city soon witness a new spectacle, that they would see
African captives led into it in triumph by the Assyrians, to the
no small terror of the magnates of Jerusalem who were trusting
in Africa; it appeared to him thus although the siege was
prolonged through three years (just as later Psammetich
besieged the same fortress for a period of twenty-nine years,
Herod. ii. 157). He was very unwilling to speak further
openly upon the matter; during that time he appeared publicly
only in the garb of a captive, without mantle or shoes, in order
that all who were struck by his strange appearance might receive a hint of something new which lay in the mind of Yahvé
and was about to take place, as the prophet foresaw in his own
soul and prefigured in his person as the commencement of the
thing itself. But when the fortress was taken, and the fulfilment of his anticipation accordingly drew much nearer, and
when the prefiguration which the prophet had given without
speaking had accomplished its end, the spirit then urged him
to speak plainly concerning the matter, with the view of

afresh exposing the folly of trusting in Africa and especially in Egypt, as had been more particularly explained in the foregoing piece.

If we knew in what year Ashdôd was captured, we should be able to determine the exact date of this piece. Or if Egypt only had been spoken of, we might have supposed that it was originally an appendix to the previous book, ch. xxviii.-xxxii., designed to prove in another form what was there said. But since the Ethiopians also, of which there was not a word said, ch. xxviii.-xxxii., are mentioned, and moreover, according to ver. 4, with greater honour than the Egyptians, we consider the piece belongs more properly to this book; and as a fact it is separated from xvii. 12—ch. xviii. merely by the later introduction of the piece, ch. xix.

XX.

1   In the year when Tartan came to Ashdôd, sent by Sargon the king of Assyria, (and he besieged Ashdôd then and took it): ‖ in that time Yahvé spake by Yesaya the son of 'Amôss thus : " Go and loose the prophet's mantle from thy loins, | and thy shoe draw off from thy foot!" ‖ and he did so, went naked and barefoot. ‖ — Then said Yahvé : As my servant Yesaya hath gone naked and barefoot three years, | as a sign and a portent concerning Egypt and concerning Kûsh : ‖ so will the king of Assur lead away naked and barefoot the captives of Egypt and the exiles of Kûsh, youths and old men; | while those bared at
5 the buttocks are the shame of Egypt. ‖ Then will they be alarmed and ashamed of Kûsh their hope, and of Egypt their boast, ‖ and the inhabitant of this coast saith on that day : behold so fareth

our hope to which we fled for help to save us
from the king of Assur : | and how should we
escape ! ‖

It is a merely prefatory remark, ver. 1, and made in order to
dismiss the narrative concerning Tartan, that he took the city
after a siege, which is subsequently, ver. 3, said to have lasted
three years, whilst ver. 2 returns to the commencement of
ver. 1. Yet the complete understanding of the subsequent
verses, ver. 3 sq., is assisted by the knowledge of the fact that
the siege was finally successful. We had a similar case above,
vii. 1.—The prophet's mantle, beneath which nothing more was
worn than a short undergarment, or shirt, is called, ver. 2, a
saq, because like the mourning garment it was made of coarse
black hair, comp. Zech. xiii. 4; Matt. iii. 4; Rev. xi. 3; whoever wears nothing more than a shirt is in ordinary language
said to be naked.—The second member of ver. 4 is clearly intended to express something which has very special reference
to the Egyptians, who, acc. ch. xviii., were considered to be
much more contemptible and base in the estimation of the
world than were the Ethiopians ; it must therefore be taken as
a special sentence describing how the Egyptians were led
captive in a still more lamentable and humiliating manner than
the Ethiopians. The captives belonging to a wealthier and
superior nation may very well make a better appearance with
regard to behaviour and clothing even in captivity. The
general, somewhat contemptuous use of *they*, or *one*, with which
Yesaya really means the magnates of Jerusalem, is peculiar to
this prophet, as is also the similarly disdainful appellation, *this
people*, ver. 5; i. 29; xxxi. 6; xxviii. 7. But when Yesaya
immediately speaks, ver. 6, of the inhabitants *of this coast*, it
follows from the entire force and context of this and all other
oracles, that he especially intends thereby really the magnates
of Jerusalem again, yet inasmuch as the remaining inhabitants
of the coast of Palestine, the Phœnicians and Philistines who

were not less oppressed by the Assyrians, might also share this hope, Yesaya was able to use a more general word here, the immediate reference of which was not obscure.

On חֲשׂוּפַי, ver. 4, see § 211 *c.*

APPENDAGE. THE ASSYRIAN AND JERUSALEM.
Ch. xxxiii.

The following oration really belongs to the last times of the trial which befell Jerusalem from the Assyrians, 711 B.C. Sancherib, who was also probably exposed to considerable danger from Africa, in anger determined no longer to spare Jerusalem. The ambassadors whom Hizqia had sent with petitions for mercy to Sancherib, as he was occupying the remaining fortresses of the land one after another, had been repulsed although their rich presents had been received, and it could no longer be concealed that the Assyrians intended not simply to humiliate Hizqia as they had done before, but to drive him from his throne and occupy Jerusalem as a military post of their own after they had led away captive its strongest inhabitants, vv. 7, 8 ; 2 Kings xviii. 14-17. But in proportion as the Assyrians became violent and insolent and everything approached the climax of a terrible crisis, the prophetic voice was raised against them as well as against all the unrighteous powers of the earth, and the nearer and more certain was the approach of a great judgment upon all the injustice of the earth foreseen to be ; from the midst of earnest cries to Yahvé for help in this terrible time, the threat against the prevailing injustice and the hope of deliverance and Messianic blessedness arise with the greater strength, and precisely in such moments of the most extreme trial does it become most clear what an inexhaustible supply of enthusiasm and confidence was contained in the religion of Yahvé for its confessors even in those later days, comp. vv. 5, 6, 21-24. This is at least the case as

long as there is a zeal which is directed against their own
shortcomings, as our prophet shows very forcibly vv. 13-16.

Inasmuch as the matter which the prophet intends to include
within the limits of his oration has grown still more varied by
the addition of the last named particular, it falls into five
strophes of somewhat larger size than common, the last only
forming a briefer conclusion.   In the first the prophetic threat
forthwith pours itself forth in a full stream, together with a
prayer and remembrance of the eternal hope, vv. 1-6; but in
the second, vv. 7-12, the prophet looks round about him and
describes the hopeless condition of the affairs of the time,
while as a flash of lightning there also darts through him the
truth, that there lies in the impossibility of the long duration
of these things the true pledge of the divine interference against
all injustice, not merely the injustice of the distant heathen
nations, but also, which the third strophe deals with, that close
at hand, that which still prevails in Israel itself, vv. 13-16;
till the oration after it has thus poured forth its violent feeling
in both directions, gives itself up in the last two strophes to
hope and calm, cheerful confidence in Yahvé vv. 17-24.

Whether, however, Yesaya himself wrote the oration is very
doubtful: though much of it as regards single words and its
entire spirit reminds us of Yesaya, other marks as strongly
point to another author.   Even in single words there are
observable differences; the poetic style is sought rather in
external characteristics, *e.g.*, in the use of particles אַף ver. 2,
כִּי אִם ver. 21, בַּל six times vv. 20-24* which Yesaya does
not use, in the use of יְשׁוּעָה, vv. 2, 6, the occurrence of which
three times in ch. xii. is no proof that this chapter is by
Yesaya, אֱנוֹשׁ, ver. 8, notwithstanding viii. 1, etc.   Equally
different is the entire imagery which here meets the hearer.
Still more perceptibly do we miss here the elevation and the
brief but wonderfully forcible figurative language, in a word,

---

* בְּלִי which is only found xxxii. 19, is in any case different.

the majesty of Yesaya's style; even his long full sentences
dwindle here into small detached and tripping ones; the character of the strophes also departs somewhat from his. And
precisely the most characteristic words and thoughts of Yesaya,
which he repeats everywhere else with an easy and pleasing
variation, are not found here. We may most naturally suppose,
therefore, that this was the oracle of one of Yesaya's disciples,
which met with a similar treatment to that of ch. xxiii.,
belonging to another disciple, which found its way as an
appendix into his fifth book.

1.

XXXIII.

1 O devastator who art not yet devastated, and
thou robber who art not yet robbed : | as soon as
thou hast finished devastating thou wilt be devastated, as soon as thou art at an end with robbing
thou wilt be robbed! || — Yahvé be gracious unto
us, in thee we hope, | be their arm every morning,
yea our help in time of need! || At the sounding
thunder nations flee, | at thy rising peoples are
scattered: || and your booty is gleaned away as
locusts glean away, | as grasshoppers run one
5 runneth thereupon. || — Exalted is Yahvé, for he
inhabiteth the height, | hath filled Ssion with justice
and righteousness, || so that the security of thy
times is a store of deliverances, of wisdom and in-
sight: | the fear of Yahvé — that is his treasure. ||

2.

Behold fearful cry without — | the ambassadors
of peace weep bitterly; || laid waste are the high-
ways, the wayfarer idleth; | he hath broken the

covenant, scorned cities despised men ; the earth
fadeth and faileth, Lebanon is ashamed and languishing, ‖ Sharon hath become like the desert, and
10 Bashan and Karmel become bare. ‖ — " Now will
I arise " saith Yahvé | " now exalt myself, now
lift up myself ! ‖ conceive ye dry sticks, ye bring
forth dry stubble : | your spirit is the fire that
devoureth you, ‖ and nations become burnt lime, |
cut off thorns, kindled with fire ! ‖ .

3.

Hear ye that are far off what I do, | and know
ye that are near my might ! ‖ In Ssion sinners
tremble, a shaking seizeth the unholy : | " who
will protect us from the devouring fire, who protect
15 us from the eternal burnings ? " ‖ He who
walketh justly and speaketh uprightly, | he who
despiseth the gain of oppressions, he who shaketh
his hands from taking a bribe, | he who stoppeth
his ear from hearing murder, and closeth his eyes
from beholding evil : ‖ he will inhabit high places,
rock-fastnesses are his defence ; | his bread is given,
his water never faileth. ‖

4.

The king in his glory will thine eyes behold, |
they will see a far-stretching land ; ‖ thine heart
will muse on the terror : | " where is he that
counted, where is he that weighed ? where is he
that counted the towers ? " ‖ The barbarian nation
shalt thou not see, | the nation of a dark inaudible
speech, of stammering tongue without sense. ‖

20 Thou shalt behold Ssion as our festive city, | thine
eyes shall see Jerusalem as a safe pasture, as a tent
that roameth not | whose pins are never drawn out,
and none of whose cords are ever rent: ‖ but we
have Yahvé there as a Majestic One, instead of
broad rivers [and] streams, | wherethrough goeth
no oared ship, neither passeth it a majestic fleet. ‖

5.

For Yahvé is our judge, Yahvé our arbiter, |
Yahvé our king: he will help us. ‖ Thy ropes [O
Ssion] hang slackly, they hold not the socket of
their mast, they spread no flag: | yet then will
robbed booty be divided abundantly, the lame take
some plunder ; ‖ and no inhabitant saith " I am
sick! " | the people that dwelleth therein is for-
given its sin. ‖*

1. The real truth concerning the Assyrian (although he will
himself not see it) is, that he who continues without hindrance
to rob and plunder incessantly, will find not only a limit put to
his power to rob (and how quickly that may take place !), but
as soon as he reaches this limit he will succumb to the same
doom which he desires to prepare for all other nations, and
which the enraged nations will turn against himself !—It is
true, that in this dark time, while the commencement of that
crisis is still invisible, almost the only thing that can be done
to sustain the courage is prayer to Yahvé, ver. 2 : but if it is
true that at no time has any nation been able in its perversity
to resist Yahvé's openly declared will and judgment, ver. 3,
the divine thunder will smite the Assyrian also with terror at the
proper moment, so that he will be an easy prey to those nations

---

* Germ. : *ist vergebener schuld,* a close rendering of the Hebrew idiom. See
§. 288 *b*, Gesenius §. 135.—*Tr.*

2. 17

which he barbarously plundered, and which will then run upon
him carrying off everything in greedy haste like locusts, ver. 4.
And there is a second consolation in the fact, that Yahvé is not
merely, as was said, ver. 3, exalted beyond all human injustice,
but has also as a historical event established in Ssion a living
fountain of justice, ver. 5 : yea, no other than that hidden, inexhaustible fulness of spiritual powers which are still ever
active in Ssion, this precious treasure and resource supplies the
best pledge of a favourable turn to be given to the present
calamitous times, ver. 6.   The repeated sudden change of
person addressed is very uncommon, and is possible only when
there is great agitation of feeling, ver. 1 ; vv. 2, 3 ; ver. 4 ;
ver. 6.

2. What a scene presents itself on all hands! Even the
ambassadors which were sent to the Assyrian, with the
humblest petitions and largest presents, to sue for peace, are
weeping (having been rudely repulsed by the Assyrian), crying
aloud for fear in the open streets, ver. 7 ; no one ventures to
appear again in public (Judges v. 6), since the Assyrian acts in
plainest defiance of all former treaties and promises, considering neither towns nor human life, ver. 8 ; yea, the whole land
appears to faint away at such cruelties as it must be witness of,
and its most verdant and blooming portions are destroyed as it
were from terror ! ver. 9.   It appears that the announcement of
ver. 7 was the latest news that had been heard : and it is as if
one heard immediately after the ambassador's mournful report
regarding the entire condition of the land.—But it is precisely
such a revelation of human injustice which most clearly shows
the necessity of a speedy divine judgment; now will Yahvé
arise as in the days of old! ver. 10, comp. Ps. xii. 6.   If that
which the Assyrians are now about, what they cherish in their
inmost hearts and desire to carry out, is nothing sound and
living, but like scorched dried grass, then that which they
finally bring to pass must be like dry stubble, worthless stuff,
which can withstand no fire, but will be devoured by it in a

moment, and their own ungodly spirit, their own aims and efforts, will be the fire to devour them, ver. 11, comp. i. 31; xxx. 13 (for the figure of the paronomasia, Ps. vii. 15; Job xv. 35): whole nations will be unable to withstand this devouring fire of trial and punishment, ver. 12, comp. 2 Sam. xxiii. 6, 7; Amos ii. 1.

3. Not merely they who are afar off, the Assyrians and all Heathen, but also they who are near, the people of Jerusalem, must give heed to this threat, ver. 13. For in Ssion itself there are those who must tremble at the threat, or at least at the fire of the judgment when it comes, and already the prophet hears their trembling cry of lamentation, as they will then pray for protection and succour from the devouring, incessant fire, ver. 14. But the only answer that can be given to them is, that only he who keeps himself pure in his whole life and in every respect, enjoys the true eternal protection, as if he were in an impregnable and constantly well-supplied fortress, vv. 15, 16, according to Ps. xv. 2-5.

4. However, when these unhappy members of Ssion are put out of view, there remains in it an eternal, secure hope, which enables it calmly to anticipate the storms that now threaten it from without. Though King Hizqia is now deeply humiliated and his land is terribly overrun by the Assyrians, and its capital is threatened, yet the king will be seen in his glory and the land in all directions freed of its enemies, and lying open, ver. 17, and with a proportionally greater joy will men then remember the present time of terror, rejoicing that the Assyrian is no longer there who numbered the people, to determine the tribute, who rudely weighed the heavy tribute which had been brought (to see whether it was not too small, like Brennus at Rome), and counted the towers of the capital to see whether they were not too many, ver. 18, comp. Ps. xlviii. 13, 14; the nation of wild barbaric language and habits, with which a Hebrew could never have friendly intercourse, will not again be seen, ver. 19. On the other hand, Ssion shall be seen as our festive

17 *

city, visited from all sides and full of festal joy (comp. iv. 5), and as an abiding tent that does not move from place to place, ver. 20; and then we shall have Yahvé himself, as the All-Powerful One, in the redeemed and regenerated Ssion, a better defence than broad streams and trenches which surround the fortress; if other cities have such fortifications, Nah. iii. 8, Ssion does not then need them, and possesses a bulwark over which no proud, hostile fleet can come, however dangerous it may be to other cities though they may be surrounded with mighty rivers, ver. 21, comp. Ps. xlvi. 5-8.

5. For Yahvé is ultimately our all, and our hope in him will not deceive, ver. 22: if Ssion now is like a ship with slack and rent ropes, ruined by storms, without mast or flag, still a higher courage will then suddenly take possession of all hearts, even of those who are weak and sick; a pure, sin-destroying spirit seizes all, and with a view to the immediate object—the victory over the robbers, vv. 23, 24, the discourse thus recurring at the end to its commencement, ver. 1; in other respects like Joel iii. 1; Ps. xxxii. 1.

Ver. 1. The reading כַּנְּלֹתֶךָ might be retained if it could be shown that הנלה from נלה = Arab. *nāla* has the meaning of *to attain, to arrive at the end, to come to an end :* but it is safer to read כְּכַלֹּתְךָ in this case also acc. § 244 *b*.

On ver. 7. Instead of אֶרְאֶלָּם (which would be "if I look upon them," and cannot be retained, because לָהֶם is never contracted into לָם, were there no other reasons against it), the punctuation should not be אֲרִאֵלָם "lion of God," acc. xxix. 1, which strange expression would not accord with the character of the ambassadors of peace, but אַרְאֵלָם as an adjective, § 162 *b*, from ראל = רעל Arab. *ra'ila, to fear,* a meaning which the LXX., although they had a very inadequate idea of the whole context, still kept the memory of; the subject מלאכי שלום is not introduced before the commencement of the second member, as xxiii. 11 and elsewhere.

On ver. 14. גּוּר to be host, = protector, helper, properly who will be to us a helper, *i.e.* keep from us the devouring fire, comp. Arab. *ajāra;* אֵשׁ is like a second object, construed acc. § 283 *b.*

Ver. 19. נֹּעֵז, or rather נֹעֵז, must be the same as לוֹעֵז, acc § 51 *b,* Ps. cxiv. 1, comp. Ez. iii. 5.

Final Words against the Assyrians.
Ch. xxxvii. 22-35, comp. 2 Kings xix. 21-34.

Yesaya was otherwise very active even in this critical time; indeed his unshaken steadfastness, founded upon confidence in Yahvé, now first won its greatest victories and became a most powerful means of saving the whole kingdom. The former discourse proves with what unsubdued divine energy and purity of insight he met the Assyrians at the last moment, when threatened by the Africans they demanded with furious threats and taunts the surrender of Jerusalem : it also proves how by the same means he sustained the hope of both the sadly distressed king Hizqia and his people. The discourse before us is without doubt genuine, but not written down by Yesaya himself and placed by him in any of his books, but was only subsequently received into the state annals as it had been preserved in the memory of contemporaries. We find it, there-fore, in such a form as would be dictated by the moment, without the customary division into strophes or other expen-diture of art. After a somewhat lengthy exposition of what is to be said to the insolent demand of the Assyrians, vv. 22-29, the discourse is occupied with consoling Hizqia and his people, vv. 30-35.

XXXVII.

22　Despiseth thee derideth thee the virgin daughter
　　Ssion, | behind thee shaketh the head the daughter

Jerusalem ! ‖ — Whom hast thou reviled and blas-
phemed, and against whom lifted up thy voice, |
that thou raisedst on high thine eyes, against
Israel's Holy One ? ‖ By thy messengers hast thou
reviled the Lord, | that thou saidst : " by the driv-
ing of my chariots I ascend the mountains' height,
Lebanon's distant parts, | and hew down its tallest
cedars, its best cypresses, and come to its utmost
25 lodging-place its fruitful forest ! ‖ I dig and drink
foreign water, | and dry with the tread of my sole
all streams of the Land of Distress !" ‖ — O hast
thou not heard how long ago I made that, from the
days of old how I created it? | now have I brought
it and it is—that I laid waste defenced cities into
bare stone-heaps, ‖ and their inhabitants with short
arms were dismayed and ashamed, | became grass
of the field and green herb, blades of the roofs and
blight before the stalk cometh.— ‖ But thy sitting
down and going in and out I know, | and thy rage
against me : ‖ just because thy rage against me and
thy godlessness is come into mine ears, | so I put my
ring into thy nose and my bridle into thy lips, and
bring thee back into the way in which thou camest.‖
30   And this is to thee the sign : that ye eat this
year what hath dropped out and in the next year
what groweth of itself, | but in the third year sow
ye and reap, and plant vineyards and eat their
fruit ! ‖ For the residue remaining of the house of
Yuda striketh root downwards, | and beareth fruit
upwards ; ‖ for from Jerusalem will an aftergrowth
go forth, and a residue from Mount Ssion : | the

zeal of Yahvé of Hosts will do this! || — Therefore thus saith Yahvé of the Assyrian king: he will not enter this city, nor shoot thither an arrow, | not advance against it a shield, nor throw up against it a rampart ; || in the way which he came will he 35 return | and not enter this city, saith Yahvé, || and I protect this city to save it, | for mine own sake and for the sake of David my servant. ||

xxxvii. 22-29. Thou threatenest with the most insolent words the honoured, unconquered, and inviolate virgin-city, xxxvi. 8-10: but she, on the certainty that thou rather wilt soon be compelled to shamefully raise the siege, already derides thee, shaking her head in derision at thy retreat! ver. 22.— But with regard to the chief thing, thy many blasphemies of Yahvé as a powerless God, xxxvii. 7 sq., 15 sq., 10-13, I ask thee, *whom* has thou really reviled with thy blasphemous words against the Exalted One? ver. 23, comp. lvii. 4. Yes, thou hast, it is true, really reviled Yahvé by thy proud boasting, as if thou hadst accomplished all thy grand deeds by thine own power and attained thy desire, as if thou hadst ascended and laid in ruins by the mere driving of thy chariots the magnificent Lebanon, with its everlasting cedars, a mountain so hard to climb and to hold, the symbol of the entire glory of Kanáan (Hab. ii. 17), as if thou advancing further through the desert towards Africa wert able at thy pleasure to call up water from the earth in strange territory, and by the mere tread of thy soles to dry up all Egyptian waters as a punish-ment, vv. 24, 25, comp. x. 13, 14. And dost thou not at once perceive the grievous folly of all this? hast thou never heard the truth, that Yahvé alone, long ago in the ancient times, per-formed all that potentially in his mind, and has now caused it to come to pass actually? *he* commanded to destroy defenced cities, *e.g.* those mentioned vv. 12, 13, into waste heaps of ruins—

and forthwith it was done, and the people, abandoned by him, powerless and helpless, passed away rapidly like perishable grass, or as when the blight destroys the young corn while it is still standing! vv. 26, 27. But how little thy wretched anger and thy boasting injures Yahvé, thou wilt soon discover from the fact, that he who fully knows all thy inclinations and deeds, thy wrath against him and thy dreadfully impious careless-ness (comp. xxxii. 9), will deal with thee as with a wild animal, will tame thee, and compel thee to retreat with thy purpose unattained! vv. 28, 29.

Thus closely are vv. 23-29 connected with each other. In-stead of עבדיך, ver. 24, 2 Kings has more correctly מַלְאָכֶיךָ, acc. vv. 9, 10; instead of בְּרֹב רִכְבִּי it is better to read בְּרֶכֶב רִכְבִּי "by the *mere driving* of my chariots," for the smaller the expenditure of effort the expression indicates the better, as in the corresponding בְּכַף פְּעָמַי (which Wellsted, *Travels in Arabia,* Vol. I. p. 281 sq., explains erroneously). מְלוֹן, ver. 24, is also a better reading than the second מרום, and the addition of זרים, ver. 25, is indispensable. *Land of Distress,* a poetic adaptation of the Hebrew name for Egypt, which becomes current precisely at this period, xix. 6; Mic. vii. 12.

Vv. 30-35. The sign of the truth of the Messianic promise which Yesaya now gives without solicitation to the people, ver. 30, is very much like the previous one, vii. 14-16, and contains substantially the same idea, only that in the present case it is more closely connected with the existing condition of affairs. This year there is nothing but what has dropped out to eat, in the next year what has grown of itself, and in the third un-hindered husbandry and the most splendid harvest! In this triple enigma lies the entire course of the immediate future, and in its truth a pledge from Yahvé of the future. The meaning of the enigma is evident. It must have then been autumn, and an autumn when no proper seed-sowing or garden⁻

ing could be reckoned upon, inasmuch as the Assyrian armies
had occupied and devastated, or, in any case, thrown into a state
of alarm, the whole land, so that in that year at most only a scanty
harvest could be looked for from *what had dropped out, i.e.* of
corn from the grains of the last harvest that had accidentally
fallen ; for the year following that the prophet is still without
hope of complete quiet in the land, he might fear that the
Assyrians would not so soon leave the land entirely, and besides,
according to the prevailing prophetic conception, a great change
must first take place in the people themselves, a decisive sepa-
ration and destruction of the wicked, which is not possible without a still more severe national calamity ; and as the seventh
fallow year must be succeeded by a further year of fallow, the
same is necessary for the restoration of the state to its true condition, a figure which was evidently in the mind of our prophet
(comp. *Alterthümer,* p. 502 (424), accordingly he anticipated in
this far more important case a second year would pass without
tillage, in which therefore only what grows of itself (*freigewach-
senes*) could be eaten, in patient expectation on the part of the
few who had grown equal to the severe trial, until a small number
of regenerated ones, after the destruction of all that was un-
sound and corrupt in the state had taken place, should begin
from the third year a new and blessed life, and the Messianic age
should commence at Ssion in accordance with the ancient promises, as the prophet, vv. 31, 32, himself explains in his usual
manner, comp. ix. 5, 6. The application to the case under
consideration follows naturally, vv. 33-35 ; with which the discourse comes back to the point from which it started, ver. 22
sq. However unhappy life may be during the next two years,
people will manage to subsist until the happier time, and
Ssion, whence that time must proceed, cannot be destroyed,
nay, cannot be even seriously besieged !

VII. YESAYA'S LAST BOOK.

The Conversion of the Egyptians and the Heathen generally.

Ch. xix.

Accordingly Yesaya witnessed the overthrow of the Assyrian supremacy and the restoration of his country; he saw the grand and glorious times, with the anticipation of which his heart had expanded, the ideal description of which he had so often eloquently sketched, and the possibility of which his own faithful and persistent labours had prepared. And although the fulfilment of the prophetic hope was not at that time quite so perfect as the prophet had desired and foreseen in the fore-castings of his heart, and the appearance of the Messiah especially and the consummation of the divine kingdom were delayed, still a great illustration of the divine rule in history had been again given, many wrongs had been redressed, and confidence in the final fall of all heathenism and in the omni-potence of the spiritual God of Ssion had been restored. Comp. *Dichter des Alten Bundes*, I *b*, p. 132 sq. 3rd. ed.

In the oracle concerning Egypt, ch. xix., we possess a very important memorial of the later life of Yesaya. The piece presents some few peculiarities which do not occur in the previous pieces (the particle אַךְ ver. 11, comp. however, xvi. 7; the orthography, קָמָא ver. 17 instead of חִגָּה, §. 173 *b*, comp. however, the earlier instance, Num. xi. 20); and the entire discourse suffers from a prolixity of expression quite unusual by Yesaya, instead of starting with sudden energy and rolling on in a bold and compressed stream. At the same time, we have here in all other respects the peculiar language, expressions, and thoughts of this unique prophet so clearly present, that there is no reason to doubt its origin from Yesaya, and the somewhat less brilliant colouring of the whole piece, the subdued fire of the oratory, must be ascribed simply to the considerably greater age of the prophet.

The historical indications also point to a considerably later period as the date of this piece. It shows no trace of the Assyrian supremacy; and although the internal dissensions in Egypt at that time would have supplied the best opportunity for an Assyrian invasion, and Yesaya would, therefore, in any earlier oracle have threatened the Egyptians with the approach of the Assyrians still more than he did in ch. xx., yet here Assyria is not represented as even distantly dangerous to Egypt. It is true Assyria is significantly mentioned vv. 23-25 : but not at all as in earlier pieces : it is here humbled and no longer far from repentance and the knowledge of Yahvé. On the other hand, the humiliation of Assyria already appears to belong to a somewhat distant past. We may, therefore, reasonably suppose that an interval of ten years has occurred between the last of the previous pieces and that before us.

Unhappily the *data* which would be most decisive for the view to be taken of this piece, the details of the history of Egypt at that time, are not at hand. The piece pre-supposes dangerous internal commotions, revolts, and difficulties in Egypt : in their causes at all events these must have been the same as those of which the Greeks give some accounts, the movements under the Priest-King Sethôs, the Dodekarchy, Her. ii. 141, 147, 151 ; Diod. i. 66 : but the detailed accounts of the time in which Yesaya could speak as he does are wanting.

But it cannot be doubtful how a prophet ought to treat such an event as that of the threatening internal struggles and calamities of Egypt, and what hopes it must create in him at a time when his own country is externally victorious and prosperous. If the ancient land of science and philosophy, which nevertheless still holds fast to the folly of the most varied idolatry and superstition, was visited with serious dangers, if its entire condition, both its moral condition as a state and

(which, as the ancients conceived, is very closely connected
therewith) its material condition, was most profoundly convulsed, and was in danger of dissolution, the prophet obtained
a gleam of light to irradiate the gloom from the fact alone
that he conceived the eternal, true, great Spirit, Yahvé, as at work
here also, with a view to destroy by his power ancient error
and strikingly to make the nation which was in its wisdom led
astray attend to his eternal truth. Yahvé, therefore, now makes
himself felt to the Egyptians who hitherto have desired to
know nothing of him: he comes as in a flying cloud into the
land to confound and to chastise it, yet not merely to destroy
it, but in order that it may turn at last to the true Helper and
Saviour when it has vainly sought help in its distress from all
the false remedies which it has hitherto used. And at this
final prospect and hope the prophet's heart leaps for joy. It is
true that he foresees that a single chastisement will not at once
accomplish the great work ; that Egypt which has been hostile
from the earliest times will only gradually acknowledge Yahvé
in the right way and worship him with true reverence : but it
is clear to his mind that that which is in itself necessary and
divinely reasonable must be attained to, that finally Egypt as
well as Assyria will fear Yahvé, and the religion of Yahvé will
throw the higher bond of brotherly unity and of equal divine
blessing around the three kingdoms of Israel, Egypt, and
Assyria, which had so long regarded each other with mortal
hatred. This great conviction is nowhere else uttered so
magnificently and clearly as here : but those times were of the
kind which favoured the conception of this free and blessed
hope, comp. Ps. lxx., and Yesaya was the great prophet whose
mind was able to rise to this free height, and he it was who
was able to close his long life with this most happy anticipation as his most becoming legacy to posterity.

The piece forms five symmetrical strophes of medium size
the first describes the general spiritual condition of Egypt, as
it at present is and as it will develop itself ; the second and

third describe more particularly how its sufferings, increasing from the lowest to the highest stages, will involve everything and with growing severity; until the two last linger at greatest length and most fondly by the pictures of the divine solution of this confusion and calamity and of the glorious end which must follow.

High-oracle concerning Egypt.

XIX.　　　　　1.

1　　Behold Yahvé rideth upon a swift cloud and cometh to Egypt, | and Egypt's idols shake before him, and Egypt's heart melteth in its bosom. || For I arm Egypt against Egypt, so that they fight every one against his brother and every one against his friend, | city against city, kingdom against kingdom; || Egypt's spirit is emptied within it, and its counsel I destroy, | so that they apply to the idols and to the ghosts and to the ventriloquists and to the soothsayers : || but I deliver Egypt to a hard master, | a fierce king will rule over them ; saith the Lord Yahvé of Hosts. ||

2.

5　　Then the waters fail from the sea, and the river drieth up parched up ; || the rivers become stinking, low and dry the streams of the Land-of-Distress, | bulrush and reed sicken ; || the fields by the stream, by the border of the stream, | and every seed-plot of the stream drieth up, is blown away and gone. || —Then the fishermen sigh, and all mourn who cast the hook into the stream, | and they who spread the nets over the water's surface

are cast down ; ‖ they are ashamed who prepare
10   combed flax, | and they who weave cotton ; ‖ and
its foundations are broken up, | all hired labourers
are sad of soul.

3.

Fools only are the princes of Tanis, Pharaoh's
wisest counsellors are a stupefied council ; | how
can ye say to Pharaoh : " I am a son of wise men,
a son of ancient kings !" ‖ Where then are thy
wise men ?   Let them tell thee | and know what
Yahvé of Hosts hath counselled concerning Egypt! ‖
The princes of Tanis are befooled, the princes of
Memphis are deceived, | and the Egyptians leadeth
astray the cornerstone of its castes. ‖ — Yahvé hath
mixed in its midst a spirit of giddiness, | so that
they lead Egypt astray in all its action, as a
15   drunken man staggereth in his vomit, ‖ and Egypt
hath no deed | which the head might do and tail,
palm-branch and rush. ‖

4.

On that day the Egyptian will be like a woman, |
will tremble and shake at the swinging of the hand
of Yahvé of Hosts which he swingeth over him, ‖
and the land of Yuda will be to the Egyptian a
terror : as oft as he thinketh on it he will tremble |
at the counsel of Yahvé of Hosts which he con-
cludeth concerning him. ‖ — On that day there will
be five cities in the land of Egypt, speaking the
tongue of Kanáan and swearing to Yahvé of
Hosts : | City-of-joy will one be called. ‖ On that day

Yahvé will have an altar in the midst of the land
of Egypt, and a pillar by its border for Yahvé ; ||
20 and it will be for a sign and for a witness to Yahvé
of Hosts in the land of Egypt | so that when they
will cry to Yahvé because of oppressors, he sendeth
them a helper and champion and rescueth them. ||

5.

Thus Yahvé maketh himself known unto Egypt,
and the Egyptians acknowledge Yahvé on that
day, | serve with sacrifice and gift, and vow vows
to Yahvé and pay them ; || Yahvé smiteth the
Egyptians, smiting and healing them, | so that
when they turn to Yahvé he is intreated of them
and healeth them. || —On that day there will be a
highway from Egypt to Assyria, the Assyrian
cometh to Egypt the Egyptian to Assyria, | and
the Egyptians pay homage with the Assyrians. ||
On that day Israel will be the third to Egypt and
to Assyria, | for a blessing in the midst of the
25 earth, || wherewith Yahvé of Hosts blesseth it
saying : | "blessed be my people Egypt, the
work of my hands Assyria, and my inheritance
Israel." ||

1. Egypt must now feel the mighty arm of Yahvé : he rides
as it were upon a swift cloud and at once Egypt with its idols
totters in wild alarm, ver. 1, comp. ii. 8 ; viii. 6. The particular
indications of this are (vv. 2-4) the breaking out of an endless
and widely extended civil war (Egypt already consisted of several
kingdoms, of which Tanis and Memphis, vv. 11, 13, were the
nearest to the Hebrews), in which they turn in extreme perplexity to every possible class of their false gods and sooth-

sayers; but all in vain, for the final issue of this as of all
violent revolutions, will be the rise of a cruel despot (which is at
present no more than simple anticipation, as may be easily
supposed, comp. ver. 20) ix. 10; iii. 3, 4; viii. 19. It is,
therefore, not necessary to conclude that the piece was not
written before Psammétich's rise.

2. However, the more artificial the entire condition of Egypt
was, amongst other things by virtue of the character of its
soil and the manner of its cultivation, the more intimately was
the interruption of the latter associated with the divine judgment, as if nature also (vv. 5-7) shared the wrath of Yahvé,
losing her vigour and beauty, and herself manifesting wrath
against unworthy human beings, comp. xv. 6 : and this would
in Egypt especially be quickly felt. As soon as the waters of
the Nile and its innumerable tributaries fail, not only the less
essential aquatic plants, *e.g.*, the papyrus, but also the rich
fields and crops of the entire country, even close by the Nile,
are as it were blown away by the wind and vanished, vv. 5-7.
The *Land of Distress*, ver. 6, as xxxvii. 25. But all the various
castes of Egypt (ver. 13) must feel this blow, so that wise
counsel and calm self-possession will be nowhere to be found.
The lowest classes, who can continue their quiet, customary
work only as nature observes her ordinary course, will be the
first to feel it; of them primarily the fishermen, so numerous
in ancient Egypt, ver. 8 (Herod. ii. 93), then the no less
numerous weavers of all kinds, ver. 9, in brief, all Egypt's
lower classes that live by manual labour, the broad and necessary *foundations* of the state, ver. 10. Similarly the priestly
caste is called, ver. 13, the *corner-stone*, the most important
stone, in the edifice of the Egyptian castes. It is well known
that the lower classes in Egypt were nothing more than
manual and hired labourers and enjoyed none of the liberties of
political life.

3. But the higher classes also, who in many ways share the
government and support the king with their counsel, have

been thrown into helpless perplexity by the blow, the wisest
amongst them becoming as it were a stultified senate, and it is
in vain that they loudly boast of their hereditary descent from
the most famous ancient priests, sages, and kings, ver. 11 :
were they really wise, they would discern the true causes of
these calamities, therefore recognise the intention of Yahvé
and what he purposes to do with Egypt, and advise Egypt
accordingly ! ver. 12. But that they cannot do, prevented by
their petrified folly : they who by their wisdom ought to be
the strongest defence of the lower orders, really only mislead
the entire land, ver. 13. Thus it appears, therefore, as the
true prophet knows, that a higher spirit has mixed and given
to the land this spirit of giddiness and drunkenness as an in-
toxicating wine, so that the people, misled by its own leaders,
reels like a drunken man in hideous stupefaction and not a
single action proceeds any longer from the consideration and
agreement of all classes, vv. 14, 15 ; v. 22 ; xxviii. 8 ; xxix.
9 ; ix. 13.

4. Thus the alarm of the Egyptians, who find no help in
their ancient faith, the alarm caused by the swinging of
Yahvé's mighty hand of judgment, will prepare the way, as
was already said ver. 1, for true knowledge and reformation,
ver. 16, as xi. 15, comp. also iii. 12 ; and inasmuch as the
people of Yahvé represents the visible dignity and truth of
his teaching, and there can be no other living channel of com-
munication between Yahvé and the Heathen (comp. ii. 2-4),
accordingly the fear with which Egypt then remembers Yahvé
will be transferred to His holy land ; and every time it thinks
of this land, it will be reminded also of Yahvé's wonderful
purposes with regard to it, ver. 17, from ver. 12, comp. xxiii.
8, 9.—The prophetic imagination, in perfect accordance with
the state of the case, conceives the transition from this first
reverential attention to Yahvé and Yuda thus : at first the true
religion will arise only here and there in Egypt, but having by
its effects proved itself to be a firm defence and real help in

the midst of the great trials of the land, it will then spread
continually further by means of its innate power. At first,
therefore, there are in Egypt only few cities, some five (xxx.
17; xvii. 6), in which Yahvé is worshipped, perhaps by
Israelites themselves that had gone into Egypt, as formerly in
the time of Moses : but one of these cities will experience the
Divine protection in such an exceptional and marvellous
manner that it will be called *Protected*, or *Happy*, *City*, ver. 18,
comp. a very similar instance iv. 3. Or, at first Yahvé has but
one altar in the land (Ex. xx. 22-26) and that perhaps on the
frontier, where monuments, pillars (Gen. xxviii. 18 ; xxxv. 14;
Josh. xxiv. 26, 27) are often erected : but that one will be a
token and witness of him amongst the Egyptians (exactly like
vii. 11, sq.; viii. 18 ; xxx. 8 ; xxxvii. 30) that when they turn
to this solitary altar and come seeking help from Yahvé, it may
be against their despotic rulers, they do not pray to him in vain,
but receive from him a powerful deliverer, a Moses or a Davîd,
who conducts their cause successfully, vv. 19, 20.

5. Thus the happy mutual relationship between Yahvé and
the Egyptians is further developed, so that the more he makes
himself known to them as the Righteous and Holy One, the
more willingly and actively they acknowledge him as one who
desires simply to promote their deliverance and welfare by his
chastisements, and turn wholly to him, vv. 21, 22 ; Ex. vi. 3.
—And then finally has come the fair time, longed-for by all
the good, when the three lands that are now divided by hostility
will be joined together by one peaceful highway and free intercourse, when Israel, placed midway between them, has no
longer alone, as the chosen spiritual nation, the higher Divine
blessing, but shares this with the others as the third portion of
a new whole, or as a brother shares the paternal blessing with
his brothers, vv. 23-25. Intentionally the words of the same
sublime benediction with which Israel was once exclusively
blessed by Yahvé, are extended also to Egypt and Assyria.
The division of the discourse into short, loosely connected

sentences with the repetition of the phrase, *on that day*, is not more perceptible here than vii. 18-25; ii. 17-20; iv. 1, 2.

Ver. 18 obtained a peculiar importance and occasioned a good deal of controversy from the 2nd Cent. b.c. onwards in the history of the Egyptian Jews. But the suspicion which recent critics have cast upon the genuineness of ver. 18, or even of vv. 16-25, is not confirmed by closer inspection. Comp. *History of Israel*, IV. pp. 464-466.

The שָׁתוֹת *foundations*, ver. 10, are in such a connexion as in Ps. xi. 3; Ez. xxx. 4, those of the kingdom, here, therefore, where the immediate context requires that meaning, the lower classes. Neither in those cases is the word construed as a feminine.—Similarly פִּנָּה ver. 13, is construed with the plural only because the priests and other leaders of the people are understood to be meant by this corner-stone, comp. Zech. x. 4.

Ver. 16, אשר must not be construed with יד but with תנופה, just as in ver. 25 it is construed with בְּרָכָה.—Ver. 17, כל אשר must be taken in a temporal sense, acc. § 337 c, *ad fin.*, and אל closely connected with הזכיר, as Gen. xl. 14.

Ver. 18, instead of החרם, the correct reading is הָחֶרֶס, but not חרס in the purely poetic signification of *sun*, as if the historical city of Heliopolis in north-east Egypt were here intended; for a historical city does not belong in the least to this connexion; but the word must be taken pretty much as the Arabic *al-mahrūsah*, which is still used of a city to which one wishes well, properly *the well-protected*, well-preserved, happy city. One reason for the Hebrew origin of the word is that the *sun* itself received that more poetic name only as the *guardian* of the heavens.

Ver. 20, וְיִשְׁלַח might be made to depend on the verb *to pray*, acc. § 347 a, with the signification, *that* he *may send* to them: in that case והצילם need not form the apodosis, but

18 *

might be the continuation of וישלח in this sense. Yet their
simple prayer for such a saviour cannot serve as a clear *token
and witness* to Yahvé : we must, therefore, be content to
understand וְיִשְׁלַח acc. § 343 b.

We must be on our guard against the supposition that עָבַד,
ver. 21, is merely an Aramaic word : in Yesaya himself, xxviii.
21, it is seen that in the loftier language it may interchange with עָשָׂה ; it is further employed here, as in ver. 23,
rather with the signification of sacrifice attaching to it. In
addition to those already incidentally supplied, a number of
other proofs may easily be found for the antiquity of this piece
and its origin from Yesaya. For instance, nothing is a
greater sign of Yesaya's authorship than the frequent mention of יָעַץ, *to counsel*, עֵצָה *counsel*, vv. 3, 11, 12, 17 :
but the idea of ver. 12 is reproduced as early as "Isa."
xlvii. 13. Further, the entire piece opens to us the clearest
view of the ancient Egyptian affairs previous to the times of
Psammétich, and is of unique value as a historical memorial of
them.

———————

We have recognised Yesaya's own hand in the arrangement
of his writings as far as the fourth of his books. In the
subsequent books all clear signs of the great prophet's work in
this direction are wanting. His fifth book, according to all
existing indications, remained without any connexion with the
collective work which he had himself already arranged. His
sixth and seventh books were subsequently added to it : the
chief portion of the sixth was appended to the longer pieces,
but the short pieces concerning Ethiopia and Egypt, xvii. 12—
xviii. and xx., as well as the older pieces concerning Damascus
—Samaria, xvii. 1-11, were inserted between the pieces concerning the foreign nations in the third book, and the latest
piece concerning Egypt, xix., before the short piece concerning
Egypt, xx. By this means without doubt the foundation of
the larger book of Yesaya's with its two halves was laid, this

book appearing still as ch. i.-xxiii., according to its later form of publication. But in this fusion of the sixth and seventh books with the previously existing larger book of Yesaya's, we cannot discover the hand of the prophet himself.

It was above clearly shown that much of Yesaya's writings has been lost. Many longer or shorter oracles of his were evidently inserted by later prophets in their publications with such verbal faithfulness that we are still able to recognise them certainly enough by the most vivid traits. The subsequent prophet especially, whose work is preserved in "Isa." xxiv.-xxvii., closes it, xxvii. 9-13, with lines which exhibit unmistakably enough in every sentence and almost in every word the characteristic spirit of this greatest of all literary prophets.

3.—'OBADYA.

1. The oracle concerning Edom, which has come down to us under the name of 'Obadya, cannot have originated, in the form in which we now have it, before the period of the Babylonian Captivity. The destruction of Jerusalem with the entire dispersion of the nation is clearly presupposed, in fact, particularly described, vv. 11-14, 19-21 : acc. to ver. 20 the prophet who published the book was himself in the captivity when he wrote it. In the disastrous days of the destruction of the city and the temple, the Idumeans had wreaked their ancient tribal hatred upon Israel to their hearts' content, as is minutely described vv. 11-15.* This is the sole occasion of this piece which threatens the Idumeans with their just punishment. From all appearances, it was written not long after the horrible events. We do not find it intimated that a definite danger had already threatened to fall upon the Idumeans : but as certainly as any base and underhand procedure in the end produces its

* Comp. further *History of Israel*, IV. 270, 274 (III. 802, 806 ; V. 105 sq.) *Dichter des A. B. Ib.* 345 sq.

own punishment, the prophet foresees the necessity of the
Divine chastisement of all such shameful wickedness and the
accompanying victory of the true Divine kingdom. From the
midst of the innumerable sufferings of the captivity and the
complete ruin of the external Divine kingdom, there rises here
the severe censure of the haughty kindred nation, and the
invincible hope of the victory of the true kingdom of Yahvé
and also of the restoration of the fallen Davîdic rule, which
seemed to be inseparably connected therewith.

2. At the same time, further enquiry shows with equal clearness that this later prophet made use of a piece concerning
Edóm which had been written by an earlier prophet. More
than a half of the present piece, vv. 1-10, 15-18, in respect of
matter, language, and style, points very clearly to one or more
of such older prophets. An additional consideration of greatest
importance is that at very nearly the same time Yéremyá,
xlix. 7-9, used the older piece vv. 1-10 as his own oracle concerning Edom, very much of it recurring in this passage of
Yéremyá from vv. 1-9 of our book, but nothing from vv. 11-14,
19-21, which most plainly belong to the later prophet. It is also
very probable that the two later prophets had before them the
same older piece. We can, with a good degree of certainty,
discover from the present book of 'Obadya, with its very
vigorous and unusual language, both the meaning and occasion
of the ancient piece. Our book quotes it at its commencement, in the least altered form, although with slight abbreviation.
A portion of Edóm, probably the capital Petra, had been unexpectedly attacked by enemies, completely sacked, and robbed of
its chief inhabitants by deportation; these enemies had just
before been Edóm's allies, and it was no evidence of the foresight and prudence of the Idumeans that they had suffered
themselves to be thus deceived by confederates. But the want of
superior wisdom justly appeared to our prophet as the more
humiliating, inasmuch as that nation was at that time often
boasting of its special and superior wisdom and culture in com-

parison with Israel.* And inasmuch as that prophet in respect
of language and artistic arrangement is clearly a contemporary
fellow-countryman of Yesaya, it is a fortunate co-incidence that
we are able to trace distinctly enough the historical occasion
of this unexpected calamity of the Idumeans.† But this first,
although more transient stroke, fallen upon this people which
was so proud of its precipitous rocks and fortresses, seemed to
the later prophet not only to confirm the earlier prophetic
threats against this nation, which had long since degenerated
in matters of religion, but also to be a prognostic indicating
how little Edóm would be able to stand at the impending great
day of judgment. From such a commencement the threatening
oration of the older prophet addressed itself to Edom, as we
see it here reproduced in almost exactly its original form, vv.
1-10.

When, however, we go on to examine the words, vv. 15-18,
we cannot, it is true, maintain that they formed a constituent
part of this older oracle of 'Obadya's concerning Edóm. Edóm
is indeed mentioned in them, ver. 18, but the entire complexion
of the language is not the same in these verses. It is also
clear that Yéremyá did not find these words in 'Obadya's
oracle concerning Edóm. There is very much in the complexion of the words that points to Yôél, comp. with ver. 15,
Yôél i. 15; iv. 7, 14;—with ver. 16, iv. 17;—with ver. 17,
iii. 4 ; iv. 17; and since Yôél, iv. 19, likewise speaks at least
incidentally against Edóm, we might suppose that he was the
original author of these verses.‡ Yet we know how much
subsequent prophets were in the habit of quoting Yôél's words ;
and the complexion of the words, ver. 18, points rather to

---

* See *History of Israel*, IV. 192 (III. 695 sq.).

† *History of Israel*, IV. 159 sq. (III. 650 sq.)

‡ In the *Jahrbb. der Bibl. Wiss.* IV. p. 47, is briefly remarked, how perverse the
recent attempt is to make 'Obadya the oldest prophet from whom we possess
literary remains ; and although the attempt has since then not been quite abandoned, it does not seem necessary at present to say more about it in this place.

a prophet resembling him whose oracles are preserved in "Zech." ch. ix-xi. In any case our later anonymous prophet has also used older pieces in vv. 15-18, since the words concerning Yuda and Yoseph, *i.e.*, the two kingdoms of Israel, ver. 18, do not in their primary signification accord with his own words, ver. 19. The conclusion, *surely Yahvé hath said it*, ver. 18, compared with the formula נאם יי, vv. 4, 8, may also be referred to an earlier origin, see *ante* p. 131.

3. In as far, however, as the condition of Edóm was at the time of the later prophet essentially the same, inasmuch as it still inhabited the same precipitous rocks and strong fortresses with the same love of robbery, the same confidence and the same hatred of Israel, he could present his own prophetic views as only a reproduction and further amplification of the ancient piece, and still himself publish it under the name of 'Obadya. And thus the description of the condition of Edóm occupies the first strophe, vv. 1-7, with hardly any change from the ancient piece, whilst the second strophe holds out the threat of the great judgment-day of the future, also on account of the quite recent cruelties towards Israel (and at this point the later prophet inserts his entirely new description) vv. 8-15, and the third makes the transition to more general prospects, vv. 16-21.

The heading :

Vision of 'Obadya.—Thus spake the Lord Yahvé concerning Edóm :

looks as if it, together with the entire piece in its present form, had been taken from a larger work of our prophet's, in which he had given a collection of Oracles concerning foreign nations. He knew quite well from the sources of his collection that the piece concerning Edóm, which he wished to place as the superstructure above his own, was by a prophet 'Obadya: and we have no reason to doubt the historical accuracy of his knowledge.

1.

A notice we heard from Yahvé, whilst a messenger was sent amongst the nations "arise and let us rise against her to battle !" ‖ Behold small have I made thee amongst the nations, | despised art thou greatly ; ‖ thy heart's haughtiness deceived thee, who inhabiteth in rock-clefts his proud dwelling, who saith in his heart, " who shall cast me down to the earth ?" ‖ Although thou wentest as high as the eagle, and if among stars thy nest were placed : | thence I cast thee down! saith
5 Yahvé. ‖—If thieves come to thee, if devastators by night— O how art thou destroyed!—they will surely steal what they require ; | if vinedressers come to thee, they will surely leave a gleaning : ‖ but O how are they of 'Esau searched, | examined are his chambers ! ‖ Unto the border all the men of thy covenant drove thee, deceived thee overcame thee the men of thy peace of thy bread, | spread under thee a net ;—there is no more any understanding in him ! ‖

2.

Surely on that day, saith Yahvé, will I make sages disappear from Edóm, | and reason from 'Esau's mountains ; ‖ then thy heroes despair, Tæmân ! | that every one from 'Esau's mount
10 may be destroyed without battle. ‖ For the cruelty against thy brother Yaqob will shame cover thee, | so that thou wilt be destroyed for ever. ‖ *On the day when thou stoodest lurking, on the day when foreigners carried away his wealth, | and barbarians entered into his gates and over Jerusalem cast*

lots | *—then art thou also as one of them !* ‖ *—But feast not thine eye upon thy brother's day on the day of his calamity, and rejoice not over the sons of Yuda on the day of their destruction,* | *and enlarge not thy mouth on the day of distress !* ‖ *enter not into my people's gate on the day of their misfortune, neither feast thine eye upon his affliction on the day of his misfortune,* | *and seize not upon his wealth on the day of his misfortune,* ‖ *nor stand at the crossway to destroy his fugitives,* | *nor surrender his escaped*

15 *ones on the day of distress !* ‖ For near is Yahvé's day upon all the nations, | as thou hast done will it be done unto thee, thy work returneth upon thy head ! ‖

3.

For as ye drank upon my holy mountain, will all the nations immediately drink, | *yea drink and gulp down and become as if they had not been !* ‖ But upon mount Ssion will be deliverance and it will be holy, | and they of the house Yaqob will occupy their possessions ; ‖ then the house Yaqob will be fire, and the house Yoseph flame,| but 'Esau's house for stubble, by those kindled and devoured, | so that none escapeth of the house of 'Esau ; surely Yahvé hath spoken it. ‖ — *For they of the South occupy the mount of 'Esau, and they of the Plain the Philistines,* | *and they of the mountains occupy the fields of Ephráim and*

20 *the fields of Samaria, and Benyamin Gilead :* ‖ *and the banished ones of this coast of the sons of Israel the cities of the Kanáanites unto Ssarephath,* | *and the banished ones of Jerusalem which are in Sepharad occupy the cities of the South ;* ‖ *and helpers come unto mount Ssion to judge the mount 'Esau,* | *and the kingdom becometh Yahvé's.* ‖

1. The present calamity has not befallen Edóm without Yahvé's will : for, vv. 1-4, it was preceded by very serious transgressions on the part of Edóm, *e.g.*, haughtiness and confidence in external assistance. Long ago, therefore, the prophets of Yahvé also anticipated such a crisis ; and before the present calamity occurred, they heard the Divine announcement that Edóm must be chastised (Isa. xxi. 1-10), while at the same time the cry, as in consequence of a signal and call from heaven,

or as by an angel, winged its way through the nations, that the movements against Edóm must now begin, ver. 1. The oracle which the prophets long ago heard ran, vv. 2-4 : Edóm which had hitherto enjoyed such a high reputation amongst the nations shall be deeply humiliated amongst them, because its own haughtiness deceived it, and it was so profoundly foolish as, by its trust in rocks and fortresses, to bid defiance to Yahvé the eternal, righteous God!—How wonderfully that oracle just then received its fulfilment is described by the prophet, vv. 5-7, in his peculiar manner, as if everyone who considers the character of this calamity must come to the same conclusion, that a higher hand is here at work. For if this had been a common attack, like those which nomadic nations are accustomed to make, Edóm would not have been so completely plundered, or so barbarously treated; thieves steal only as much as seems good to them, vine-dressers similarly always leave at least a gleaning: but, alas, how is Edóm wholly destroyed, completely robbed and ransacked! (Since the last particular is properly the chief thing, it breaks into the first sentence, ver. 5, with the words, *O how art thou destroyed!* in the very middle of this long sentence). And how marvellous that Edóm must be thus deceived precisely by its nearest friends and allies (Ps. xli. 10), thus caught in the net and made to see its nobles go into captivity and exile! Such being the state of things, there can be no other conclusion than that in Edóm there is really very little higher perception and foresight left, that in the great impending trial it will, therefore, succumb in shameful confusion and perplexity (Job xii. 24, 25), this conclusion being followed out in the commencement of the next strophe. The direct address is abandoned in the last member of ver. 7, the discourse turning away, as wearied from displeasure; the opposite is equally possible, "Zech." xiv. 5.

2. Yea, in the future also, on the great general day of punishment, Idumeans will similarly end in shameful confusion, and their proud warriors be overcome even without a battle, from

pure despondency (in some such way as Isa. xxii. 3, *ante* p. 159),
because the heinous transgression of cruel family hatred cleaves
to them unpardoned, vv. 8-10. Yet as the main theme of the
later prophet has been thus approached, he takes it up, ver. 11,
with his own words, and describes how certain it is that Edóm
on the day of the destruction and sacking of Jerusalem acted
toward his brother as only some foreign, wild barbarian could,
vv. 10, 11 ; it is true it stood only *opposite*, *i.e.* neither near
nor far off, waiting and lying in wait, with a view to indulge
quite safely its desires as soon as the best opportunity should
offer, Ps. xxxviii. 12 : but precisely such a neutral position is
baser than an openly hostile one, and as a fact Edóm did Israel
greater injury thereby than if it had acted openly, as appears
from the detailed description, vv. 12-14.—But let it beware !
let it not perform such shameful actions as it has here actually
performed ! The Divine voice of justice and the anticipation
of eternal retribution thus address it reprehensively, 12-14 :
for the general judgment day is near to it also, ver. 15. With
great emphasis the time of calamity is mentioned in the long
record of such evil deeds, at the end of every sentence, vv. 12-
14, since it is precisely at the time of the calamity of a brother
that such treachery and malicious joy is doubly culpable.

3. In fact, the general day of judgment will soon come
upon all nations, and as its consequence the redemption of
Israel from evil and restoration of the Davîdic kingdom : then
will Edóm's fate be also determined !—The great judgment
held upon the mount Ssion, where the sons of Israel emptied
the cup of suffering just described, vv. 11-14, is only as the
commencement of the universal judgment ; as they drank the
cup in Ssion, all nations shall forthwith drink the cup in their
countries (comp. Jer. chap. xxv.), but the latter, inasmuch as
they are morally quite different from the sons of Israel, drink
their cup in another way and with other consequences, namely,
so that they quite gulp down the dregs of the cup, Ps. lxxv. 9,
therefore become totally insensible and dead, as if they had

never been, Job. x. 19. Especially in the new strophe, it follows as a matter of course that the sons of Israel are addressed
in ver. 16.—In contrast with the fate of the nations, there will
be in Ssion, when this great general judgment takes place, a
refuge and salvation (as is said vv. 17, 18, in conformity with
Joel iii. 5, and other earlier oracles) ; and this mountain which
is at present desecrated will again become holy, the Israelites
will again take possession of their possessions, and animated
with new zeal and fire easily burn up Edóm as ripe and sapless
stubble, Nah. i. 10.—The new kingdom, that is, will be
restored (as the prophet's imagination goes on to depict it,
vv. 19, 20), at least as far as the ancient territories which are
at present held by the Idumeans to the north and the west are
concerned, so that the Israelites which still dwell in the
extreme south of Yuda inhabit the *mount 'Esau, i.e.,* the most
ancient territory of the nation in the extreme south-east, the
Israelites of the south-western plain by the sea inhabit the
neighbouring Philistia, at present Idumean, they who are at
present dispersed about the *mountain, i.e.,* further north in
mountainous Yuda, inhabit the middle of the country, Ephráim
and Samaria, and the Benyaminites the districts beyond the
Yordan; then those who are dispersed further north by the
Mediterranean, to whom our prophet himself belonged, take
possession of the coast as far as Sarepta, which was formerly
Kanáanitish but then Idumean territory, other exiles from
Jerusalem, on the other hand, who were living furthest to the
north, in Sepharad, take those southern cities of Palestine which
had become vacant by the above movement to the extreme
south of Edóm, comp. Zech. vii. 7 ; whilst in Ssion all the
helpers, *i.e.,* acc. Judg. ii. 16, the great heroes and judges of
the nation, then assemble also for the purpose of judging, *i.e.,*
ruling over, the then subjugated Edóm, and the rule of Yahvé
is consummated, the ultimate goal is reached.

Whoever is able to catch the true force of prophetic utterances generally, will perceive that the words of the whole first
strophe, vv. 1-7, yield a suitable sense only when they are
interpreted as has been indicated above, but that then they are
also quite worthy of an older contemporary of Yesaya. The
very commencement, v. 1, shows that although the words are
very similar to those of a Yesaya, they are from a prophet
possessing very marked characteristics : and this prophet will
never be understood unless the two following particulars are
borne in mind. (1) שמועה, in the connexion in which it here
stands, must have the same signification as Isa. xxviii. 19;
and (2) the context requires that the *messenger* should be an
angel, as if the very ancient and genuinely Hebrew feeling
made its appearance again in this case, as it was formerly
expressed Judg. v. 23. Only in the present instance it is
blended with the genuinely prophetic feeling in quite a new
manner : at the same moment in which the prophets receive
an announcement from above which they may further publish,
each in his own way, an angel is sent from above to arouse the
nations, so that they then say amongst themselves with marvellous unanimity, *Arise and let us, etc.*—With regard to שׂים,
ver. 4, see § 149 *f.*—That לחמך , ver. 7, must be connected,
contrary to the accents, with the preceding words (since it
supplies no clear sense if connected with those that follow),
appears also from the consideration, that then the two previous
verbs completely correspond in the rhetorical rhythm and
poetical structure of the sentences to these two nouns similarly without an *and.*

Ver. 9, מקטל can signify *without battle,* acc. § 217 *b* : if
that cannot be doubtful, it suits well the sense of the foregoing
member, whilst if they were connected with ver. 10, *on account
of the battle on account of the cruelty against thy brother, etc.,*
a pleasing climax would scarcely be produced.

It is clear enough from the whole connexion that the words,
vv. 11-13, refer to something in the past which Edóm ought

not to have done, comp. § 136 *f.*: but when it is said, nevertheless, ver. 11, *then art thou also as one of them*, as if it were in the present, it is because the horrible nature of the thing, *per se*, is before the mind rather than its temporal relations : a usage often found in such cases.—On תִּשְׁלַחְנָה, ver. 13, see § 246 *a.*

The figure, which notwithstanding its great brevity is manifestly brought prominently forward at the opening of the last strophe as of great importance, ver. 16, bears every appearance of being an echo from Jer. ch. xxv.; and there, ver. 27, its strong colouring also occurs, only that it is in each case represented by a different word (as in the similar passage, Ps. lxxv. 9), which must, however, bear essentially the same signification.

Ver. 19, the word החר has dropped out after the second ויר‍שו, as the LXX. shows : we have then in the *mountainous*, *i. e.*, northern Yuda, the otherwise missing link between the *Négeb, i.e.*, the southern slope of Yuda and Benyamin. But ver. 20 it is necessary to read with the LXX., אֶת־אֶרֶץ, or better אֶת־עָרֵי, before כנענים instead of אשר. On the ground of its orthography alone, comp. vv. 11, 13, חֵל cannot stand for חיל, and *host* would be here in all cases meaningless, since it was by no means merely people of the army only who were exiled. It appears to be used as a difference of dialect instead of חול *sand*, sand in the meaning of coast; with הזֶּה this prophet points to the district where he lived with the exiles here intended. But *Sepharad* according to this context would be naturally looked for further to the east of this coast; at the same time, supposing this reading to be correct, no one has yet succeeded in discovering the name anywhere else than in this passage notwithstanding the recent ingenious discovery of a similar name upon a Persian cuneiform inscription ; it is perhaps an early copyist's error for סְפָרָם or שפרם (שפרעם), a place nine miles south-east of ʻAkkô, where at all events in later times many Jews lived, comp. Joh. Schwarz, *das heilige Land,* p. 138 (p. 96 *b* of the Hebrew edition) ; in Reland's *Palæstina,*

p. 999, compared with the *addenda*, the word is merely forgotten; Niebuhr's *Reisen*, Book 3, p. 69.* With regard to
another possibility which would amount essentially to the same
thing, see *History of Israel*, IV. 162, *note* (III. 655). What has
been subsequently made of this *Sepharad*, is to us more a matter
of indifference : we might suppose it was *Hispiratis*, now called
Sbêr, or Ispir, between Armenia and Kappadokia (comp. Vivien
St. Martin in the Nouv. Annales des Voyages, 1847, May, sq.,
and Études de Géographie ancienne I., p. 250); the later Jews
themselves in the East made of it the Bosporus and the surrounding countries, especially the city of *Kertsch* (as is now
known from the Qaraitic literature), in the West they made of
it Spain as of the foregoing צרפת Gaul : but these are all
absolutely unhistorical conjectures. Whoever really understands the words, vv. 19, 20, will perceive that nothing else is
here described than the manner in which the Yudeans who were
still found dispersed in the ancient Kanáan may drive the
Idumeans both from their possessions in the north, whither
they had then advanced, and from the older ones; and so far
the passage has great historical value. We see here more
plainly than anywhere else what districts the Idumeans had
then under the protection of the Chaldeans taken possession
of; and other scattered indications of the same fact do not
contradict this geographical sketch. We also see what a
number of Yudeans still dwelt in a scattered way in ancient
Kanáan, although it might be in captivity.

---

* Perhaps the author refers to Niebuhr's *Reisebeschreibung*, ii. table 31.   *Tr.*

4. MIKHA.

1. Mikha comes before us as a younger contemporary and fellow-countryman of Yesaya's. The powerful oratory of the great prophet, which was fearlessly directed against the whole of Jerusalem and Yuda, is heard from the lips of Mikha with almost the same force ; the matter is very similar, in particular ideas, thoughts, phrases, and peculiarities of style, there is considerable likeness, only in Yesaya one seems always to hear the powerful original.

There is only one circumstance by which he is obviously distinguished from Yesaya, which also probably assigned to him a very different sphere of activity. According to the heading, i. 1, which in this respect agrees with Jer. xxvi. 18, he is from Morésheth, without doubt the same small town of Yuda that he himself mentions under the name of Morésheth, near Gath, i. 14. In fact, many indications betray the inhabitant of the lowland country. The complexion of Mikha's language itself is distinguished from that of Yesaya by many peculiarities of the kind which might be looked for from an inhabitant of the district bordering on the ancient Philistinian boundary as distinguished from the language of the capital. The chief point, however, is, that while Yesaya has everywhere the capital primarily in view and discourses and labours in it alone, Mikha has as clearly the country before him as the immediate sphere in which his imagination and thoughts move, although he is compelled to speak most concerning the capital owing to its decisive importance. It is especially the towns of the country that he sees smitten by the great calamity which his imagination pictures as coming upon the land, and he lingers longest by the description of their position, i. 10-15. And in his Messianic conceptions, while he follows the more definite and distinctly out-lined elaboration of them which we first meet with in Yesaya, he gives prominence to the country of Bethléhem by the side of Jerusalem in a way quite peculiar to himself, as if in this particular also he were unable to let go the country as his sphere of vision with its antithesis to the capital, iv. 8 ; v. 1.

2. We know from Yesaya how the internal condition of Jerusalem assumed an increasingly deplorable form until some time after Hizqia had ascended the throne, and how the most unworthy magnates nevertheless found prophets who were base enough to flatter them. It is against such destructive internal injuries of the kingdom that Mikha also contends. He raises his stern, fearless voice against the degenerate magnates of the time, particularly, as it appears, against one of the most injurious of them, ii. 5; iii. 10, perhaps the Shebnâ described by Yesaya, xxii. 15, 16 ; against the false prophets, against all the ungodly and destructive tendencies of those days, wherever and in whatever form they appeared. The increasing confusion in the internal affairs of the kingdom, and the impenitent, thoughtless life of the masses, may long have seemed to the prophet to be a preparation for an early Divine chastisement and a calamitous overthrow; and just then a new phenomenon appeared on the horizon of the time, giving a firmer outline to all future prospects.

For it follows with certainty from the opening of Mikha's book, that at the time when it was written the Northern kingdom was approaching its end with rapid strides : the Assyrians were probably already advancing to the final siege of Samaria. This decisive event must have greatly affected the prophets : the devastating tempest whose approach over the holy land they had long ago anticipated from afar, was already as close at hand and in as threatening a form as was possible ; the Southern kingdom was now more seriously threatened with the prospect of seeing the storm break over its borders also, which had been hitherto but little affected by it ; and a solemn picture of Divine chastisement, from which no thoughtful man could turn his eyes, was presented to all as a terrible warning. How natural it was for a prophet of Yuda to find in that event the occasion for his orations, is shown by the piece Isa. xxviii-xxxii, which belongs to the same period although according to all appearances it is a little earlier; it combats the same vices, though from another point of view and in connexion with a special question; especially is the same multitude of false prophets opposed as in Mikha's book.

When this event, occurred, therefore, the Divine tempest, which had so long been threatening in the distance, seemed to the prophet to be quite near and certain to descend with unsparing violence upon the holy land, and particularly upon Yuda, for the purpose of laying bare all false greatness in its nakedness and weakness. He can anticipate even for Yuda and Jerusalem, because the basis of good in the kingdom was corrupted, nothing but the severest chastisement, indeed the entire overthrow of the existing kingdom and the luxurious capital together with the temple, and beholds the realisation of the Messianic hopes only as proceeding from the ruins of the present irremediable state of things. Precisely this serious view of the present, this expressed necessity of a destruction even of the temple at Jerusalem, notwithstanding the certain truth of the Messianic expectations, is the chief peculiarity of this prophet, and according to the remarkable testimony of Jer. xxvi. 18, comp. iii. 12, it was also considered as such even in ancient times. Mikha, unlike Yesaya, who as living at the centre of the kingdom could better study and understand foreign affairs, did not occupy himself with the relations of the kingdom to Assyria and Egypt: but with the more unerring aim his words strike at the internal vices of the land, the covetousness of the powerful, the unrighteousness of the judges, the corruption of the false prophets.

3. The plan of the book, with this subject-matter and scope, follows naturally partly from the ultimate occasion of it, partly from the violent conflict with the false prophets in which Mikha was involved. He must hold forth the threat of a tempest of Divine chastisement, which is rolling up from Samaria over the

19 *

whole of Yuda also : but he must threaten this in conflict with
the false prophets, who, in order to flatter the degenerate
magnates, painted the future in splendid pictures of prosperity
and would hear nothing of a Divine chastisement of these
magnates. He is, therefore, compelled both in his threats and
his Messianic promises to prepare the way in opposition to the
false teachers, before he utters the pure doctrine, no longer
disturbed by them, and attempts the true mediation and reconciliation in the midst of this darkness and confusion on the
basis of the eternal, Divine truth. When, therefore, (1) beginning with Samaria, but soon passing to Yuda alone, he has
sketched in language of unusual agitation the certainty of the
threatening tempest of Divine anger against the perversities
of the magnates of the Southern kingdom, ver. 1, he collects
himself (2) to prove more particularly precisely this certainty
from its causes, especially with reference to the evil magnates
and their prophets, vv. 2, 3 ; that finally (3) he may show that
he, no less than the false prophets, is indeed able to promise
eternal prosperity and salvation and to sketch sublime Messianic pictures, but it is with quite another meaning and under
other conditions than is the case with the false teachers, chaps.
iv. and v.

These are the three genuine portions of this book of
Mikha's : each of them differs from the others with respect to
its entire tone and character, so much so that the structure of
the strophes takes in each case a peculiar form ; and yet the
same fundamental thought connects them indissolubly together.
With these three portions the book is completed and finished,
and both well arranged and closely connected in its various
strophes. The following chapters, vi. and vii., on the other
hand, form an entirely different piece, and belong (as will be
shown below) to another prophet.—Similarly the heading, i. 1,
cannot have come from the hand of the prophet in its present
form :

I.

1   The word of Yahvé which came to Mikha of
    Morésheth in the days of Yotham Ahaz Hizqia the
    kings of Yuda, which he spoke as seer concerning
    Samaria and Jerusalem.

This heading may correctly assign roughly the time at
which Mikha lived : but his book does not fall so indefinitely
in the time of these three kings; it must, on the contrary,
have been written in the reign of Hizqia, shortly before the
destruction of Samaria, which is also shown by the trustworthy
historical reminiscence, Jer. xxvi. 18.   The meaning of the
historical note of the heading, compared with Isa. i. 1, must
be that Mikha did not commence his prophetic labours until
after the reign of Uzzia, and was, therefore, younger than
Yesaya: in this sense it is not superfluous.   As little could
Mikha himself speak of Samaria and Jerusalem as equally the
subject of his book, since it properly deals with Yuda only,
and Samaria is mentioned only briefly and in passing at the
commencement: so that this note is intelligible only as the
opinion of an early reader who found Samaria mentioned in the
opening of the book.   It is further remarkable that in the
ancient historical note in Yéremyá, the name of the prophet
has a somewhat different, and, as it appears, more ancient
orthography, *Mikhaya*, LXX. Μιχαίας (*K'thîb*).—The real date
of the heading is discussed Vol. I. p. 94; comp. *Jahrbb. der
Bibl. Wiss.* V., p. 247 sq.

1.—The Judgment of God.

Ch. i.

Mikha is compelled to hold out the threat of the certain
coming of the Divine judgment with its punishments, of which
he has a foreboding.   He must threaten Yuda and Jerusalem
with these punishments; although they may not be overtaken
by them so soon as Samaria, they will not escape.   He must

especially threaten his own country with them, although it is
against his will, and even with lamentation and sighs, compelled by the truth, the causes of the punishments being painfully clear.   And who must not be most deeply moved at the
certainty of the ruin of his own people ?   Mikha at all events
is unable to repress the most profound agitation as soon as his
mind comes to confront the consideration of this ruin : accordingly, the first section of his book is entirely occupied with
this extreme agitation.   Mikha must pronounce the threat of
the certain coming of the Judgment upon both kingdoms : let
all nations on the earth below and Yahvé himself from above
witness the truth of the threat which he will pronounce ! ver.
2.   But he must proclaim that Judgment upon both kingdoms,
as he has so clearly seen it, both as to the nature of its coming
and its necessity, vv. 3-7.   Now, however, the thought approaches more particularly that object, upon which from the
first it tends to rest, namely, Yuda : O how profoundly is the
prophet moved at the closer view of the terrible calamities
which will befall the numerous cities and villages, great and
small, of Yuda ! vv. 8-16.   Thus the entire discourse unfolds
itself by successive outbursts in strophes of increasing length,
until the third and last at once takes more the form of a simple
lamentation, which obeys entirely the necessities of its own
peculiar tone and measure, whilst the oracle properly speaking
with its Divine *I* seems to subside.

1.

Hear all ye nations, and give heed O earth and
her fulness ! | and let the Lord Yahvé be against
you for a witness, the Lord from his holy
palace ! || —

2.

For behold Yahvé goeth forth from his place, |
cometh down and treadeth upon the heights of the
earth, || and the mountains melt under him, the

valleys cleave asunder | like wax before the fire,
5 . like water poured into an abyss. || — Through
Yaqob's guilt [is] all that, and through the house
of Israel's transgressions! | — who is Yaqob's
guilt? is it not Samaria? | and who is Yuda's
Heights? is it not Jerusalem? || Therefore I make
Samaria into a ruin-heap of the field, into vineyard-
plantings, | and pour into the valley her stones,
and her foundations I lay bare ; || and all her
carved-images are broken up, all her harlot's-
presents burnt with fire, and all her images I
make a desolation! | for from harlot's hire were
they gathered, and unto harlot's hire shall they
return. ||

3.

For this cause let me lament and wail, go bare-
foot and naked, | let me raise a lamentation like
jackals, a cry like the ostriches, || because incurable
are her wounds, | because it cometh unto Yuda,
reacheth unto the gate of my people unto Jerusa-
10 lem! || In Gath [*Tellby*] tell it not, in 'Akkô [*Weep-
ton*] weep not! | in Bæth-leaphra [*Dustton*] *rolled I
myself in dust!* ||

Pass by thou citizen Shaphîr [*Fairtown*] with
shame uncovered! | the citizen Ssaanan [*March*]
is not marched forth; the lamentation of Bæth-
haéssel [*House of Union*] taketh from you its
stand, || because about good trembleth the citizen
Maroth [*Bitter*], because evil hath come down from
Yahvé to Jerusalem's gate! || Bind the chariot to
the horse thou citizen Lakhîsh [*Horsham*], | thou

beginning of the sin for the daughter Ssion, because
in thee were found Israel's transgressions. ||

Therefore wilt thou [O Ssion] give a relinquish-
ment of Morésheth-Gath [*Possession near Gath*], |
the houses 'Akhzîb [*Liespring*] become a lie to
15 Israel's kings! || yet will I bring the heir unto
thee thou citizen Maresha [*Heirby*], | unto Adullam
[*Cave of wild Beasts*] will Israel's splendour come! ||
Make thyself bald [O Ssion] on account of the sons
of thy delight, | make thy baldness large like an
eagle, that they are gone into exile from thee ! ||

1. Let not merely all the nations of the earth and all that
moves upon it hear the truth of the following severe discourse,
but let also Yahvé himself become a witness against you of the
truth of this threat, ver. 2 ; Isa. i. 2 is followed, but in an
original manner.

2. For the prophet cannot keep silence with regard to
the dreadfully threatening tempest, which is clearly before
his mind in the manner of its approach.   The entire
creation takes part, a mysterious horror runs through everything, and the prophet has the plainest presentiment that
Yahvé will descend in storm and tempest and encamp upon the
heights of the mountains, so that they even melt like wax
before fire under his weight and his burning anger, and the
valleys rend asunder with a crash, as when a waterfall thunders
into an abyss, vv. 3, 4 ; Ps. xviii. 8 ; Amos iv. 13.—Is it asked,
why all this happens ?   It is clear that the perversities of the
two communities and kingdoms are the guilty cause of the
provocation of this Divine anger ; but in the two kingdoms it
is only the two capitals which represent as persons, as it were,
the entire sin of these kingdoms, the unfaithfulness of the
Northern and the Heights, *i.e.*, the idolatrous Bamoth-cultus
(*History of Israel*, III. 306 (III. 418), *Alterthümer* 301 (260)),

of the Southern kingdom, which Mikha compresses into a few emphatic words, ver. 5, in order that he may quickly pass to the chief point, comp. "Isa." xlii. 18, 19. Accordingly Samaria will be first overtaken by this tempest, vv. 6, 7, it will be wholly destroyed, so that on the mountain where it now stands is seen only a few stone heaps in the midst of the field, and new plantations of wine, comp. iii. 12, and all its various kinds of idols will be destroyed by the conquering enemy ; but with the last particular the real cause of the ruin of this great and luxurious mercantile city is touched ; for the end bears the character of the commencement, as Samaria has collected its treasures and power from the numerous rich presents to its idols, or thereby that it seduced the whole land to its idolatry, Hos. ix. 1, its treasures accordingly will be again brought as offerings to the idol-temples of its conquerors, becoming again harlot's hire. In this way the last phrase which has the ring of a proverb, explains at the same time the preceding bold denomination of the costly images as *presents of harlotry.*

3. It is not with joy that the prophet announces the horrors of such a destruction ; he is compelled to weep over it, especially as it will roll nearer and nearer over Yuda and Jerusalem and not Samaria only. Yet notwithstanding his grief, he foresees only too clearly that the destruction will come ; therefore he falls here into a long elegy, he cannot restrain himself, he requests only to be permitted to lament aloud, as jackals and ostriches howl, Job xxx. 29. Jerusalem may give up its splendour and mourn most deeply over its own desolation ! But all towns of the lowland country also, where Mikha lived, must feel the terrible blow : wherever the prophet turns his eye, he foresees calamity, every name of a place reminds him of its disaster, which is also the general disaster of the whole land, and accordingly paronomasiæ follow one upon the other. This gloomy, burdened elegy pours forth its grief in three symmetrical strophes of three verses each. (1) Vv. 8-10, the mourner is at present quite unable to overcome his own tumultuous

feelings, because he sees that her, *i.e.*, Jerusalem's (which is not yet mentioned by name) wounds are *sick*, *i.e.*, incurable, that nothing will be spared; in the hostile border cities, where the enemies lie in wait with malicious joy, in Gath (quoted from 2 Sam. i. 20) to the south and 'Akkô to the north by the sea, let not the serious hurt be made known even by too loud weeping! Yet the prophet cannot control himself, in Bæthleaphra (or Ophra in the tribe of Benyamîn, Josh. xviii. 23, which might at that time belong to Yuda), which by its very name reminds him of the dust, he has as good as rolled himself in the dust, *i.e.*, been overwhelmed with sorrow.—(2) Vv. 11-13. Prepare yourselves, but with fear and trembling, ye towns of the lowland country, the lamentation cries to the chief of them in somewhat calmer language. Thou Shaphîr, who according to thy name shouldst be *Fairtown* (which is, however, elsewhere *Shamîr*, Josh. xv. 48), pass by, led away captive, accordingly with no fair aspect, without clothes or covering! Isa. xx. 4, comp. xlvii. 2; Ssaanan, Josh. xv. 37, which from its name ought to *march to war* with courage and full ranks, has not marched forth against the enemy, Amos v. 3, but holds back in fear and trembling; from you, ye cowards, the lamentation of Bæth-häésel, *i.e.*, House of Union (probably the same small place that is called *Assél*, "Zech." xiv. 5), takes its stand, its rise, owing to its nearness; for, on account of the threatening loss of good, Maroth also trembles, the place (otherwise unknown) whose very name calls to mind bitter calamity, the evil of Jerusalem is indeed unalterably determined; thou Lakhish, a city whose name calls to mind *rékesh*, *i.e.*, *horse*, especially a *war-horse* (comp. *Hist. of Israel*, III. 260 (III. 356)), flee with horse and chariot as soon as thou canst, since thou, moreover, as the city of Yuda which worshipped idols even before Jerusalem (a fact which is mentioned here only) art most deserving of thy fate!—(3) Vv. 14-16. If this is so, the lamentation concludes returning to Jerusalem, then must thou, proud, luxurious capital, relinquish the city Moré-

sheth near Gath, although even its name seems to promise
that it shall become thy *possession* ; the city Akhzîb in Yuda,
Josh. xv. 44, and that bearing the same name in the Northern
kingdom on the Phœnician border, in Greek *Ekdippa*, the kings
of Israel will lose, the signification of the names of these cities,
Falsespring, i.e., deceitful water, Job vi. 15, being thus confirmed. To the city of Maresha also, in the south of Yuda, a
new heir will come, taking it into his own possession, destroying and dividing it, although its name seems to denote *heir*, or
secure possession, comp. ii. 4 ; away as far as the cave 'Adul-
lam in the most southern desert Israel's splendour will go, its
proud magnates that they may hide in the cave on their flight,
Isa. ii. 19; therefore mourn only, Ssion, over the exile and
captivity of thy luxurious inhabitants, for grief tearing off all
thy hair as the eagle which loses hers annually! Hos. ix. 11 ;
x. 5, 8.

The first words, *hear it all ye nations !* occur also in the history of the elder Mikha. 1 Kings xxii. 28 ; but the connexion
is in the two cases quite different.

It might appear strange, especially after the corresponding
passage concerning Jerusalem, iii. 12, that the ground of
Samaria shall become new vineyards, i. 6, and yet it is quite
correct, for the ground upon which Samaria was built had
been undoubtedly originally planted with vines, as the bare
mountains of Jerusalem could not have been, so that it only
appeared that what had formerly existed must again recur.—
On קִבְּצָה, ver. 7, comp. §§ 93 *a*, 131 *d :* without doubt the
passive force accords best with the structure of the two verse-
members, Mikha immediately afterwards, ver. 9, construes a
similar plural with the fem. sing., and a similar variation of the
gender with the two verse-members is shown in the same verse
in the case of בָּאָה and נָגַע and iii. 2 in טוֹב and רָעָה
K'thib.

Reland had in his day concluded from the LXX that in ver.

10 בְּעַפַּוֹ should be read instead of בָּכוֹ ; as regards all the
following places, the sense of the whole passage requires that
they must be looked for in the kingdom of Yuda, Akhzîb,
ver. 14, being no complete exception to this. *I rolled
myself in dust* is certainly strange, since everywhere, and
especially in ver. 14, the address of others, wherever the
use of paronomasia allows it, is here most natural : yet the
Q'rî, *roll thyself* (O woman) ! cannot be said to supply an easy
meaning, inasmuch as neither the city of this member nor
Jerusalem can very well be addressed. Probably Mikha simply
retained the entire sentence from some older book.

The results of a comparison of ver. 13 with ver. 5 with
regard to the guilt of the town of Lakhîsh are given *History
of Israel,* IV. 147 sq. (III. 634 sq.) : the transgressions mentioned in ver. 13 and ver. 5 must correspond, and then it is
clear from ver. 5 which at least in general are intended.

With reference to Akhzîb, ver. 14, it is needful only to
remember, in order to understand the paronomasia, that probably numerous witty sayings had long been in circulation
with regard to this duplicate Akhzîb, one of the cities being
claimed by the king of Yuda, the other by the king of the
Ten Tribes. The plural *houses* really points to the two cities
of the same name, since nothing is said either in this
or in any of the other sentences of the houses of a single
city, and it is not easy to conceive why this city should not
like all the rest be called simply Akhzîb; a single city might,
however, be called בֵּית אַכְזִיב. *The kings of Israel* also point
to the same fact, since if the Yudean Akhzîb merely had been
intended, the *king of Yuda* would have been named instead.—
It appears also that all the places mentioned here are still re-
cognizable as belonging to the kingdom of Yuda, with the
exception of מָרוֹת, ver. 12; but perhaps this is only a later
form of the name מַעֲרָת, Josh. xv. 59, LXX. Μαγαρώϑ,
Josh. xv. 37 צַאנן, ver. 11, is written צָנָן (incorrectly
pointed צְנָן).

2. Tʜᴇ Pʀᴏᴏғ ᴏғ ᴛʜᴇ ɴᴇᴄᴇssɪᴛʏ ᴏғ ᴛʜᴇ Jᴜᴅɢᴍᴇɴᴛ.

Ch. ii. and iii.

But the discourse rises again from this elegy to its full prophetic force and character, to indicate much more fully than was done i. 5, the proof of the necessity of the approach of that judgment and at the same time the causes that must bring such great misery upon the kingdom. The discourse turns, therefore, to the violent magnates in Jerusalem. The first of the five symmetrical strophes of medium length has really done with them: yet inasmuch as these crafty people, relying upon evil prophets as their flattering friends, pretend to find a libel of themselves in the words of the true prophet, Mikha is compelled, from the second to the fourth strophe, to make some side blows, before he can return in the fifth and last straight to the chief subject of this threat.

II.

1.

1 O they who meditate vanity and prepare evil upon their couches, | when the morning dawneth to execute it, because—it's free to their hand ! ‖ and covet lands—and rob them, houses—and take them, | and do injustice to the man and his house, to men and their inheritance ! ‖ —Therefore thus saith Yahvé : behold I meditate an evil upon this family | from which ye will not draw your necks nor go upright ! because it is an evil time. ‖ On that day will proverbs be taken up concerning you, and there will be *wailed* the *wail* " the *worst* is come ! " saying

"Laid waste laid waste are we:
  the heritage of my people is measured with
      the line! |

O how withdraweth he from me—
  he allotteth to the rebel our lands! ||

5   Therefore wilt thou have no one who may cast the
line by lot in the community of Yahvé. ||

2.

"Preach ye not!" preach they, | "they shall
not preach concerning this! the revilings never
cease!" || —What a word, thou house of Yaqob!
is then Yahvé become impatient, or are these
his doings? | do not my words mean well to
him who walketh uprightly? || And long ago they
set up my people for an enemy, away from the
garment ye strip off the mantle | from those passing
by quietly, those averse from war! || the women
of my people ye drive from the house of their plea-
sure, | from off their children ye take my adorn-
10   ment perpetually. || Arise and be gone! for this is
not the restingplace, | because of pestilent im-
purity and incurable pestilence! ||

3.

If a man walking in wind and deceit should lie
    "I will prophesy to thee of wine and of sweet-
III. drink!" | he would be the prophet of this
1   people! || *—But I say: hear now ye heads of

12   * [*Gather gather will I thee all Yaqob, will bring*
together the remnant of Israel, | *join it together as*

Yaqob and judges of the house of Israel! | (Is it
not your business to know justice?) ‖ ye who hate
good and love evil, | who have plucked off their
skin from off them and their flesh from off their
bones, ‖ who have devoured my people's flesh, and
their skin from off them have flayed and their bones
broken, | and deal it out like what is in the pot,
like meat in the midst of the caldron! ‖ (—then
will they cry unto Yahvé yet he will not hear
them, | he will hide his face from them at that
time, according as their deeds are corrupt !) ‖

4.

5   Thus saith Yahvé concerning the prophets who
mislead my people, | who bite with their teeth and
cry peace, but whoever putteth nothing into their
mouth against him they hallow war: ‖ Therefore
will ye have night without a vision, and it will be
dark to you without divination! | Yet if the sun
goeth down upon the prophets, and the day
groweth dark upon them: ‖ then the seers blush
and the soothsayers are ashamed, all of them cover
their lip-beard | because they have no answer from
God. ‖ But I am full of power with Yahvé's

sheep of a fold, as a flock in the midst of its pen, | *so
that they roar with men !* ‖ *The breach-maker
advanceth before them,* | *they break through and
pass on — the gate and go out through it,* | *and the
king passeth on before them and Yahvé at their
head !"* ‖⟧

spirit, and of judgment and manliness, | to pro-
claim to Yaqob his guilt, to Israel his sin! ||

5.

Hear now this ye heads of the house of Yaqob
and ye judges of the house of Israel, | ye who
10   abhor justice and twist all that is straight! || thou
that buildest Ssion with blood | and Jerusalem
with wrong, || the city whose heads pass judgment
for bribery, and whose priests teach for gold and
whose prophets divine for silver, | and yet lean upon
Yahvé saying " is not Yahvé in our midst? no evil
will come upon us!" || Therefore for your sake
will Ssion be plowed as a field | and Jerusalem
become ruins, the temple-hill forest-heights! ||

1. ii. 1-5. The transition from the previous section something similar to Isa. v. 8, while the course of the new section is
quite different. Woe to those who in their leisure and repose
follow no other thoughts than how they may carry out predatory excursions and do injustice against the weak and helpless,
and who then carry out all their desires as soon as possible
(when the morning light comes after the black silent night of
intrigue and evil projects), forthwith seize what they had
wickedly coveted, do wrong both to the man and his property
—and all for no other reason than they have the power to do
it, or think they have! vv. 1, 2. Accordingly the punishment,
which is already preparing in Yahvé's secret mind, will correspond to the sin : those haughty men who at present bear their
necks so high and insolently, Ps. lxxiii. 6, 7, shall in vain wish
to raise themselves from the calamity which is coming upon
their necks ; and they who rob others of their property, having
become a general laughing-stock (Hab. ii. 6), shall wail forth
the wailing cry (*nehî*, Amos vi. 10, comp. ver. 13) " it is done,"

all is lost ! (*nihya* is here used for the sake of the paronomasia,
comp. γέγονε Rev. xvi. 17), the mighty God, whose name
we now dare hardly take upon our lips (Amos vi. 10), has laid
us waste, our lands are already being measured out afresh, we
are wholly deprived of our inheritance, and how ? alas he allots
it to the hostile conqueror (the Assyrian) ! Amos vii. 17.   (*The
Rebel* is here the heathen, unlike Jer. xxxi. 22).   Thou wicked
man, whoever thou art, comp. iii. 10, wilt be for ever driven
out of the community of Yahve in such a way that in the
future, in probably better times, thou hast not even a descen-
dant who might cast the measuring-line with a lot, *i.e.*, who
might be able to claim a portion, a piece of land at the new
distribution of it, Jer. xxix. 32, Ez. xiii. 9.

   2. ii. 6-10.   It is true, these people will not have discourses
of that kind ; they cry, " prophesy not !" as if they were
themselves prophets ; and add : " people ought not to prophecy
about these things, these affairs of the magnates ! the revilings
(as they choose to call the words of truth) never come to an
end !" comp. Amos vii. 16.   But, the prophet breaks in with
dignified displeasure, what language is this you are using !
Has Yahvé become passionate or revengeful, so that he were
able even to do what ye charge him and his discourses with, as
if he desired to revile ? on the contrary, do not his words
always deal kindly with him who walks uprightly ? ver. 7.
And such wicked accusations are thrown out against him
whilst the helpless, the poor, notwithstanding that they are
Yahvé's people, are constantly treated in the most shameful
manner, as if they were even enemies (Job xvi. 12), the
travelling cloke is stripped off from wholly peaceable, harmless
travellers and their gold taken away, for miserable reasons, *e.g.*,
on account of small debts of poor people, women are taken
away as pledges and cruelly driven out of their houses, or
their necessary clothing, the adornment which their God Yahvé
had given them, is stripped from the children as a pledge ! vv.
8, 9. comp. Ez. xvi. 14.   No, that is beyond all bounds !   Ye

2   20

have thus pronounced your own condemnation: begone from
my land into exile! as was already said ver. 5; here ye may
no longer tarry in luxurious repose (acc. Isa. xxviii. 12), on
account of the infectious, pestilential impurity which cleaves to
you, and because this pestilence is incurable, i. 9; vi. 13.

3. ii. 11—iii. 4.   And truly, if one constantly habituated to
wind and deceit should mendaciously prophesy to them fair and
flattering promises, that they would always live in such an
intoxication of joy and pleasure (Isa. v. 11, 12), he would be
the prophet according to this people's own heart! ver. 11.
The two following verses contain promises of great happiness:
Israel again united into one great flock, so that for multitude
they make loud noise, and like sheep in a too small fold are
unable to keep within their ancient boundaries, force their way
under a great hero, one who breaks through, a conqueror,
from one captured city into another, with Yahvé as their
leader, Hos. ii. 2 [i. 11]; Ex. i. 10; these lying prophets
depict to the people nothing but such glowing pictures of
approaching prosperity and great victories.   Nevertheless, it
seems Mikha himself, or another early reader, wrote these
words of one of the prophets, whom he really had in his mind
at first only in the margin, as an example of their false prophecies; they are not absolutely necessary in the context, and
they also destroy the structure of the strophes.—Mikha's prophecies are of another kind: all the more openly he summons
these magnates and judges to hear the Divine sentence against
these false prophets, which he is about to pronounce; he summons them to hear this because they as the heads of the nation
ought most of all to hear the Divine sentence, Hos. v. 1, they
who are the opposite of what they ought to be, fleecers of the
people, who slaughter it, divide it amongst them, and devour it
as a delicacy, Ps. xiv. 4, Rev. xvii. 16, who, however, will one
day, when the Divine judgment arrives, call vainly to Yahvé in
the same proportion as they now commit wickedness, ver. 4.
Thus this strophe, having started from a mere parenthetical

sentence, ver. 1 *b*, finishes without being able conveniently to commence the stern utterance against the pseudo-prophets, which they must hear; this is left, therefore, for the following strophe.

4. iii. 5-8. The false prophets, who in sacred phraseology proclaim peace or war according as something is given them to bite (eat) or not, shall be suitably punished, inasmuch as the day of trial suddenly deprives them of the light of the eye and the mind, and no more receiving any oracle they must maintain an ignoble silence, Isa. xxix. 10, 11 ; comp. lii. 15 : whilst, on the other hand, a true prophet like Mikha always finds in the spirit of Yahvé sufficient strength, judgment and manliness to bring before even the whole nation, when it is needful to do so, as at present for instance, its guilt and deserved punishment.

5. iii. 9-12. The magnates of the realm, who desire to pay no attention to justice, and prefer to pervert all uprightness, are therefore called upon to hear this public censure of the false prophets and proclamation of the truth, especially must the rich man hear, who although he rebuilds Jerusalem, yet does it with the blood of the oppressed, ver. 10. Because all kinds of leaders of the people in Jerusalem are corrupt, although they imagine that they have Yahvé's favour, and make a show of their reliance upon him ((just as Amos ix. 10) : on this very account, the conclusion of all these words is, will Jerusalem together with the temple become ruins, just as was the case with Samaria, i. 6.—Mikha probably intends by the one magnate of iii. 10; ii. 5, the Shebnâ of Isa. xxii. 15 sq.

---

ii. 1, אוֹר must be taken acc. § 238 *b*.

With regard to the dirge נְהִי, see *Dichter des A. B. Ia,* p. 42 sq. It must, however, be observed that a complete

20 *

dirge follows the first detached note of lamentation נִהְיָה,
which is rendered *the worst is come* simply on account of the
paronomasia.* The dirge consists of two brief lines, the first
member of each of which is shorter than the second when the
correct reading is restored. According to the present reading
a paronomasia might seem to lie in the words יָמִיר and יָמִישׁ,
and the translation would have to be *the heritage of my people he*
(Yahvé) *changeth*, causing it to pass into other hands as if by
exchange or sale; and the next clause *O how doth he remove*
(which would mean almost the same as changeth, or selleth,)
it from me? a lamentable inquiry followed by the answer: he
allotteth it to the enemy! But the idea of changing would be
thus too briefly and unintelligibly expressed; and, following
the LXX., a far better meaning is obtained if יְמוּד is read and
בְּחֶבֶל is then inserted: preparations are already making to
redivide our fields; and how? They are to be given to the
enemy by lot! This was probably an existing popular song:
on which supposition it may be best explained how the prophet
himself, v. 5, goes on to make the application of it to the case
before him, and the first strophe may therewith hasten to a
close within its proper limits.—In any case this dirge which is
sung by the exiles themselves is wholly different from the
gnomic song, i.e., satirical song, ver. 4 *a*, which others will
strike up.

As to הֶאָמוּר, ver. 7, see § 101 *b;* in Arabic also the *Alif*,
i.e., *ă* prefixed to a noun can have the force of the vocative, as
Hamâsa p. 745, 5. As in Gen. iv. 7, הטיב may also signify to
mean well, descriptive of the intention and feeling; and upon
הַיָשָׁר הֹלֵךְ see § 335 *a*.

The long censure, ii. 8, 9, begins forcibly with אֶתְמוּל, which
bears here the meaning of *long ago*, as in Isa. xxx. 33, and
closes with לעולם, which has nearly the same force. But it

---

* The author translates the words וְנָהָה נְהִי נִהְיָה und winseln wird man
winselnd " weh ! vorbei !"—*Tr.*

should also be observed that this second strophe closes, ver. 10, with substantially the same threat as the first, ver. 5.

It is time it should be generally understood that the words of vv. 11, 12, can have no place here save in the sense which has been above given to them. In appearance the genuine prophets prophesy the same thing : and yet what a difference, as soon as one attends more minutely to the passage ! When we hear the Messiah called boldly *their king,* as if such glorious things could be looked for from any king that was then living, we are quite unable to recognise that Messiah who is described by Yesaya and Mikha. Or we have only to compare the commencement of this luscious prophecy as to the future *gathering* of the whole nation with what Mikha, iv. 6, 7, says as if in designed contradiction of it, to comprehend how far he was from being able to approve of these words.

iii. 12, it is remarkable that Ssion as the bare hill on the south is still accurately distinguished from Jerusalem as the entire ancient city exclusive of the hill of the temple and also from this hill itself, comp. *History of Israel,* III. 121 sq. (III. p. 165 sq.

---

3. The Promise.

Mikha also can utter glorious promises concerning the Messianic times and their great happiness, as well as any lying prophets : he is able to proclaim them more powerfully and in a more beautiful form then they, for he does not utter them in flattery to existing magnates, but from the most living faith, the deep conviction that such times of consummation must at last arrive. And as the previous threat had to be very severe, he now the more gladly summoned all his powers to depict in grand glowing pictures the bright side also, which every true prophet cherished in his anticipations and views of the future. Yet while Mikha can present as bright promises as those false

teachers, there is a great difference which separates him entirely
from them. He does not in the midst of these elevating
eternal hopes overlook the real condition of the present time with
all its profound defects and corruptions, and is, therefore, unable
to give himself up without reserve to those hopes. Confident of
the consummation of the true community as older prophets had
already promised it, and full of the fair hope of the appearance
of a new Davîd who will far excel even his great predecessor,
he looks into the impending serious troubles of the Davîdic
kingdom not without confidence, it is true, indeed, with
defiant courage; but at the same time he cannot in the Divine
spirit hide from himself the fact that the existing vices and
transgressions can only serve in the immediate future to increase
for a time the sufferings and dangers that are already assailing
the kingdom, yea, that the destruction of Jerusalem itself and
the exile are necessary; nor can he avoid seeing that the longed
for Messianic age will not come save by the removal of these
existing obstacles in the way of a better state of things. So
different from the view of his opponents, so joyous and at the
same time so serious is this form which Mikha's anticipations
assume. It is in this part, therefore, that the book reaches its
climax, with a rapid change of very various feelings and truths,
which pour themselves forth in four large strophes of 7-8
verses each, the last one only being somewhat shorter. At the
commencement the prophet places the same glorious description of the Messianic age from an older prophet that Yesaya
also, ii. 2-4, placed at the head of one of his books; this portion
of the book is thereby worthily introduced, the eye is at once
directed into an entirely different region, into the pure, bright
realm of blessed hope; but the passage appears to be very
happily chosen for the further reason that it treats of the same
Ssion with which the previous piece had closed, thus bringing
the opposite prospects into immediate contrast. But after the
Messianic hope has been in the first strophe brought forward
in its pure and simple beauty, the second glances with higher

courage from this point upon the impending sufferings as the necessary transition period to that glory, which the third then calmly takes up once more and describes exhaustively; till in the fourth the great condition and limitation under which all such promises are alone to be understood is supplied.

1.

IV.

1   " And then at the end of the days will the mountain of the house of Yahvé be placed upon the summit of the mountains, and it is exalted before hills, | so that to it the nations flow, ‖ and many nations go and say ' come, let us go up to the mountain of Yahvé and to the house of the God of Yaqob, that he may teach us of his ways and we go in his paths !' | for from Ssion will go forth the doctrine, and Yahvé's word from Jerusalem. ‖ Then judgeth he between many nations, and giveth decision to numerous Heathen afar off, | so that they forge their swords into hoes, and their spears into pruning-knives, | nation against nation raise not a sword, and learn not war any more, ‖ and dwell each under his vine and under his fig-tree, by no one made afraid : | surely the mouth

5   of Yahvé of Hosts hath spoken it. ‖ — If all the nations go, each one in the name of his God : | then let us also go in the name of Yahvé our God for ever and ever ! ‖—On that day, saith Yahvé, will I gather that which is lame and that which is scattered abroad bring together, | and what I only injured, ‖ and make that which is lame a remnant, and that which was chased away a numerous

nation, | and Yahvé reigneth over them upon
mount Ssion from henceforth and for ever. ‖ But
thou Tower-of-the-flock, thou hill of the daughter
Ssion— | unto thee will arrive and come—the
former rule, the kingdom of the daughter Jerusalem! ‖

2.

Now wherefore criest thou [O Ssion] so loudly? |
is there no more any king within thee, or hath
thy counsellor perished, that trembling seizeth
thee as a woman in travail? ‖ O tremble and
be in labour daughter of Ssion as the woman
in travail! | for now wilt thou go forth from the
city dwell in the field and come unto Babel:
there wilt thou be set free, there will Yahvé
redeem thee from the hand of thy enemies! ‖

Yea now against thee many people may have
assembled, | they who say " may she be dese-
crated, and on Ssion shall our eyes feast!" ‖ But
they know not Yahvé's thoughts and understand
not his purpose, | how he hath brought them toge-
ther—as sheaves to the floor! ‖ Arise and thresh
thou daughter Ssion! | for thy horn will I make
iron, and thy hoofs will I make steel, | so that
thou crushest many nations | and sacrificest to
Yahvé their plunder, their wealth to the Lord of
the whole earth. ‖

Now press together thou daughter of the press!
Siege may they have laid upon us, | with the staff
may they have beaten the judge of Israel upon

V.
1   the cheek! ‖ Yet thou Bæthlehem-Ephrátha,
small to count among Yuda's provinces: | from
thee will one go forth for me to become ruler over
Israel, | and his origin is from antiquity, from
primeval days. ‖

3.

Therefore will he give them up until she that
beareth hath brought forth | and his remaining
brothers return to the sons of Israel: ‖ then he
standeth there and shepherdeth with Yahvé's power,
with the majesty of the name of Yahvé his God; |
but they settle down, for then he will be great
unto the ends of the earth! ‖ And this will be
peace: | when the Assyrian cometh into our land
and when he treadeth our lofty-edifices, we set up
against him seven shepherds and eight anointed
5   men; ‖ they shepherd Assyria with the sword, and
the land of Nimrod in its gates; | thus he deli-
vereth from the Assyrian, when he cometh into our
land and when he treadeth our border. ‖ Then will
the remnant of Yaqob in the midst of many nations
be as dew from Yahvé, as showers upon herbs, |
which waiteth not for mortals neither tarrieth for
sons of men; ‖ or the remnant of Yaqob will be
among the Heathen, in the midst of many nations |
as a lion among the beasts of the forest, as a
young-lion among the flocks of sheep, | who when
he passeth by trampleth and robbeth with no
deliverer. ‖ Let thy hand be lifted up over thy
oppressors, | and all thy enemies will be cut
off ! ‖

4.

But then on that day, saith Yahvé, then I cut
off thy horses from thy midst, | and destroy thy
10   chariots, || and cut off the fortresses of thy land|
and demolish all thy fortifications ; || I cut off the
enchantments out of thy hand, | and magicians
thou will not have, || I cut off thy graven-images
and statues from thy midst, | that thou no more
doest homage to the work of thy hands; || I pluck
up thy idol-groves from thy midst, | and cast
down thy fortresses, || and execute in wrath and in
fury vengeance | against the nations which did not
hear. ||

1. On vv. 1-4, see the commentary on the passage in Yesaya,
ante, p. 22 sq. The transition to the prophet's own words,
ver. 5, is like Isa. ii. 5 : if every other nation reveres its God,—
follows his commandments and hears his oracles, then we also
will for ever follow Yahvé and his ancient oracles, *e.g.*, precisely that oracle concerning the Messianic times which is here
quoted, and which Mikha further elaborates in his own way.
Yes, then in that glorious time (but not at present as the false
prophets say, ii. 12, 13), will Yahvé gather together again as
the nucleus of a great new nation all the fragments of the
widely scattered, banished, and halting flock of Israel, which
he was once himself compelled to injure by punishment, so
that then the true eternal Theocracy begins, never again to be
destroyed, vv. 6, 7. But that which is here of peculiar importance and original is, the addition which Mikha, following in
Yesaya's steps, joyfully makes to the ancient promises, ver. 8,
that the former wide Davidîc rule shall return by the Messiah,
who, having sprung like Davîd from Bethlehem, rules in Ssion,
to the unimportant place called the *Tower of the Flock,* between

Jerusalem and Bœthlehem, Gen. xxxv. 21 (comp. *M*. Sh'qalim
6, 4), as also to Ssion, comp. further v. 1.

2. It is true, severe sufferings must come upon the community henceforth in the intermediate period until the blessed
time arrives, as the prophet foresees with equal clearness : but
if that great hope is once firmly established, how can Ssion
despair ?   Let these sufferings come, they must be borne ; but
they cannot hinder the fulfilment of that eternal hope, must, on
the contrary, really hasten it !   With this exalted, defiant
courage, the prophet beholds certain distinct classes of these
approaching afflictions.   In agitated language he proceeds from
the extreme limit of the future which here occupies him back
to the present, observing three stages.   This he does in order to
present at each stage the contrast of the corresponding still
greater hope.   (1) Vv. 9, 10. The prophetic glance beholds
Jerusalem, *i.e.*, the community, already as good as annihilated,
already as without king and counsellor, Hos. iii. 4 ; x. 3 ;
xiii. 10, 13, lamenting aloud as if attacked by the most violent
pangs of a travailing woman, that is, at that time when the
existing Jerusalem will really be destroyed, acc. iii. 12.   But
Divine confidence with higher courage demands of her in a
tone of surprise and reproof, wherefore she cries so loudly ?
whether her king and counsellor is lost that she trembles like
a woman in labour ?   And then, as if after a moment's thought,
the Divine confidence replies : O no ! the true king is never
absent from thee !   Be in labour, agonising in extreme pain,
this birth-crisis of a new age must be gone through : for thou
must go into exile, sent to Babel by the Assyrians, but there
the hour of birth (of the Messiah and the regenerated community) as well as of true redemption arrives !—(2.) Vv. 11-13.
Coming back somewhat nearer to the present, the prophetic
glance beholds Ssion already surrounded by conquerors, eager
to destroy and delighting in her humiliation ; but, cries Divine
confidence, let them surround the holy city, full of unholy
thoughts and deeds, the more violent their rage and the more

they collect around the one holy place to desecrate the last sanctuary of the earth, so much the more easily and irresistibly can
they be reached with one blow by the Divine punishment. This
is a turn of events which is as little anticipated by them as it is
firmly resolved upon in the Divine councils (for the summit of
wickedness is the place for its fall), so that it may really be
said, that Yahvé has collected them all around Ssion to punish
them with greater ease, just as sheaves are conveyed together
to the threshing-floor to be threshed. The victory is thine,
the harvest is ready for threshing, arise and thresh, strengthened
by higher power (Hos. x. 11), devoting the precious plunder of
the vanquished thankfully to Yahvé as to him who rules over
the heathen also! A twofold anticipation that reminds us of
Isa. xxix. 1-8, which nevertheless does not cancel the punishment of iii. 12, as also appears from Isa. xxxii. 13, 14, because
it is precisely Jerusalem as the community of true religion
which has received a higher signification.—(3.) Vv. 14, 15.
The prophetic glance beholds that in the immediate future the
Assyrians will still further treat the gentle king Hizqia with
his people in a disgraceful manner (as they had already treated
him thus), and that in the closely besieged city only a poor
little flock of people must crowd closely together like a flock
in a thunderstorm (that is, according to the other anticipations
of this book, before the city shall be quite taken and destroyed,
its inhabitants led away captive). But press, cries the higher
confidence, close together in your distress, thou daughter of
the press, *i.e.*, those who art at other times accustomed to
press and drive together others (Gen. xlix. 19), and it is to be
hoped wilt in the future again press upon and conquer others,
press and crowd together both now and for some time to come,
as a flock at the time of tempests, and bear up patiently; the
Messiah will yet certainly come! Thou little Bæthlehem, who
canst scarcely make a district in Yuda (Zech. ix. 7), thou art
not too insignificant in the sight of Yahvé, no more than Davîd,
thy shepherd's son, was formerly too insignificant in his sight,

from thee the Anointed of Yahvé, a second and greater Davîd, will go forth, himself sprung from the ancient, venerated Davîdic royal line ! The Davîdic house, compared especially with the changing dynasties of the northern kingdom, could at that time be justly called *ancient,* since, in fact, the antiquity of those times had in general not yet become of such an extent as we now consider it ; comp. Amos ix. 11 ; Isa. xi. 1 ; xxiii. 7.

3. The combined sense of the two previous strophes shows that the Messianic prosperity will by no means come immediately, nevertheless it is still certain and how glorious ! Yahvé, it is first said, will *give them up,* surrender them to their enemies, until she who bears has brought forth, *i. e.* (since the oracle Isa. vii. might already be used as a model in Mikha's time) until the as yet unknown mother in Davîd's house shall have given birth to the exalted child from whom the better time takes its rise, the Messiah, and his brothers that remain from the great trial, the Israelites, shall return, awakened and strengthened, from the exile to the few who will still be living in the sacred land, just as formerly the march out of Egypt was the sign of the beginning of a better age, Isa. xi. 11, 12. When these two happy events take place in conjunction, then the full splendour of the Messianic prosperity begins to shine, the Messiah, on the one hand, reigning with Yahvé's all-embracing power and in his exalted name, and the people, on the other, attaining to durable repose, iv. 4, Amos, ix. 14, because from that time Yahvé's name will be revered amongst all nations, ver. 3. Peace is the proper end and the distinctive feature of the Messianic time : yet it does not consist in indolent subjection, but will be thereby prepared, that then not only is the one Messiah great and glorious, but an inexhaustible number of great leaders and princes support him, repelling in his own land every attack which the Assyrian, for instance, might again make, and conquering the gates, *i. e.,* the boundaries and frontier fortifications (Nah. iii.

18) of the land of Nimrôd (Assyria); for the Messianic prosperity does not consist in there being no danger of any kind,
but in its being warded off by a number of great men, worthy
of the Messiah, before it becomes destructive, and the speedy
return of peace, vv. 4, 5. Zech. ix. 16; x. 4.; Isa. xxxii. 1,
sq. And as reviving dew and rain falls everywhere in innumerable drops from Yahvé alone without waiting for the will of
men, so the Messianic people will then be found unexpectedly and as if rained from heaven everywhere dispensing
refreshing doctrine and knowledge amongst the heathen,
without the heathen being able wholly to keep them off, ver.
6, comp. Ps. cx. 3 : these Messianic people being but a few in
the wide world, but these few like lions whose simple appearance suffices to put all small animals of the forest and field into
a state of alarm, ver. 7. So let it be and so must it be; arise
Israel and conquer ! ver. 8.

4. But all the glorious things which have been promised in
these three strophes cannot co-exist with the numerous perversities that now prevail : these perversities must, therefore, be
all first abolished in the great judgment-day ! Thus with sad
seriousness and brief threatening language, the discourse
returns to the burden of the first two main sections. There
are especially two quite universal perversities of the nation
which cannot remain : trust in false resources and vain help,
which in real danger give no assistance, horses and chariots,
castles and fortresses, vv. 9, 10 ; and the false direction of
faith, superstition of various kinds, vv. 11, 12. Hos. iii. 4 ;
the first and the second perversities will be destroyed on that
great day, when severe judgment is passed upon all disobedient
nations, whether they are Israel or heathen, vv. 13, 14. Thus
there are three pairs of verses here, the verses of each of which
are more closely related, whilst in the third and last instance
the matter of the first two pairs is only briefly reiterated and
finally concluded. But both in regard to the horses and the
needlessness of defenced cities, it is nothing more than a

reminiscence of the primitive times of this community under
Moses that crosses the mind of our prophet, comp. *History of
Israel*, II. 130, sq. (II. 187).   And as Mikha with respect to
the Sanctuary, (see *ante*, p. 291) is more advanced in his view
of the future than even Yesaya, so with regard to fortified
cities and the curse (iv. 13 ; v. 14, comp. *Alterthümer*, p. 101,
sq. (86 sq.)) there is no other prophet who goes so far back as
he into the times of Moses.   And yet it should be carefully
noted that he says at the last, only those nations shall meet
with a double portion of his wrath who did *not hear :* accordingly the Divine truth must previously be clearly preached to
them, and in that case all nations become equal in that manner
implied in i. 5, even if this refers primarily to what was said,
v. 6, 7.

· Apart from the fragment of Yôél's (see Vol. I. p. 114), the
style of this section differs somewhat from that of the two
previous sections.   The phrase וְאַם וֹּ, iv. 6 ; v. 9, does not
occur in ch. i.-iii. (nor, indeed, ch. vi. vii.) : at the same time,
it is elsewhere very frequent only in the case of certain prophets, as 'Amôs, Yéremyá, Hezeqiel, other prophets, even
Yesaya, using it more rarely.   Further, the representation of
a city as a daughter pervades ch. iv., v., but not ch. i.-iii., where,
on the contrary, i. 8-16, the city is called a *citizeness*, see Vol.
I., p. 189, when figurative language of this description is used
of it ; at the same time, just as this latter figure is found only
in the particular piece i. 8-16, as being there specially appropriate, so in the section before us the figure of the *daughter
Ssion* might with peculiar propriety be preferred and kept up
where the discourse rises to the pure height of Messianic prospects ; in conjunction with this figure, the name of a city,
beginning with *house* or *tower*, is also used poetically as a masculine, iv. 8 ; v. 1.   While these peculiarities might suggest
doubt of Mikha's authorship, there is much that supports it.
The choice of אָסַף and קָבַץ, together with the entire thought

of iv. 6, 7, is unmistakably intended as an allusion to the words of ii. 12, 13, which is at the same time a confirmation of the opinion that Mikha did not himself invent those words of the false prophets, although, nevertheless, he alluded to them ; just as iv. 7, he clearly uses the expressions גוי עצום and הר ציון (comp. also ver. 13) with iv. 1, 3, in his mind. Further, the thought and form of expression of iv. 13 is very similar to ii. 10; in this respect also that both bring a small strophe to a rapid close. The frequent use of שָׂדֶה, i. 6; ii. 2, 4 ; iii. 12 iv. 10, which Yesaya, *e.g.* rarely uses, and the construction of the plur. עֵינֵינוּ, iv. 11, comp. *ante*, on i. 7, similarly point to Mikha.—There would be more reason to doubt Mikha's authorship if the prophecy of the complete destruction of Jerusalem, iii. 12, contradicted that which we find here, iv. 8—v. 3 : but, in fact, there is no more a complete contradiction here than there is between Isa. xxix. 1-8 and xxxii. 12-14, see *ante*, p. 224, and the only difference between Yesaya and Mikha is, that the latter describes the temple-hill also as quite waste during the interval.—At all events, Mikha's book could not have closed originally with the two portions i.-iii., inasmuch as they contain no Messianic outlook ; and, on the other hand, iv.-v. belong incontestably to the same limited period of time. At most, therefore, we could do no more than suppose that a piece by some contemporary prophet had got into the place originally occupied by the lost piece of Mikha's : but after all is said, these three portions, i.-v., are not so dissimilar as to compel us to accept this supposition. We shall find it otherwise in the case of vi., vii.

In iv. 8, the unusual agitation with which everything is expressed in a great sentence, with its double start, direct address, predicate, subject, is very remarkable : hence here also the accentuation places its great distinctive accent exactly in the middle of the whole verse immediately after the first predicate, as if the verse really consisted of only two halves. Mikha's reason for mentioning here the *Tower of the Flock* especially, though it is elsewhere so little referred to, would most likely become clear if we were in possession of all the Messianic Oracles ; for he plainly makes particular reference to many older Oracles of this class. As it is we must content ourselves with the consideration that both this tower and Bæthléhem had been alluded to in the ancient Patriarchal History.

But the agitation of the discourse evidently rises still higher in the following strophe, iv. 9—v. i. : not a line of which can be understood unless this unusual emotion of the inmost heart at the thought of the Messiah, of his possible, certain coming, and also of the terrible sufferings which precede it, is comprehended, and unless the three stages in which the thought moves backwards from the furthest future of these Messianic events in a gradual approach to the present, are clearly distinguished. At the same time, the discourse is plain enough when it is properly understood. Upon each of these three stages there are three steps through which the thought moves with great agitation : the recognition and painful sense of a profound trouble ; the consideration of it ; the sudden, joyous, yea, defiant rise above it. Thus a struggle goes on between the most unshaken hope and Divine confidence and the clear truthloving gaze into the most serious complications and miseries which have already partly begun and must further ensue : and however difficult the victory of the former over the latter may be, it is nevertheless won. In this respect the passage is quite peculiar, and has a marvellous beauty of its own.—With regard to וְהַחֲרַמְתִּי, ver. 13, see 190 c : since Mikha, as was above remarked, affects nice variations in the two members of a verse, this difference from the preceding וַהֲדִקּוֹת may be intentional.—*Judge*, iv. 14, instead of *king*, only in imitation of ancient and venerated language : the same consideration that immediately produces the solemn combination of Bæthléhem and Ephráta, v. 1.—As to צָעִיר לִהְיוֹת, v. 1, see § 285 *d*.

It is clear that with the exception of the incidental thought,

iv. 9, the full transition to the Messiah is not made before the
end of the strophe, iv. 14, v. i, afterwards to dwell, at the
beginning of the following strophe, v. 2 sq., on the consideration of his bright picture.   It is at this point that the entire
discourse reaches its climax, and the Divine light and exalted
repose, which has been won in that struggle of most various
anticipations and feelings, shines forth undisturbed at the commencement of the third strophe.   But with whatever brevity
Mikha here brings together the things that concern the Messiah,
we cannot help seeing that he is able to speak of him and of
those who are most nearly connected with him with such brevity
as we find him doing in ver. 2, only because he is referring to
things which were at the time generally known : what those
things were is indicated *ante*, p. 81 sq.—As, however, Mikha's
greater contemporary is always willing to give *signs* in matters
that are difficult to perceive, see *ante*, p. 13, Mikha also adds
here v. 4, 5, at least in words, a new mark by which the
glory of the Messiah and his age may be recognized ; for it is
necessary to take the first words, ver. 14, *and this is their salvation*, or *peace*, in such a sense that the following supply an
example of the salvation and peace which he will bring ; the
word וְהִצִּיל, ver. 5, may also be referred to the Messiah, and
not as in Isa. xix. 20, since nothing compels us in our passage
to suppose God is intended.

The fortresses, עָרִים, v. 10, properly *cities*, because originally all cities were in high situations (an Aramaic *Tell*, as the
ancient sites of those cities are still recognized by such *levelled
hills*) and fortified, Isa. xxxii. 19, or, in any case, usually fortified, Num. xiii. 19.—It was shown above that there is no
ground for doubting the correctness of the reading עָרֶיךָ, ver.
13 ; on the contrary, the cities are very properly mentioned a
second time in conjunction with the idol-groves.

III. YESAYA'S IMMEDIATE SUCCESSORS.

1. AN ANONYMOUS PROPHET.

"Mikha," ch. vi., vii.

Inasmuch as prophecy greatly flourished and was exceedingly influential at the time of Yesaya, and a great number of glorious prophets gathered around him, it is the more surprising to find this field so barren immediately after his death. But we have already indicated the explanation of this phenomenon, Vol. I., p. 53. We should be without even a single complete piece from this gloomy period, did we not possess the small but beautifully finished piece which, appended to the book of Mikha as chaps. vi.. vii., usually passes under his name. If we were to endeavour to connect this piece closely with chaps. i.-v., we must proceed in the following manner. The promise, we should have to say, has not become finally predominant in the strophe v. 9-14, but has at last given way for threatening again : and yet the book ought surely not to begin and close with threats, without mediation or reconciliation, the genuine prophetic spirit not seeking to remove by doctrine and explanation the hindrance which in the present stand in the way of what is good, or to mitigate the severity of the threatening. We must, therefore, suppose that Mikha presents in this extremely instructive piece the best mediation which the prophetic spirit could attempt in the darkness and confusion of the time, this piece certainly laying bare to us with rare clearness the depths of the love of the genuine prophetic spirit. The nation shall not be threatened and condemned merely, as at present : it shall also be heard in its self-defence before the eternal judge, and not be finally condemned before it comes

21 *

itself to feel that it is no longer able to defend itself even
before the freest and most favourable tribunal : and for this
purpose a solemn trial (*processus*) is here commenced.   Yet
when carefully weighed these considerations are not satisfac-
tory.   Not only is it undeniable that the piece, chaps. i.-v.,
correctly understood, is with its three sections so complete in
itself, after the manner of the prophecy of Yesaya's time, that
there is nothing further wanted, but there are other reasons
of quite another kind against the integrity.

For, first of all, we are in these chapters translated into quite
different times.   There is in them no further any trace of the
stirring and elevated times of Yesaya's activity.   The community which still gathered around the temple and a national
prince (vi. 9), has become very small and retired from external
affairs, very faint-hearted and exceedingly fearful, vii. 11, 12 ; vi.
6, 7 : but the petty, degraded, selfish, faithless thought and feeling of individuals towards each other has become proportionally
greater, which is precisely what is to be expected from a nation
that is suffering from increasing calamities from without and
threatening to sink ever deeper into a condition of internal decay,
vi. 10 sq., vii. 1-6.   The distance of this time from that which
is clearly manifested in Mikha, ch. i—v, is perceptibly great :
indeed, we seem to be placed in those times which are familiar
to us from certain Psalms (comp. *Dichter des Alten Bundes* I *b*,
p. 152 sq.), Yéremyá, Habaqqûq, and other productions of the
7th cent. B.C.   We feel here the effects of the cold, biting
wind which king Manasse brought over the kingdom of Yuda :
it is also plain from vi. 16 that the idolatrous tendency which
this king favoured had long been prevailing ; and the more
religious hardly ventured, acc. vi. 9 *b*, to name the king quite
openly.

If it would be of itself conceivable that Mikha, supposing
him to be young when he wrote ch. i-v, had lived to these
times and was thus the author of ch. vi., vii. also, this possibility vanishes as soon as we remember that the language is

quite different in the latter piece. We have here nothing of
the elevated force which is still met with in Mikha ch. i—v. as
an echo of Yesaya's lofty eloquence: the style of the piece
before us already approaches very nearly that of Yéremyá.
In details also the complexion of the language of our prophet
is so entirely different that we nowhere perceive the peculiarities that prevail in the former chapters. Even where at
first sight a similarity appears to exist (as in the structure of
the sentences, vi. 10 *b*—12, compared with iii. 10, 11), it
vanishes on a closer comparison.*

The form and art of our piece is also so essentially different
that on that account alone we can hardly suppose that we have
the same author here. This is the first prophetic piece with a
purely dramatic plan and execution that we have met with,
leaving far behind it those first essays of dramatic description
which have previously come before us. It looks as if our
prophet had been no longer able in any way to appear and
speak publicly in Jerusalem. And how could he have done
that during the reign of Manasse? Accordingly, with the
most vivid clearness and firmest confidence, he has traced out in
his spirit the entire relation subsisting between Yahvé and his
people, and feels himself called upon as a prophet to interpose
as it were; but what had with clearness and certainty
appeared to him as a prophet in the fire of wrestling thought
and believing vision, he reproduces forthwith in an artistic
form as an author as distinct from a public speaker. That the
most severe Divine judgment must come upon the nation as it
now is, and that a Messianic Israel can arise only upon the ruins
of the present hopelessly lost nation, are positions he holds as
firmly as all the earlier prophets of those centuries: and how
righteous this punishment must appear even to him who has to
bear it, this prophet graphically describes under the figure,
which had often been used by his predecessors, of a judicial trial

---

* The addition of אשר, vi. 12, producing a decisive difference.

between Yahvé and his community. But the great proceedings of unequalled character, which the prophet has already clearly beheld in his spirit, and in which he must take most exciting part as mediator between the two contending parties, he depicts in a drama, which could not be more animated, more true, more full of feeling, or more profoundly exhaustive notwithstanding its great brevity. The entire piece proceeds amidst changing voices : and there are not fewer than ten voices that are heard one after the other. But since the prophet still retains the ancient artistic form of the strophe, the whole falls into five strophes which are also five acts, thus completing all that has to be said and giving it a perfectly rounded form. We shall, however, subsequently see how this piece, which notwithstanding its new form is still very simple, was afterwards imitated with much more elaborate art.

This piece accordingly can have been appended to the book of Mikha only by accident, as it were : but it is possible that the younger prophet himself appended it on the publication of a new edition of Mikha's book.*

VI.

1.   1.

(The Prophet) :

Hear now that which Yahvé hath to say!— Arise contend before the mountains, | and let the hills hear thy voice! ||—Hear ye mountains Yahvé's contention, and ye unchanging foundations of the earth! | for a contention hath Yahvé with his people, and with Israel will he dispute. ||

---

* Comp. *Jahrbb. der Bibl. Wiss.* XI. 29 sq.; *History of Israel*, IV. 207 (III. p. 716).

(YAHVÉ) :

My people! what have I done unto thee and
wherewith wearied thee? | answer against me! ||
Surely I led thee up from the land of Egypt, and
from the slaves'-house I redeemed thee, | and sent
5   before thee Mosé Ahron and Miryam. || My
people! remember what Moab's king Balaq advised, and what Bileam son of Be'or answered
him*—in order to acknowledge Yahvé's righteous
ways! ||

(THE PEOPLE) :

Wherewith shall I come before Yahvé, bow my-
self before the God of the height ? | shall I come
before him with burntofferings, with calves a year
old? || taketh Yahvé pleasure in thousands of
rams, in ten thousands of rivers of oil? | shall I
give my firstborn as my guilt, the fruit of my
body for the expiation of my soul? ||

(THE PROPHET) :

He hath proclaimed to thee O man what is good; |
and what requireth Yahvé from thee but to do
justice and to love kindness† and humbly to walk
with thy God ! ||

2.

Hark Yahvé calleth to the city (surely it is sal-
vation to fear thy name !): |

---

* *From Shittim unto Gilgal.*

† Germ. *huld.* See a valuable discussion of the meaning of חֶסֶד in the author's
last work, *Die Lehre der Bibel von Gott,* Vol. II. p. 207 sq.—*Tr.*

(YAHVÉ) :

Hear O community and who appointeth her! ‖
10   Are there still in the house of the unjust the trea-
sures of injustice | and the accursed waning mea-
sure? ‖ are they innocent with scales of injustice |
and with a bag of deceitful stones? ‖ —she whose
rich men are full of violence, and whose inhabi-
tants speak lies | since their language is deceit in
their mouth! ‖ So I also smite thee incurably! |
amaze thee on account of thy punishments: ‖ thou
wilt eat but not be satisfied, since thy raging-
hunger remaineth in thee; | and remove but not
rescue, and what thou rescuest will I give to the
15   sword! ‖ thou wilt sow but not reap; | thou wilt
tread olives but not anoint thee with oil, and must
—but drink no wine! ‖ And 'Omri's statutes are
kept, and the whole work of the house of Ahab—
in whose counsels ye go | in order that I make
thee a horror and her inhabitants a hissing, to the
end that ye bear the shame of my people! ‖

3.

(A GODLY MAN) :

VII.

1   O woe is me that it is with me as at fruit-har-
vests, as at the vintage-gleaning: | there is no
cluster to eat, nor early-fig which my soul desired! ‖   The good have disappeared from the
land, and the upright among men are no more; |
all lie in wait for blood, one hunting the other in

the net. ‖ ˙ On account of the misdeed of the
hands—to make it good—the prince is besought
and the judge for payment: | and the great-man
speaketh his self-conceit, and so they wrest it. ‖
The best of them is as a bramble-bush, the upright
from a thorn hedge: | —the day of thy outlookers,
thy punishment is come: now will their confusion
take place! ‖

(A Second Godly Man):

5   Trust not a friend, confide not in an acquaint-
ance, | from the wife of thy bosom* guard the
utterances of thy mouth! ‖ For the son ridiculeth
the father, the daughter riseth up against her
mother, the daughter-in-law against her mother-
in-law, | the enemies of every man are the people
of his house! ‖

4.

(The Community):

But I will look out unto Yahvé, will wait for
the God of my salvation: | my God will hear
me. ‖ Rejoice not my enemy† over me! for I fall
I rise again, | when I sit in darkness, Yahvé is my
light. ‖ Yahvé's anger will I bear, because I have
sinned against him, | until he conduct my cause
and execute my right, bring me forth to the light
10   that I look upon his righteousness, ‖ in order that
my enemy may see it and shame cover her, she

---

* Gem.: *von deiner busenvertrautin.—Tr.*
† Germ.: *meine feindin.—Tr.*

who said unto me "where is Yahvé thy God?" |
my eyes will feast on her, now will she be as mire
of the streets for treading upon! ||

(Yʜʜᴠᴇ́):

It is a day for building thy walls; | that day—
distant is the date! || At that day—then will men
come to thee from Assyria and the cities of the
Land-of-Distress, and from the Land-of-Distress
unto the River, from sea to sea and mountain to
mountain! || But the land will become a desert on
account of its inhabitants, | in consequence of
their deeds.

5.

(The Prophet):

Pasture thy people with thy staff as sheep of thy
heritage, solitarily inhabiting a forest in the midst
of Karmel! | may they pasture in Bashan and
15   Gilead as in the days of old! || as in the days when
thou marchedst forth from the land of Egypt | cause
it to see wonders! || May nations seeing that be
ashamed at all their might, | putting the hand upon
the mouth, with deafened ears! || may they lick the
dust like the serpent, as the crawlers of the earth
quake forth from their enclosures, | unto Yahvé
our God may they tremble, and fear before thee! ||
Who is a God like thee, that forgiveth guilt and
passeth by transgression to the remnant of his
heritage, | retaineth not for ever his anger, but
delighteth in grace! || he will again have pity upon

us, tread down our iniquities; | wilt cast into the
20   depths of the sea all their sins, || wilt bestow faith-
fulness on Yaqob, grace on Abraham, | which
thou hast sworn unto our Fathers from the days of
old ! ||

1. After the prophet has announced an utterance of Yahvé's
(alas, what other utterance is it than that of a just controversy
or contention with his people !) and referred the people to the
mountains as umpires, ver. 1, he calls upon the latter also to
hear his complaint in the dispute of Yahvé's which is just
about to be opened, ver. 2.

In the complaint which follows, vv. 3-5, it is as if omnipotence
laid aside its own nature and for the moment put itself on a
par with men ; its purpose is to provoke the defence of the
accused, and it reminds the nation but briefly of the great
benefits and proofs of favour which once formed and preserved
them—in order that the nation may recognize the *righteous-*
nesses, i.e., the righteousness which manifests itself in such
various ways, or the righteous thoughts and deeds of Yahvé ! as
is added at last with a certain emphasis. The people are briefly
reminded of all the great events of the good times of old,
commencing with the exodus from Egypt, ver. 4, especially of
the remarkable prophecies of Bileam, ver. 5, which are already
conceived in full accordance with the description of the events
that took place in connexion with Balaq, Num. xxii.-xxiv.
The following words, *from Shittim to Gilgal,* are probably
an ancient marginal observation, intended to serve as a reference
to the last portion of the Pentateuch where the history of
Bileam might be found, comp. Num. xxv. 1 ; xxxi. 8 ; Josh.
iv. 20.

In the presence of the word of pure truth, denial is of no
avail in this trial : now that the nation ought to answer, it can
find no justification of itself, vv. 6, 7. But still, as hitherto,
possessed by an indolent, slavishly timid spirit, it cannot rise

to true insight, or even to the power of true contrition and
repentance, but proposes in a slavish sense, as if Yahvé
demanded eternal sacrifices, to give every possible material
atonement,—yea, even the sacrifice of its own dearest children
if Yahvé should demand them ! since man estranged from
the Divine life is more willing to sacrifice any external object,
were it at other times his dearest possession, than to give up
his own fainthearted, confused thoughts, and to live to Yahvé
alone. And human sacrifices were as a fact not uncommon at
that time.

The highest voice is wholly unable to make a direct reply to
this crude, inexcusable error of the poor-spirited nation ; the
plaintiff, against whom the defendant has not been able to
produce anything at all, disappears naturally, and instead of
Yahvé the prophet only answers as the mediator, correcting
the serious error in a few words, ver. 8 : it has long ago been
clearly proclaimed to the people by the ancient lawgivers and
prophets what Yahvé really demands of it, and what simple,
but great, universal and necessary demands these are ! comp.
Luke xvi. 29. Zech. vii. 9, 10 ; viii. 16, 17, 19.

2. But, as a sudden peal of thunder, the distant, terrible
voice of Yahvé vibrates through the prophet. After the proceedings of the accusation have come to an end, Yahvé has
again resumed his position of judge, and irrespective of anything further, pronounces the judicial sentence which, according
to strict principles of justice, must follow the accusation,
together with the reasons for it, vv. 9-16. And as if the
prophet were collecting himself from the first shock of the
terrible sound, he first inserts the words : *yet surely it is salvation to fear thy name !* i. e., it now appears that it is really not
a vain thing to fear thy name, whilst the unrighteous must
tremble. The severe words of the judge are addressed to the
community (properly the *tribe*, Yuda) *and him who appoints it,*
calls together and guides it, whoever he may be (but of course
the king is intended). And since a good judge never gives

judgment without supplying his reasons, the Divine voice
enquires, whether the injustices of all kinds ought still to go
on? (vv. 10, 11; comp. Amos viii. 5). This enquiry is put to
that community which, as this voice well knows, is full of
cruelty towards the helpless and of cheating and lies, and
which would have done better if instead of those cowardly
subterfuges it had previously confessed with true penitence
openly before the omniscient accuser, these great transgressions
which the judge must now publicly charge it with. If Israel,
therefore, on its part is incorrigible, then Yahvé also has on his
part to smite it as good as incurably with these words of judgment, although it may be horrified at the punishments which
are here apportioned to it, ver. 13. These terrible punishments are, that it shall work and live in vain, tortured as it
were by ravenous hunger in the midst of eating, Job xviii. 12,
13, and that it shall have followed the projects and laws of the
godless· kings, 1 Kings xvi. 25, only to be destroyed, to serve
for ridicule to the world, and to bear not the honour but the
shame of a people of Yahvé! For the greater the honour of
being Yahvé's nation is, when this honour has once been
recognised in the world, the more profoundly are they despised
who have lost this honour.

3. Is this Divine punishment, then, if it really comes as has
been above proclaimed, too severe, and not fully deserved
even according to the nation's own conscience? Alas, let only
the sincere and true voice of the nation be listened to! What
are the simple and truly godly men of the people, of whom
there are always some, thinking and saying? A time always
comes when their voice also may be heard loudly enough; and
after that former voice, which might be public, but was nevertheless half hypocritical, half mean-spirited, vi. 6, 7, has for good
reasons become silent, this of the truly godly among the people
may be heard more distinctly. Accordingly the voice of such
a man is now heard, a man who, notwithstanding his strong
desires to do so, was unable to find a just man in the land:

it happens to him as if in the gleaning of fruit and grapes, as poor people are accustomed to do, he had sought in vain for any refreshing fruit, Hos. ix. 10 ; there are, as is explained in detail from ver. 2 onwards, no more any who are well-pleasing to Yahvé in the land, Ps. xii. 2 sq., their only endeavour is to get the advantage of each other, to ensnare and capture, even if it were by sanguinary means, ver. 2 ; but the magnates and judges, who ought to check the growing injustice, promote it from selfish motives, are prepared for gold to stamp the evil deed as a good one, if they are requested to do so, speak only their own conceit and pervert *it, i.e.* the judgment which they pronounce, ver. 3 ; even those who are comparatively the best among them are like thorns, owing to their prickly, false sides, hard to touch and handle, ver. 4 *a*; Ps. lviii. 10 ; Nah. i. 10.   Here in the midst of this sad but true experience, the man himself is seized by the conviction of the necessity of those punishments of the nation, so that he cries out, ver. 4 *b*: the day of thy outlookers, the day which thy attentive prophets who are ever looking out into the future (Is. xxi. 11, 12 ; Hab. ii. 1) long ago announced, thy examination and punishment, is here ! now will their confusion commence, so that the people who knew how to protect themselves by thorny tricks become now, when seized by higher punishment, themselves confused and helpless !—And then a second equally solitary godly man of this kind is heard complaining, that even amongst friends and nearest relatives mutual faithfulness has disappeared, ver. 6, comp. Jer. ix. 3 ; xii. 6.

4. But if such pure voices, although they may come but from solitary souls, begin to be heard in due time, their sincerity and truth may happily be once more operative in the entire community.   In a community which, like this, is that of the true religion, in spite of all declensions there always remains not only the eternal hope, but also an indestructible foundation of good ; for if in its present form the community perishes irremediably, it rises again in the future in a purified

and nobler form. Still the germ and possibility of the future
regenerated community already exists in the present one, however much it may be repressed and hidden; otherwise the
new community could never arise : the future attainments are
present aspirations. Accordingly there is now heard as from
an entirely different quarter, the voice of the community; it
is heard in confiding prayer to Yahvé, resolved to bear whatever punishments are due for former sins, and patiently to wait
till the day of redemption may arrive, deeply humbled, yet not
without hope or just pride; for, to set over against its own
unworthiness, it knows that its enemy [Heb. *'ôyebeth; Germ.
feindin*), that heathendom which is at present so haughty and
eager to destroy, cannot go on for ever to conquer, but the day
of the punishment of the Assyrians and of the redemption of
the believers who are oppressed by them, must also come, vv.
7-10. And who could help at once giving in his agreement
with such immortal thoughts and new endeavours after reformation !

And, behold, the Divine answer which has been thus
prompted and provoked, as if a point of honour had been
touched, is no longer simply like the former severe rebuke,
seeming to leave no room for hope : as in the rapid flight of
glorified and transporting outlook, it promises a glorious day
of restoration, a day whose date, however, is still far off, since
the land in consequence of its grievous transgressions must
first suffer its punishment, vv. 11-13. The discourse, vv. 11,
12, is composed of partial hints and abrupt words, brief and
disconnected in the extreme, and yet clear to the attentive
hearer.

5. But here, by way of rapid conclusion, is the fitting place
for the prophet's especial and separate utterance : as he began
the entire piece, vi. 1, 2, and spoke in the middle of it the
decisive word between Yahvé and the nations, vi. 16, it is still
more necessary that he should here speak once more to close
the entire proceedings. For though in the present, upon the

actual earnestness of which everything finally depends, he is
too weak to ward off the threatening Divine punishments and
sufferings, there is still left to him the power to wrestle in
earnest believing prayer for the Divine mercy, and to make im-
portunate intercession on behalf of his country : and in strong,
wrestling prayer he gathers together all that further agitates
his prophetic heart, and thereby finally stills all his desire and
aspiration.   May Yahvé as the good shepherd guide his people,
his community, which can after all never be separated from him,
as though it were a retired, protected little flock in the forest of
fair Karmel, Num. xxiii. 9 ; Deut. xxiii. 28 ; but may this
flock also again take possession of all its former territory, the
land since lost beyond the Yordan, Zech. x. 10 !   Yet such
wishes can now be realised only by something like a repetition
of the ancient deliverance from Egypt :   may this time of the
exaltation of Israel, when the Assyrians, who are now so
haughty, and other heathen, trembling forth with shame from
their fortified castles, submit to Yahvé (Ps. xviii. 46 ; lxxvi. 5,
11), not be too far off !—Truly, there is no other God from
whom such things could be looked for with trustful confidence !
In the true spiritual God there is this also included, that his
eternal purpose is only the good, simply salvation and life :
wherever, as is the case in this community, the genuine Divine
spirit has been operative from ancient times, he is ever work-
ing there in the abolition of guilt and promotion of reconciliation, and thus he will overcome by his omnipotence the errors
and sufferings of the present, complete the work which had
long ago been commenced and promised in this sacred community, vv. 18-20.

The main thing here, as in every drama, is to catch the right
voices and their right alternation ; and unless this is done an
interpretation must be in the highest degree uncertain.   Thus,
e. g., it is as important, as according to the plan of the drama

it is correct, that the prophet himself speaks immediately three
times only, but in each case at the proper place : as a voluntary
mediator he begins and closes, and speaks as such in the middle
also at the proper place. But that the words vii. 1-6, are not
meant to be taken as his may also be seen from the simple fact
of the allusion to the prophets and the judgment-day long ago
announced by them. With regard to the *five acts,* comp.
Dichter des A.B. I *a,* p. 69 sq.

vi. 2. The translation of איתנים [Germ. *ewig gleichen*] is
a free adaptation of its primary meaning.—*Wearied thee,* vi. 3,
so that from vexation and satiety thou leavest me and goest to
other Gods.

If the words from *Shittim unto Gilgal* belonged to the
original text, we should have to suppose that the prophet
wished to refer to the narratives of the last portion of the
journeyings of Israel under Moses : at the same time, although
this is another distinction of our prophet compared with Mikha,
Yesaya, and still older prophets, that he makes frequent allu-
sions to the ancient histories, we cannot think he would in this
connexion make a purely learned reference of such a strange
and especially of such a superfluous nature. We must consider
that the prophet, though he is a writer and not a speaker, dis-
plays great artistic effort.

Instead of יִרְאֶה, vi. 9, it is simplest to read יִרְאָה, or
rather the first form must be so understood, acc. § 173 *f,* so
that שמך is governed as the accusative by this infinitive.—The
use of the third person sing., ver. 11, when the subject of the
verb is indefinite, Germ. *man,* our *we, they, people,* is found
again in our prophet, vii. 3, 12.

אֲשֶׁר, vi. 12, refers back to מטה, ver. 9, for its ante-
cedent ; הָאוּזכה, ver. 11, must stand for הֲיִזְכֶּה, acc. § 53 *c,*
comp. הָאָשׁ, ver. 10 ; the waning measure, literally the
declining, wasting measure, which by the deceit of the seller
grows less and less.

vi. 16, one might be at first sight disposed to read וַיִּשׁ

instead of וַיִּשׁ׳, since וַתֵּלְכוּ follows : but this is not necessary, and the simple present is really most suitable at the commencement of this sentence. From the tone of the commencement of the strophe, ver. 10, one may conclude that either our prophet or another had a short time before spoken loudly but in vain against these injustices of the market. With regard to צוּד with חֵרֶם, vii. 2, comp. § 283 *a* and Hab. i. 16, 17.—It is clear that the construction of the sentence, vii. 3, is considerably involved : and since our prophet, as was remarked vi. 11, often uses the third person sing. when the subject is indefinite, שׁוֹאֵל may be taken to mean *they request the prince and the judge;* for that אֵת is not necessary in this case before חַשֹּׁר, follows from § 277 *d*. The participle is used as in ver. 6, but can afterwards change into the regular verb וַיְעַבְּטוּ.* First the subordinate official and the judge are bribed, then their unjust sentence is confirmed in the further appeal to the magnate, *i.e.*, the higher official, and thus the *perversion* (עבט) of the matter is complete. But precisely because these three persons co-operate to produce the final result, the sing. changes at the end into the plur., ויעבטו.—The expression *from a thorn-hedge*, vii. 4, is only a stronger way of putting *like* a thorn-hedge, just as *from nothing*, "Isa." xli. 24 is only a stronger form of *as nothing.*—The brief word *out-looker*, scout, for *prophet* in ordinary discourse is quite new here and "Isa." lvi. 10, as appears from the passages collected vol. I. p. 28 sq.

It appears from the entire plan of the drama that the words vii. 11-13 are put into the mouth of Yahvé : the prophet speaks again vii. 14. But inasmuch as this prophecy, vv. 11, 12, is not intended to take place before a distant period, it takes the form of a few supernatural, mysterious hints, only indicating with a few vague outlines far off events, these outlines growing more and more indistinct and losing themselves

---

* The author writes the word three times with מ.—*Tr.*

in the mists of the future. Particular words are also exceedingly graphic: יֵרַחַק חֹק, ver. 11, how deep and mysterious is their sound ! And so the solemn prophecy proceeds almost without interruption. At the same time, a little consideration reveals the meaning of the words. The existing Jerusalem must fall: it shall be restored in the future, but how far distant is that still ! Restored but made more glorious than before, so that from the widest circuit all again flock back to it who can be considered as its citizens, from the north-east unto the south-west, and again from the south-west to the north-east, from sea to sea and mountain to mountain! And it is evident that such passages as Isa. xi. 11, 12 ; xxvii. 12, 13 ; Amos viii. 12, *et al.*, are in the mind of the writer, only that the close especially, *mountain to mountain*, has a much more general force. *The date,* חֹק, is, therefore, in this connexion *its date,* that of the day just mentioned, §. 309 *b ;* יוֹם הוּא, ver. 12, is still shorter than יוֹם הַהוּא, ver. 11, comp. §. 293 *a*, and הָר הָהָר still shorter than יָם מִיָּם, comp. Nah. iii. 8 and §. 349 *b.* Word-painting of this description by means of extreme brevity is of late origin, and is hardly met with earlier than in our prophet. The rapid change from the feminine to the masculine suffix in ver. 11 and ver. 12 might seem to show that the community is addressed in ver. 11, and Israel in ver. 12 : but there is no reason for this, and from the whole context it is evident that it is the community only that is addressed.— The subjoined condition, ver. 13, like Mic. v. 9-14, or still more like Isa. xxxii. 19, 20.

vii. 15 אַרְאֶפוּ must stand for הַרְאֶפוּ acc. §. 122 *a*, since the imperative only is here suitable.

---

2. OTHER ANONYMOUS PROPHETS.

From such we have at all events unmistakeable fragments. Oracles like " Isa." xl. 1; liii. 1 sq. ; lvi. 9 sq.; lvii. 1 sq., bear every mark of an origin from Manasse's days, have great similarity to the piece which has just been explained, although plainly to be referred to other prophets, and their tone is such that they could have arisen only in a time of still greater temptation and trial of the faithful. But it will be best to treat of them subsequently.

The following table may be useful in as far as it gives a bird's-eye view of general results as regards the order of the origin of the component portions of the book. But it is purposely general in its information. No exact dates, but only larger periods have been indicated, and the order rather than the year of the origin of each piece may be gathered from it. The supposed date might have been prefixed to each piece, but in more ways than one such precision might mislead in a table of this kind. Besides, the new light of Assyrian inscriptions may considerably affect the dates of certain pieces of the book, while they are not likely substantially to alter the order of their succession.* Nor is the table intended to save the reader the trouble of consulting the works of the critics whose arrangements have been given. He will find the table positive where the critic is often doubtful; he will also find a piece placed not quite accurately for some reason or other. But it is believed that legitimately and cautiously consulted, the table will be instructive.

At first it was intended to add a column giving the arrangement adopted by Ewald in the first edition of his work (1840), but when it was drawn up it presented so few really important variations from that of the second edition that it seemed almost superfluous, and when placed in a bare table might rather mislead than instruct. In the first edition Ewald separated the productions of Isaiah into three great groups, and doubted the possibility of a complete restoration of their original form. In the second edition, he no longer considered this an impossibility, and discovered the seven books of this volume. But this discovery produced no very important change in the order of the pieces. Ch. vi. was in the first edition placed before the piece, ii. 2-v. 25 ; xvii. 1-11, before vii. 1-ix. 6 ; i. after the foreign oracles, xxi. 11-17; xx. before x. 5-xi. 16. The pieces xxi. 11, 12, xxi. 13-17, were treated as two oracles, Isaianic throughout.

The non-Isaianic pieces are italicised in the columns.—*Tr.*

---

* I learn from Mr. Cheyne that he has seen reason since 1870 to alter his opinion with regard to the chronology of some of the prophecies included in the book of " Isaiah." The Assyrian discoveries have been the cause of this change, so far as the genuine portion of Isaiah is concerned, and it is to be earnestly hoped that Mr. Cheyne will take an early opportunity of expounding their bearing on the prophecies of this book.

CHRONOLOGICAL ARRANGEMENTS OF THE BOOK OF "ISAIAH."

	EWALD.*	GESENIUS.†	KNOBEL.‡	KUENEN.§	CHEYNE.||	REUSS.¶
Post 897	xv., xvi. 7-12 xvi. 1-6	xv., xvi. 12?	xv., xvi. 12	xv., xvi. 12	xv., xvi. 12	xv., xvi. 12
UZZIA.						
JOTHAM.			xvii. 1-11 xvi. 13, 14 xxi. 13—17 xxi. 11, 12 ii.—iv.		ix. 8—x. 4 v. 25-30	
AHAZ.	ii. 2—v. 25 ix. 7—x. 4 v. 26-30	vi. ii.—v. vii. 1-16, 17-25 viii. 1—ix. 6 xvii. 1-11 ix. 7—x. 4 xiv. 28-32	vi. v. vii. viii.—ix. 6 i. ix. 7—x. 4 xiv. 28-32	ii.—iv. v. vii. xvii. 1-11 ix. 7—x. 4 xiv. 28-32	ii.—v. 25 xvii. 1-11	i. ii.—iv. v. vi. xvii. 1-11 vii. 1—ix. 6 ix. 7—x. 4
HEZEKIAH.	vi. 1—ix. 6 xvii. 1-11 i. xiv. 28-32 xvi. 13-14 xxi. 11, 12 xxi. 13, 14 xxi. 15-17 xxii. 1-14 xxii. 15-25 xxiii. 1-14	xxiii. 1-18 x. 5—xii. 6 xiv. 24-27 xvi. 13, 14 xxviii.—xxxiii. xvii. 12—xviii. 7 xx. xxi. 11, 12, 13-17 xxii. 1-14	xxviii. { x. 5—xii. 6 { xiv. 24-27 xxiii. xix. xx. xxix. xxx.—xxxii. xvii. 12—xviii. 7	xxi. 11, 12 xxi. 13, 14 xvi. 13, 14 xxviii. xix. xx. xxix. xxx.—xxxii.	vi. 1—ix. 7 i. xiv. 28-32 xvi. 13, 14 xxi. 11, 12 xxii. 13-17 xxii. 1-14 xxii. 15-25 xxiii. 1-14	x. 5—xii. 6 xiv. 29-32? xxviii. xxix. xxx. xxxi. 1—xxxii. 8 xxxii. 9-20 xxxiii. xx.

	*	†	‡	§	‖	¶
HEZEKIAH	xxviii.—xxxii. x. 5—xii. 6 { xvii. 12—xviii. 7 xiv. 24-37 xx. xxxviii.? xxxvii. 22-35 xix.	xxii. 15-25	xxii. 1-14 xxii. 15-25 xxxiii.	xxii. 15-25 xxii. 1-14 x. 5—xii. 6 xiv. 24-27 i. xvii. 12-14 xviii. xxxiii.	xxii. 15-18 ? xxviii. xxix. xxx. xxxi. xxxii. 1-8 xxxii. 9-20 x. 5—xii. 6 xiv. 24-27 xx. xvii. 12-14 xviii. xxxiii. xxxvii. 22-35 xix.	xxii. 15-25 xxii. 1-14 xiv. 24-27 xvii. 12—xviii. 7 xxi. 11, 12 xxi. 13-17 xxiii.? xix. xxxvii. 21-35
MANASSEH	al. 1, 2 lii. 13—liv. 12 lvi. 9—lvii. 11	xix. 1-17, 21-25 vv. 18-20?				
EXILE	xxvi. 1-10 xvii. 2—xviii. 23 al.—lxvi. xxxiv.—xxxv. xxvi. 1-6	xviii.—xix. 23 xxi. 1-10 xxxiv.—xxxv. al.—lxvi.	xxxiv.—xxxvii. xxxiv.—xxxv. xviii.—xix. 23 xxi. 1-10 al.—lxvi.	xxxiv.—xxxvii. xxxiv.—xxxv. xviii.—xix. 23 xxi. 1-10 al.—lxvi.	xxxiv.—xxxvi. xxxiv.—xxxvii. xxi. 1-10 xvii. 2—xviii. 23 al.—lxvi.	xxxiv.—xxxvii. xvii. 1—xxv. 23 xxvi. 1-10 xxxiv.—xxxv. al.—lxvi.
RETURN	xxxiv.—xxxvii. xxvii. 15-18					

* The second edition (1867) of the Propheten des Alten Bundes, of which the present work is a translation.
† Philologisch-kritischer und historischer Commentar über den Jesaia. von Wilhelm Gesenius, Leipzig. 1821.
‡ Der Prophet Jesaia erklärt von Dr. August Knobel, 4te Auflage, herausgegeben von Dr. Ludwig Diestel. Leipzig, 1872.
§ Historisch-kritisch Onderzoek naar het Onstaan der Boeken des Ouden Verbonds door A. Kuenen, Hoogleeraar te Leiden, tweede Deel. Leiden, 1863.
‖ The Book of Isaiah Chronologically arranged by T. K. Cheyne, M.A. London, 1870.
¶ Les Prophètes par Edouard Reuss, Professeur à l'Université de Strasbourg. Paris, 1876.